Critical Pedagogy and Global Literature

New Frontiers in Education, Culture, and Politics

Edited by Kenneth J. Saltman

New Frontiers focuses on both topical educational issues and highly original works of educational policy and theory that are critical, publicly engaged, and interdisciplinary, drawing on contemporary philosophy and social theory. The books in the series aim to push the bounds of academic and public educational discourse while remaining largely accessible to an educated reading public. New Frontiers aims to contribute to thinking beyond the increasingly unified view of public education for narrow economic ends (economic mobility for the individual and global economic competition for the society) and in terms of efficacious delivery of education as akin to a consumable commodity. Books in the series provide both innovative and original criticism and offer visions for imagining educational theory, policy, and practice for radically different, egalitarian, and just social transformation.

Published by Palgrave Macmillan:

Education in the Age of Biocapitalism: Optimizing Educational Life for a Flat World
   By Clayton Pierce

Schooling in the Age of Austerity: Urban Education and the Struggle for Democratic Life
   By Alexander J. Means

Critical Pedagogy and Global Literature: Worldly Teaching
   Edited by Masood Ashraf Raja, Hillary Stringer, and Zach VandeZande

Critical Pedagogy and Global Literature

Worldly Teaching

Edited by

Masood Ashraf Raja,

Hillary Stringer, and

Zach VandeZande

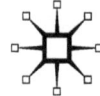

CRITICAL PEDAGOGY AND GLOBAL LITERATURE
Copyright © Masood Ashraf Raja, Hillary Stringer, and Zach VandeZande, 2013.

All rights reserved.

First published in 2013 by
PALGRAVE MACMILLAN®
in the United States—a division of St. Martin's Press LLC,
175 Fifth Avenue, New York, NY 10010.

Where this book is distributed in the UK, Europe and the rest of the world, this is by Palgrave Macmillan, a division of Macmillan Publishers Limited, registered in England, company number 785998, of Houndmills, Basingstoke, Hampshire RG21 6XS.

Palgrave Macmillan is the global academic imprint of the above companies and has companies and representatives throughout the world.

Palgrave® and Macmillan® are registered trademarks in the United States, the United Kingdom, Europe and other countries.

ISBN: 978–1–137–31975–3

Library of Congress Cataloging-in-Publication Data

    Critical pedagogy and global literature : worldly teaching / edited by Masood Ashraf Raja, Hillary Stringer, and Zach VandeZande.
        pages cm—(New frontiers in education, culture, and politics)
    Includes bibliographical references and index.
    ISBN 978–1–137–31975–3 (alk. paper)
    1. Literature—Study and teaching. 2. Critical pedagogy. 3. Literature and society. I. Raja, Masood A., 1965–

PN61.C75 2013
807—dc23   2013006084

A catalogue record of the book is available from the British Library.

Design by Newgen Knowledge Works (P) Ltd., Chennai, India.

First edition: August 2013

10 9 8 7 6 5 4 3 2 1

The editors would like to thank their contributors, their families, and their colleagues at the University of North Texas. Without their support, this book would not have been possible.

Contents

Introduction   1
Masood Ashraf Raja

Part I   Theory

1. Gender, Knowledge, and Economy: Greg Mortenson, Turning Schools into Stones   9
   Robin Truth Goodman

2. Educating for Cosmopolitanism: Lessons from Cognitive Science   25
   Mark Bracher

3. Learning to Be a Psychopath: The Pedagogy of the Corporation   47
   Kenneth J. Saltman

4. Corporate World Literature: Neoliberalism and the Fate of the Humanities   63
   Jeffrey R. Di Leo

5. Reading the "Other" in World Literature: Toward a Discourse of Unfamiliarity   75
   Swaralipi Nandi

6. Pedagogy for Healing and Justice through Cambodian American Literature   97
   Jonathan H. X. Lee and Mary Thi Pham

7. A Moving Pedagogy: Teaching Global Literature through Translation   113
   Kyle Wanberg

8. "Re-worlding" in Tsitsi Dangaremba's *Nervous Conditions*   131
   Linda Daley

9 Teaching World Systems: How Critical Pedagogy Can Frame the Global   149
   David B. Downing

10 Object Lessons: Material Culture Approaches to Teaching Global Poetry   165
   Hella Rose Bloom

Part II Praxis

11 A Gun and a Book: Teaching Naguib Mahfouz's *The Thief and the Dogs* in a Time of Revolution and Occupation   181
   Jessica Chiccehitto Hindman

12 Magical Realism: A Gateway out of America and into the World   189
   Tessa Mellas

13 Making the Familiar Unfamiliar: Teaching Origin Myths, Material Conditions, and "the Bible as Literature"   193
   Hillary Stringer

14 Cycles of Opportunity: On the Value and Efficacy of Native American Literature in Teaching World Literature to Millennials   201
   Marnie M. Sullivan

15 "The Speculation of Schoolboys": Confronting the Academy in *Ulysses*   213
   Matthew McKenzie Davis

16 Reaching for the Other in Teaching Aleksandar Hemon's "A Coin"   221
   Zach VandeZande

Afterword   227
Masood Ashraf Raja, Hillary Stringer, and Zach VandeZande

List of Contributors   229

Index   231

Introduction

Masood Ashraf Raja

The world as it was, is, or will be, is beyond common sense, beyond natural understanding: it must be taught. Didactics is not only a fancy term for teaching but is also a loaded concept, which, under certain enabling conditions, is meant to teach us the very nature of what is given to us and then perform an enabling act of transcendence from the given. The world that we live in, this world in which neoliberal capital offers itself as natural and non-referential, is also a world of unrelenting greed and heart-breaking inequalities. How must we change this world? The answer: we must teach the world as it is but also as it ought to be. We live in the belly of this monster called neoliberal capital that Ngugi, in another age it seems, had called a two-mouthed demon that steals "food from people's stores at midnight" and then visits the robbed in "robes of charity" to offer them "a calabash filled with the grain" (13) that was stolen at night. We are all complicit in its design, instruments of its logic. Yes, sadly, there is no outside to capital: we must, therefore, teach it from within and also learn, share, and teach the strategies of its ultimate undoing. For, let us not forget, every system has its own undoing woven into the very fabric of its being: the system needs this death message to remain constantly on the move, in flux. The system, thus, always has a secret at its core: true revolutionary pedagogy must seek, share, and teach this secret.

In its earlier stages, the demon of capital effaced difference to make everything in its own image and to arrogate all of world's resources to itself. Neoliberal capital, however, is a multiheaded demon and appropriates difference in the name of development to continue the northward flow of world's resources for the use and pleasure of the so-called "masters of the universe."

World literature, in all its connotations and denotations, is yet another tool in the hands of capital: to teach the world so that the new generations of northern elite can learn to negotiate the world in order to extract the maximum advantage. Knowledge for the sake of profit and appropriative drive is at the heart of this new emphasis on introductory level world literature, world history, or world culture courses. The corporatized university is the ideal place to teach the world: it has now become the university's unannounced mission to maintain the US comparative edge by producing noncritical, but aware, citizens of the world, citizens ideally programmed to serve the purposes and missions of the global corporations. Yes, teaching the world through literature so that our students know of the world, because knowledge, as Foucault has aptly taught us, is inextricably linked with power and its project of disciplining, managing, and controlling human bodies and desires. That these courses are often taught by an overworked and underpaid precariat is also aptly clear. In the end then, the practice of teaching world literature to facilitate a certain metropolitan-specific view of the world is also an emblem of current division of labor: contingent labor of the so-called cognitariat[1] is appropriated to bring the world to our classrooms. And this "deliverance of others" (Palumbo-Liu, 1) to our students instead of creating empathy only functions to normalize the preinscribed global hierarchies of the neoliberal world, a world in which inequalities are essential and where the other can enter the metropolitan academy only as an exotic appendage or as a demonized marker of otherness.

But there is, I dare say, another kind of knowledge: a knowing beyond Hegel, beyond instrumentalization, beyond western metaphysics: knowledge in the thought of Levinas and in the praxis of Freirre. Knowledge not as the master or as the child of logos but as a servant of Eros, a bringer of freedom, love, kindness, care: knowledge that enables us to live more compassionate and responsible lives, lives in concert and in constant touch with our global others; a sort of impossible knowledge that seeks the other not to master it through learning but to love it through caring and sharing. This is the worldly knowledge, the worldliness that Edward Said talked about in one of his major and more hopeful books, and that is why what we propose here is called worldly teaching. For Said, worldliness, if described succinctly, is to acknowledge that the texts and critics exist in the world and are "hence worldly" (35). Our teaching, therefore, must also be grounded in the worldliness of the text, the teacher, and the student, and it must teach the world.

In the traditional epics of my culture,[2] epics not yet included in our world literature curriculum, a hero, when confronted with a self-regulating system—called Tilism—must launch a two-pronged offensive to reduce the Tilism, to undo its logic and the binding force of its regulative and appropriative power. In the heroic realm, the hero must muster his forces and build lateral alliances to fight countless battles and skirmishes to keep the Tilism at bay, to buy more time, more leverage, while searching for the tablet that has the secret of the Tilism's final undoing inscribed on it. This tablet, this magical knowledge, is always hidden in the deepest recesses of the Tilism; one could argue that it is the *raison d'être* of the Tilism, something that needs the Tilism to hide it. But the tablet is always there, for it is absolutely necessary for a normalized system to pre-inscribe its own undoing, its own death, for without it there will be no reason for the system to grow. It is this genetic code, this pre-inscription coded at the originary moment of the system—the prescribed death—that forces the system to grow, and that must be found. For, unless the hero finds the tablet and reads the inscription aloud, the system cannot be undone: so the hero seeks the tablet while his supporters and his allies fight a thousand different battles to force the Tilism to look the other way.

So, as we muster our forces and fight our losing battles, in the classrooms, on the streets, in courtrooms against a thousand different specters of power, we are also buying time: enough time to find the tablet, the code, to undo the Tilism and write the world anew. And when, after a thousand stalemates and lost battles, we find the secret, all we will have to do is to speak the secret, to unhinge it from the interests of its masters. The mere act of saying it will undo the Tilism of capital and free us to be human, free us to live, to love, and to die in peace.

But until that moment comes, and trust me it will, as there are signs of it in the air already, we—teachers, students, activists, and the wretched of the earth—painfully aware of our own history of complicity in the projects of power, must fight on, must teach, learn, love, talk, write, and hope for a future to come, a future impossible but worthy of our hopes and dreams. True critical pedagogy, I believe, applied to the transformative potential of world literature can, at least, enable us to pose a threat to this neoliberal monstrosity that has now been globally naturalized.

What would it take for us to think the world differently, to love unconditionally, for conditions always reduce differences, and to live responsible lives? In my naiveté, I sometimes believe that world literature can help us do that, can help us train and, in Gayatri Spivak's words, enable the "empowerment of an informed imagination" (2) for our students. But when we mobilize these loaded and so-called cheesy concepts against the powerful machines of capitalism, do we not look slightly dreamy, and certainly ineffectual? But then who cares: let us fight on as Faiz Ahmad Faiz taught us: it is how you enter the field that matters / for to win and lose is entirely inconsequential.

Most of the essays in this collection come from academics: all committed to the issues of critical pedagogy and world literature, all at different levels of career trajectories. This emphasis on academics is the main strength of this collection but also its Achilles' heel: for as academics we have a mission to produce liberatory knowledge, but in the process we are also inescapably caught in the normalizing process of power, for we, after all, are also expected to teach a certain degree of functionality within the system of capital. We are, however, humanists, and thus also responsible to teach beyond the system, beyond utility; the most important aspects of our practices are, or ought to be, to think the system itself, to lay bare its normalizing practices, its seductions, and its strategies of social stratifications. In the end, our efforts too are probably doomed to failure, but who knows: as the Arab spring and Occupy movement have taught us, the young may still surprise us, may still teach us the true meaning of life and the true spirit of democratic popular public dissent.

There are two parts to this book: Part I includes theoretical writings by some leading and some emergent scholars in the field of critical pedagogy. These are all situated scholars: they are concerned with the everyday functions and consequences of informed pedagogy. Unlike their prolegomenon counterparts who exist "in a preliminary intellectual space, whose value is enhanced by being, above other things, above productive work" (Brennan, 13), these scholars respond to the world as it is, point out its flaws, its irregularities, its inequalities, and then theorize transformative strategies. These scholars are deeply interested in transformative power of informed pedagogy and neither do theory for theory's sake nor subscribe to the dicta of the "aesthetics of complexity" (9) or "fetish of intricacy" (9). I will not attempt to reduce their chapters and give you some pithy excerpts here: I hope you, the reader, will take your time to read them and then enter in a conversation with them.

Part II contains essays by the practitioners of world literature: part of the overworked global precariat; these are the people on the front, in the trenches. Theirs is a story of hope and resistance. We are honored to have them in this book, for they alone can teach us the true value of transformative pedagogy through their lived experiences.

Read together, the two parts are meant to provide you a set of theoretical and praxis-driven approaches to teaching world literature: teaching it against the grain, in opposition to the imperial imperatives of the global elite, and in the hope of changing and transforming the world.

All you have to do is *Iqra*: Read!

Notes

1. For a detailed discussion of precariat and cognitariat read: George Caffentzis, "A Critique of 'Cognitive Capital'," in *Cognitive Capitalism, Education and Digital Labor*, ed. Michael A. Peters and Ergin Bulut (New York: Peter Lang, 2011), 23–56.

2. Muhammad Hussain Jah. *Hoshruba: The Land and the Tilism*, 1883–1893, trans. Musharraf Ali Farooqi (New York: Urdu Project, 2009). (More information in: http://mafarooqi.com/hoshruba/index.html).

Works Cited

Brennan, Timothy. "Intellectual Labor." In *Cognitive Capitalism, Education and Digital Labor*, Edited by Michael A. Peters and Ergin Bulut. New York: Peter Lang, 2011, 1–21.

Palumbo-Liu, David. *The Deliverance of Others: Reading Literature in a Global Age*. Durham: Duke University Press, 2012.

Said, Edward. *The World, the Tex, and the Critic*. Cambridge: Harvard University Press, 1983.

Spivak, Gayatri. *Other Asias*. Oxford: Blackwell, 2008.

Thiong'o, Ngugi wa. *Devil on the Cross*. Oxford: Heinemann, 1982.

Part I

Theory

1

Gender, Knowledge, and Economy: Greg Mortenson, Turning Schools into Stones

Robin Truth Goodman

In April, 2011, the news hit the wires that Greg Mortenson, the author of the celebrated *Three Cups of Tea* and *Stones into Schools,* had not described his adventures building schools in Pakistan and Afghanistan with full accuracy. *Three Cups of Tea* and *Stones into Schools* are both feel-good memoirs that chronicle Greg Mortenson's heroic travel exploits in an unfamiliar and often hostile environment to bring learning to Muslim girls. In a number of TV exposés and other mainstream outlets, including a dialogue with Jon Krakauer on *Sixty Minutes* followed by a book devoted to the topic entitled *Three Cups of Deceit,* Mortenson's credibility was interrogated along with the legitimacy of the charity he founded to collect money for the school-building projects that the book describes—Central Asia Institute or CAI. Evidence had surfaced that his stay in the village of Korphe, and his promise to build a school there, did not directly follow from his failed attempt to climb the Himalayan mountain K2 in 1993 and getting lost on the descent as he had written, and he was not really kidnapped by the Taliban. Krakauer is explicit about the questionable accounting practices that Mortenson practiced and later claimed as but instances of a naïve guy who suddenly and miraculously finds himself at the head of a large business enterprise. Not only did many of the members of the CAI charity's Board of Trustees resign due to Mortenson's inadequate reporting of expenses—for example, he was using expensive private jets to travel for speaking engagements—but also money that was collected from schoolchildren in the United States to pay for "teachers' salaries, student scholarships, school supplies, basic operating expenses" (Krakauer, 41) was not spent in these designated ways. The total 2009 outlay for such school support amounted to "$612,000" (41). "Most teachers...have never received any training from CAI" and "a significant number of CAI schools only exist on paper" (48).

I am not so concerned here with the authenticity or veracity of the text but rather with questioning the desire for authenticity that the text elicits. Neither *Three Cups of Tea* nor *Stones into Schools* demands to be read as a reflection of the real. Mortenson's self-aggrandizing anecdotes often verge on the comical. For example, in *Stones into Schools*, Mortenson, encouraged by his daughter who had recently read *Where the Wild Things Are*, dashes out to Gold's Gym to buy playground equipment to provide to the schools. One day a Taliban fighter arrives, puts down his weapons, and along with his companions, "gleefully sampled the swings, the slide, and the seesaw" (201). The Taliban warrior then decides that he likes the idea of educating girls after all "but [the schools] absolutely must have playgrounds" (201). Immediately seduced upon first contact with US consumer products, the terrorist throws away local traditions, religious beliefs, and historical resentment for the sake of a friendly romp in the sandbox.

Given that Mortenson's tale is so preposterous, what is surprising is precisely the surprise with which the pundits responded to the revelation that the stories are fiction. As Katha Pollitt asks, "How did Mortenson enchant so many, including knowledgeable people?" (9). Pollitt's conjectured answer is that: "We've gotten used to a certain kind of NGO fairy tale...: Heifer International gives a family a farm animal, and in a dozen years, the profits send a daughter to college" (9). The idea of spreading education to girls promises the success of the imperialist dream while shadowing the nightmare of continued extremist attacks on girls and their schools, including insurgents throwing acid on the schoolgirls' faces, high dropout and low attendance rates, and low quality of curriculum and instruction.[1] Though certainly imperialist clichés and promises saturate Mortenson's prose, turning US military ventures in Afghanistan into miraculous acts of care, this paper argues that such girls' school narratives, as Angela McRobbie has recognized, position girls as the carriers of new economic rationalities: "The girl who has benefited from the equal opportunities now available to her, can be mobilized as the embodiment of the values of the new meritocracy" (721–722). For McRobbie, the girl under neoliberalism is "now a social category understood primarily as being endowed with capacity" (722); she demonstrates the success of the education system as a whole and, on the international plane, becomes the target of worthwhile investment aid in the form of educational aid for the production of "the ideal... subject of the new international division of labour" (729), in other words, "gender training to the long term benefit of the global corporations" (729).

Mortenson's "feel good" narrative of girls' emancipation through girls' education builds on a prior positioning of girls' schools as the crux of the struggle between colonizers and nationalist movements in other postcolonial renditions. For example, in his famous chapter on women revolutionaries, "Algeria Unveiled," Frantz Fanon interprets girls' schools as methodologically destroying the indigenous national culture. Fanon's description of girls' schools have an uncanny similarity to many of the celebratory descriptions that Mortenson, too, constructs: "Much is made of the young student's prodigious intelligence, her maturity; a picture is painted of the brilliant future that awaits those eager young creatures, and it is none too subtly hinted that it would be criminal if the child's schooling were interrupted. The shortcomings of colonized society are conceded, and it is proposed that the young student be sent to boarding school in order to spare the parents the criticism of 'narrow-minded neighbors'" (fn. 39). In keeping, Mortenson promotes the girls' school as the crux of social change in Afghanistan and Pakistan, but the culture that the schools are instituting is constantly extolled as a new economic culture, in this instance as the culture of the sweatshop: "In a disused room at the back of Hafi Ali's home, Korphe's women gathered each afternoon, learning to use the four new Singer hand-crank sewing machines Mortenson purchased, under the tutelage of Fida, a master Skardu tailor... 'Balti already had a rich tradition of sewing and weaving," Mortenson says. 'They just needed some help to revive the dying practice'" (Mortenson amd Relin, 2006: 193). Mortenson uses the schools and the girls they are meant to benefit as praise-worthy examples of such overcoming of indigenous culture, traditions, and practices, imposing in their place technological rationality and the temporality of the machine. Mortenson's girls' schools also establish a transformation into neoliberal economic relations: public sphere destruction, military benevolence,[2] and private initiative. Every instance of public involvement, for Mortenson, ends in tragedy that Mortenson's heroic construction of schools will alleviate: for example, "the few permanent government school buildings that had been reconstructed were inappropriate, having been raised directly over the footprints of the old schools, and with the same techniques that were responsible for the structural failures that had killed so many children" (*Stones,* 219). Girls in schools come to represent a naturalized relationality and cooperative ethic that exist outside of external state controls and systems' regulations, or, as Krakauer cites Mortenson, outside of "government scrutiny into our operation" (57), as unmediated market potential.

This paper argues that Mortenson's construction of girls' education as the cornerstone of imperialist policy participates in a literary tradition of a girls' school genre that develops an economic rationality through displaying a common sense about girls. In its early twentieth-century form, as Patricia Tilburg notes, girls' school narratives "became...a kind of shorthand for feminine success" with the girls' school depicted "as a powerfully modern and powerfully female public space" (77). I show here how imperialist culture has co-opted the figure of rebellion that girls' school narratives have developed, to represent the problem of the marketability of women's work. As imperialist narratives merge into the girls' school trope, women's work turns to being a display of women's compliance with regimes of capitalization. This change in the literary role of women's work for the imperialist context has migrated into the social scientific justification in policy debates over girls' education, separate schooling, and "choice."

Girls' Schools in the Social Sciences

Though feminists have been critical of the move towards same-sex education because it perpetuates harmful stereotypes (American Association of University Women), public single-sex schooling and single-sex classroom options were incorporated in the school choice rhetoric of the "No Child Left Behind" era. Under the premise that public schools were failing, single-sex schools were championed as one option that might improve achievement levels for some children. However, the research routinely shows that single-sex classrooms have no proven or provable effect on educational "success." "There remains no strong evidence," Andrew McCreary, for example, states, and there is virtual consensus about this among researchers, "for the concurrent or long-term effects of these policies and no federal structure for uniformly studying those effects" (492). As the US Department of Education's report from its "Policy and Program Studies Service" sums up, "Any positive effects of SS [single-sex] schooling on longer-term indicators of academic achievement are not readily apparent. No differences were found for postsecondary test scores, college graduation rates, or graduate school attendance rates" (xv). The research on the effectiveness and benefits of single-sex public education is inconclusive, anecdotal at best. Researchers note that single-sex schooling expanded at the same time as high-stakes testing and accountability regimes were also expanding, blending together the effects of each. "There are no guarantees," Herr and Arms analyze in the existing empirical data, "that simply separating the sexes creates an equitable learning environment or one that interrupts stereotypical and racial arrangements" (548).

Salomone pronounces that most of the disparities measured between girls' and boys' performance can be said to be due to race or economic disadvantage since "the data make clear that the convergence of race, culture, and class present a complex set of social factors that reach well beyond the conventional girl-boy argument" (113). Part of the problem in the social science perspectives is, throughout, a lack of clear articulation of the intentions of single-sex schooling and what would count as "success": whether what is sought is higher "achievement," graduation rates, indicators of future effect (such as income or employment), or equality. Because of this indistinctness in outcomes, what counts as inputs often also seems variable and arbitrary, apart from the fact that such inputs are to be isolated from other potential influences.

Though single-sex schooling has no discernable scientific evidence that it "succeeds" or analysis of what would count as its "success," in the United States, 400 public schools have arisen in 37 states and the District of Columbia (McNeil)[3] along with 445 sex-segregated classrooms for the purpose of solving "sagging test scores and behavioral problems" (Medina).[4] Though Title IX of the 1964 Civil Rights Act enacted in 1972 explicitly denies federal funding to institutions that discriminate on the basis of sex, the George W. Bush administration in 2006 loosened its provisions, allowing the expansion of single-sex classrooms and schools in order to create alternative possibilities for raising achievement and competition. Constantly trying to justify school segregation by evoking sexed bodies as evidence of different types of aptitude and, contingently, future employability, the debates about single-sex schooling produce gendered subjectivities in order to position the child's body as the promise of a potential productivity, of differential market access. I show here how the debates over single-sex schooling serve to call upon and preserve the nature of the gendered body as underscoring the division of labor under neoliberalism, and to entrench the division of labor in the pledge of advancing prosperity.

In order to literalize these differences in the sexed body as grounded in fact, researchers often turn to the body. Rosemary C. Salomone, for example, declares, "Sex is irreducibly biological with an overlay of social considerations that define gender" (120). As Munira Moon Charania notes, anxiety about all-girls' schooling resonates with a "public anxiety surrounding girls' bodies" (306), situating girls' bodies as "the symbols of both cultural continuity and cultural crisis" (307). This frequent recourse to the body in the social science literature most often passes through a reference to the writings of Leonard Sax, MD, PhD. Sax's thesis is that "girls and boys behave differently" and learn differently "because their brains are wired differently" (28). In his book *Why Gender Matters,*

Dr. Sax supports his thesis by asserting that girls have better hearing than boys because of the configuration of their ears. Sax does not then recommend separating children on the basis of hearing ability but rather recommends a wholesale embrace of gendered classrooms on the basis that girls are more easily distracted by soft noises. Such hard-wiring makes girls better at reading and boys better at math and *Grand Theft Auto* while also explaining why men are interested in pornography when women are not. Furthermore, these brain-determined differences in hearing translate, for Dr. Sax, into irreparable differences in risk-taking, attention, self-esteem, aggression, and income. In response to the special configuration of their ears, girls process emotions through the cerebral cortex where the higher language functioning is located and therefore learn better through talking while boys learn better through doing. The gender differences that Dr. Sax spots in his learning bodies build toward a core understanding that boys move and girls do not, and girls relate while boys do not. Because of their hard-wiring, a girl learns through talking, relating, cooperating, collaborating, not acting. A 2011 study in *Science* has found Dr. Sax's recommendations based on misinformation, debunked science, and stereotypes.

As McRobbie underscores, such visibility of the sexed body produces an understanding of sexed bodies and subjectivities as carriers of economic capacity in ways that suit the economic layout of the present. Such science that explains how girls learn differently often draws on feminist research—like the work of Carol Gilligan, Nancy Chodorow, and Nel Noddings—to illustrate that girls respond to situations by relating cooperatively to others rather than through abstract principles, even though these analyses are based in historicalized socialization processes rather than essential gender types. The (boy's) moving body appears in the educational setting as moving toward mastery, like manual labor—in Marx's sense—taking control over nature. As, in contrast, the girl's immobilized body indicates, on the one hand, a lack of forward motion or advancement—in other words, a site of need, an unrealized capacity, a productive delay, even a momentum destroyed, awaiting inputs; on the other hand, the girl's body is in perfect submission, inactive but ready for service.

The Literary Record: Bronte's *Villette*

The scientific treatment of single-sex schooling cannot explain its constant recourse to the body as the final justification and cause of educational difference. The literary record, however, does offer a way of reading the body as the source of educational difference. Since the nineteenth century, the girls' school plot in literature symptomatized the insecure line between women's domestic, reproductive work on the one hand, and, on the other, their inclusion in the productive economy. According to Anita Levy, early twentieth-century literary productions wove literary scenes out of the nineteenth century's "household as emptied of female labor" (51). The girls' school in Charlotte Bronte's 1853 novel *Villette*, for example, became integral to how economic realities relating to women's work were newly entering symbolic form and affecting identities. "I seemed to hold two lives," the protagonist Lucy Snowe notes to herself as she hesitates to enter the classroom, "—the life of thought, and that of reality; and, provided the former was nourished with a sufficiency of the strange necromantic joys of fancy, the privileges of the latter might remain limited to daily bread, hourly work, and a roof of shelter" (85). Her entry into the classroom proves her wrong, establishing that the work of the caretaker as well as the work of the thinker can be rendered countable in commodity form. Jennifer Ruth has demonstrated that Bronte's depiction of the proto-profession of teaching—which in both *Jane Eyre* and *Villette* develops as women's work—exhibits an ambivalent attempt to represent in marketable form a type of labor that had heretofore not been marketable. For Ruth, intellectual work like teaching in the nineteenth century had to be considered outside of the quantifiability of manual labor because of its irreducibility to time measurement, but, with the demise of a patronage system for art, intellectual products had to "embrace commerce" (284): intellectual work had to remain ungoverned by capital's determinants but were still appropriable into capital's value system.

The position of women's intellectual work as conflicted between the "natural" sensibility of household care and its production by circulating capital does affect women's bodies. In *The Professor*—Bronte's first novel, written in 1845–1846 but published posthumously in 1857, which many critics acknowledge as the rough draft of *Villette*—the professor's love interest, Frances, changes from inaction and a docile corporeality—"a corpse-like lack of animation" (89)—in a state of ignorance to an absolute mobility—"wakened to life,... she... could move with vivacity and alertness" (109)—when engaged in learning, to the point of eroticizing her acquisition of knowledge. Visibly revealing Frances's talents, these physical tensions between her domestic "quiescence" (89)—resistant to or even failing at market appropriations—and the energy of her marketable knowledge, propelled the girl's body into motion, indicating her potential as a teacher. The girl's body movement shows that she is entering, through schooling, into a relation to capital, but without a total alignment, as though the process of capitalization were still in conflict with the substance of its appropriation. In *Villette*, Lucy is similarly afflicted.

Left alone at school, with no employment or intellectual engagement over the holidays, Lucy's body literally becomes "lifeless" (173), "wasting and wearing" (174), without strength and compared to death and burial. Consumed with depression, Lucy wanders around until her body becomes immobilized, stilled in sickness, and collapses. The process of getting physically well and regaining physical and erotic vitality is the process that brings Lucy back to work at the school.

In *Villette*, this contradiction between nonmarketable and marketable forms of work is constructed into Lucy Snowe's femininity through her relation to the girls' school. In the middle of the novel, Lucy's friend M. de Bassompierre considers sending his daughter Polly to the school where Lucy teaches. M. de Bassompierre makes it clear that Polly's education is mostly for a good marriage, except if economic circumstances change, yet he also expresses admiration for what he calls Lucy's "success" and independence, the fact she is not a burden to others. By constructing women's work in a calculable form, the girls' school stages the development of women's service to the home as parallel to labor and appropriable by its terms, but sometimes anxiously or reluctantly so. Bronte shows the girls' school as producing a character—women's character in particular—*for* the market. Lucy's entry into the classroom establishes that the work of the caretaker as well as the work of the thinker can be rendered countable in commodity form.

The Girls' School as Transgression

In Modernism, the girls' school would be a temporary disruption to institutional practice, usually indicated by a type of female sexuality that fell out with convention. Even more fundamentally linked to strategic calculation, autonomous agency, and economic potential than Lucy or Frances, the girls' school in Modernism resembles the semiotic, an infantile corporeal fragmentation in Julia Kristeva's poetic language, where modern literature "attests to a 'crisis' of social structures and their ideological, coercive, and necrophilic manifestations" (15), a shattering of symbolic cohesion brought about through the "unceasing operation of the drives" (17) and primary processes but always in relation to a final closure of the socio-symbolic meaning. Both girls' animated bodies and the consciousness developed in the girls' schools are external and even antagonistic to normalization while always, as the semiotic, bringing stability to the symbolic stasis of institutional form. Girls in these accounts are anything but "relational," impossible to silence or to still, and certainly not cooperative.

This excessiveness of girls' bodies and sexualities in girls' school plots arises when women's bodies refuse the symbolic economy of women in the division of labor. One might consider, for example, Michel Foucault's 1978 "retrieved memoir" *Herculine Barbin,* where, once allowed to see inside the hidden fortress of the mid-nineteenth-century convent school, the reader learns its true secret to be that the headmistress has a penis. Once the girls' school reveals this secret, all sorts of unexpected misreadings and moral reversals ensue, as when, during a storm, Herculine, in shock from a clap of thunder, jumps out of bed into the palliative embrace of her teacher-nun Marie-des-Anges, only to find herself completely naked and visibly aroused. In the end, *Herculine Barbin* turns out to be a symbolic tragedy, where the institutional apparatuses of education, religion, law, and medicine are set in turmoil because the symbolic was wrongly assigned. This mis-assignment entailed, as one of its discomforts, "the prospect of being a *working woman*" (Barbin's emphasis; 20). Only when the designation "man" would be restored its functionality, in its proper body and for its proper job, is the convent institution again made secure.

The sexual, symbolic, and physical disorientation is often a cover-narrative for a deeper symbolic disturbance caused by the challenge of women's productive work to the sexual division between paid and unpaid labor time. Often, the sexual-symbolic problem of the girls' school plot erupts in the uneasy intersections between domestic, maternal socialization and caring functions with market value. In Dorothy Sayers's 1936 mystery-thriller *Gaudy Night,* for example, the protagonist Harriet Vane learns that the murder motive is the murderess' resentment over the loss of conjugal domesticity caused by the professionalization of women's scholarly labor in the Harriet's *alma mater,* the women's college of Oxford.

Colette is the writer who captures fundamentally the formation of girls' consciousness as economic capacity, precisely in its resistance to institutional appropriation, regimentation, and sexual control. Colette's quasi-autobiographical *Claudine in School,* published in 1900, imagines the girls' school as unabashedly in the business of training girls for the teaching profession, not predominantly for domestic or conjugal prospects as in *Villette.* Both the pleasure and the problem of the text appear through class inversions that are caused by this training but are woven through sexual play: "I had immense pleasure," Claudine characterizes her impressions of a dictation, "in hearing these daughters of grocers, cobblers and policemen meekly reciting and writing down parodies of the Romantic School" (37). Behind Claudine's sexual escapades and impish tricks, the girls' school upsets the expected correspondence between knowledge, language, and class identity.

In fact, what makes Claudine exude sexuality and pleasure, even as she does not engage in direct sexual acts beyond playful kissing of students and teachers alike, is that she seems always to know more than she should and more than either the other characters or the reader. Claudine *uses* knowledge against its intended, conventional usage and its established value. Claudine makes clear that girls, when they acquire certain kinds of school knowledge, also acquire capacities that cannot be domestically restricted: "She's not a girl you'd overlook," Claudine hears Rabastens, one of the schoolmasters, characterize her, "with that hair flowing down her back and all around her and those very naughty brown eyes! My dear chap, I believe that girl knows more things she oughtn't to know than she does about geography!" (23). She breaks the rules, sets up pranks, and misbehaves, causing havoc. Patricia Tillburg sees the main intention behind Colette's capriciousness as a way of defining as "labor" certain knowledge-practices (particularly in relation to immaterial and aesthetic production) that had not, before, found such currency or acceptance, especially for women. "I know we shall be just as absurd in twenty years' time," laughs one of her examiners at Claudine's response to a question about troubadours, "but that idea of a troubadour with a helmet and a lyre!...Run away quick, child, you'll get a good mark" (147). According to Tillburg, the girls' school during the Third Republic taught its students, including Colette, "a profound valorization of physical fitness and wage-paying craft labor that pushed uncomfortably against cultural dicta encouraging women to find moral contentment within the confines of a respectable marriage and home" (15). Colette was looking for new ways to capitalize her knowledge. What was counted as paid labor for women did not include craftwork or performance entertainment, the kind of work that Colette would later engage and try to legitimize as part of a paid economy. As in *Gaudy Night* and *Herculine Barbin,* the break from the institutional and symbolic apparatus—the excess—allows Claudine to produce meaning by setting what she knows into circulation and so to construct out of herself a mobile economic variable, a working potential of value. Girls' school literature tied Modernism's symbolic breaks to the maturing of girls' economic rationality and autonomous interest.

Into the Wild

Greg Mortenson reimagines the girls' school as participating in the work of exporting knowledge in order to defeat the impulse to violence erupting in Central Asia as "the terrorist threat." For Mortenson, "Young women are the single biggest potential agents of change in the developing world—a phenomenon that is sometimes referred to as the Girl Effect... In military parlance, girls' education is a 'force multiplier'" (*Stones,* 13).[5] Mortenson is orchestrating a reversal in the girls' school genre. The girl in the process of getting educated is no longer oppositional as an expression of autonomous interest in a break of symbolic and institutional form. Rather, the girls' school is revamped as the symbolic form of imperial state power. The girls' school is what marches into the heart of darkness to tame the wilderness and bring the violent savages into the light of civilization instead of, as in Claudine, an expression of the barbarism itself, needing to be tamed. By releasing girls into the productive landscape, the girls' school for Mortenson is able to move the developing world into capitalizability.[6] Merging with the girls' school narrative, imperialism is, here, envisioning itself as the disruption, a breaker of conventions.

In his attempts to build schools for girls in Pakistan and Afghanistan, Mortenson is constantly coming up against obstacles, *fatwas,* Taliban attacks, local traditions and resistances—just as Claudine comes up against teacher rules, examiners, and government superintendents—and mostly outsmarts them. The goal of his efforts is made particularly clear when he visits Shakeela, one of the graduates of a school Mortenson built. This is one of the very few examples that Mortenson gives of his encounters with the students who benefit from his schools. Shielding her face behind a shawl as her father compliments her, Shakeela is "poised and pretty at fifteen" (*Three Cups,* 207), and, smiling "confidently" (*Three Cups,* 207), informs the interviewer that she plans on attending medical school and becoming a doctor, though she is better in reading and language skills than in physics. As a doctor, Shakeela plans on going "to work wherever I am needed" (*Three Cups,* 208), being an "honor to the village" (*Three Cups,* 208) by serving others' needs. Mortenson's girls' schools are poised on the brink of the same cultural divisions faced by Lucy Snowe and Harriet Vane—between women's professional paid labor and family obligations, including care of the home. However, instead of women's capacity for professionalism appearing in the body as physical fitness, as in Claudine, or as uncontrollable urges and protrusions that challenge homogeneity and orthodoxy, as for Herculine, it materializes as an immobile, retiring, and obedient body, sexually both docile and inviting. The educated girl's body is no longer a destabilizing mobility, anxiously conflicted between an autonomous domesticity that cannot be reduced to its representation as calculable time and the claims of its marketability, but instead has settled into a marketable form. Girls' school tropes in *Three Cups of Tea* and *Stones Into Schools* are twisted into feel-good "success" stories of women who market their labor not for autonomous interest or professionalization or even trickery but, rather, for imperialism. That is, though taking its cue from historical literary representations of women's professionalism and its anxiously divided consciousness, Shakeela's inactive and retreating body—through which her role as "good student" and "non-terrorist" is attributed—extends the formulation of gender differences as learning about differences in the body through which the social scientific literature affirms help and cooperation in calculable terms as gendered labor-in-service.

The social scientific rendition of girls' bodies as exuding educational difference constructs girls' education as a site of intervention. Absorbed into imperialist narratives, such difference has a particular message: that girls educated for work marshal the economic capacity of imperialism's global power. The suggestion that developing countries are places of expanding girls' schooling carries with it the sense, from its literary legacy, that educated girls are poised between autonomous domestic economies and work that can be quantified as capital. The image of girls in schools redesigns ideologically the imperialist mission as adventurous men encountering helpless, eager, willing, and compliant potential female laborers who are good at cooperating. Mortenson's lie keys into a desire that girls' educational difference makes visible the potential extension of markets into the heretofore unpaid working time of women globally. The adoption of educational policy stereotypes—as feel-good success stories—into narratives about masculinity taming nature and violence in developing countries serves to make comforting imperialism's expanding labor markets despite the cultural destruction, alienation, violence, and disenfranchisement that such markets often cause to women.

Notes

1. "Reena," a 19-year-old member of the Revolutionary Association of the Women of Afghanistan, who uses this pseudo-name to travel undercover, mentions these aspects of girls' education in an interview with Amy Goodman on *Democracy Now!* "Ten Years after U.S. Invasion, Afghan War Rages on with No End in Sight" (October 7, 2011). http://www.democracynow.org/. Accessed: October 7, 2011. Annie Kelly reports in *The Guardian*, "A new report [by 16 NGOs] is warning that hard-won progress in girls' education in Afghanistan, heralded as one of few success stories of the last nine years, is increasingly under threat as international interest in reconstruction efforts ebbs away." Though expanding girls' education was originally seen as a "shining example" of the success of intervention, approximately one quarter never attend, many (especially in rural areas) have no access, and, according to the Afghan Ministry of Education, 47 percent have no actual building while 61 percent in some provinces remain closed, and there is little investment in

female teachers ("Afghan Girls' Education Backsliding as Donors Shift Focus to Withdrawal." *The Guardian* (February 24, 2011): http://www.guardian.co.uk/global-development/2011/feb/24/afghanistan-girls-education-report. Accessed: October 7, 2011).
2. Mortenson, *Stones into Schools*: "I also came away with the conclusion that the military is probably doing a better job than any other institution in the United States government—including the State Department, Congress, and the White House—of developing a meaningful understanding of the complex dynamics on the ground in Pakistan and Afghanistan" (257).
3. Meanwhile, single-sex state schools in the UK have fallen from 2500 to 400 over the last 40 years (Jackson, 227).
4. The research on test scores as a measure of predictability is inconclusive, at best. As Kenneth J. Saltman concludes from reviewing the research, "High stakes testing regimes do not achieve what they are designed to achieve. However, to think beyond efficacy to the underlying assumptions about 'achievement,' it is necessary to raise theoretical concerns. Theoretically, at the very least, the enforcement-oriented assumptions...fail to consider the limitations of defining 'achievement' through high-stakes tests, fail to question what knowledge and whose knowledge constitute legitimate or official curricula that students are expected to master, and fail to interrogate the problematic assumptions of learning modeled on digestion or commodity acquisition" (128).
5. None other than friend and hero of feminism and die-hard supporter of female intellectuals, Larry Summers, agrees: "An extensive body of recent research...has convinced me that once its benefits are recognized, investment in girls' education may well be the highest return investment available in the developing world...Expenditures on increasing the education of girls do not just meet the seemingly easy test of being more socially productive than military outlays. They appear to be far more productive than many other valuable categories of investment" (as cited in Herz and Sperling, 38). Lawrence H. Summers—formerly filling various roles in the Clinton administration's Treasury, chief economist of the World Bank, and then President Barack Obama's economic advisor—famously said, while he was president of Harvard University, that the reason there were so few professional women in science and engineering fields was because women had lower aptitudes.
6. "Unless that girl can land a job outside her home," Mortenson interprets the situation, "it is unlikely that her skills will translate into a substantial boost in her family's income...Aside from becoming a teacher, there are almost no jobs available for rural women outside the home" (*Stones*, 231).

Works Cited

American Association of University Women. "Separated by Sex: Title IX and Single-Sex Education." *American Association of University Women*, 2011. http://www.aauw.org/act/issue_advocacy/actionpages/upload/single-sex_ed111.pdf. Accessed: October 6, 2011.

Bronte, Charlotte. *Villette*. Edited by Helen M. Cooper. London and New York: Penguin Books, 2004.

Charania, Munira Moon. "Reading the Body: The Rhetoric of Sex, Identity and Discipline in Girls' Education." *International Journal of Qualitative Studies in Education* 23, no. 2 (May–June, 2010): 305–330.

Colette. "Claudine at School." In *The Complete Claudine*. Translated by Antonia White. New York: Farrar, Straus and Giroux, 1976.

Fanon, Frantz. *A Dying Colonialism*. Translated by Haaken Chevalier. New York: Grove, 1965.

Foucault, Michel. *Herculine Barbin: Being the Recently Discovered Memoirs of a Nineteenth-Century French Hermaphrodite*. Translated by Richard McDougall. New York: Pantheon Books, 1978, 1980.

Goodman, Amy. "Ten Years after U.S. Invasion, Afghan War Rages on With No End in Sight." *Democracy Now!* (October 7, 2011): http://www.democracynow.org/. Accessed: October 7, 2011.

Halpern, Diane F., Lise Eliot, Rebecca S. Bigler, Richard A. Fabes, Laura D. Hanish, Janet Hyde, Lynn S. Liben, Carol Lynn Martin. "The Pseudoscience of Single-Sex Schooling." *Science* (September 23, 2011): 1706–1707.

Herr, Kathryn and Emily Arms. "Accountability and Single-Sex Schooling: A Collision of Reform Agendas." *American Educational Research Journal* 41, no. 3 (Autumn 2004): 527–555.

Jackson, Janna. "'Dangerous Presumptions': How Single-Sex Schooling Reifies False Notions of Sex, Gender, and Sexuality." *Gender and Education* 22, no. 2 (March 2010): 227–238.

Kaminer, Wendy. "The Trouble with Single-Sex Schools." *The Atlantic* (April 1998): http://www.theatlantic.com/doc/199804/single-sex. Accessed: October 9, 2011.

Kelly, Annie. "Afghan Girls' Education Backsliding as Donors Shift Focus to Withdrawal." *The Guardian* (February 24, 2011): http://www.guardian.co.uk/global-development/2011/feb/24/afghanistan-girls-education-report. Accessed: October 7, 2011.

Krakauer, Jon. *Three Cups of Deceit*. New York: Anchor Books, 2011.

Kristeva, Julia. *Revolution in Poetic Language*. Translated by Margaret Waller. New York: Columbia University Press, 1984.

Levy, Anita. "Gendered Labor, the Woman Writer and Dorothy Richardson." *NOVEL: A Forum on Fiction* 25, no. 1 (Autumn, 1991): 50–70.

McCreary, Andrew J. "Public Single-Sex K-12 Education: The Renewal of Sex-Based Policy by Post-Race Politics, 1986–2006." *Journal of Law & Education* 40, no. 3 (July 2011): 461–497.

McNeil, Michele. "Single-Sex Schooling Gets New Showcase." *Education Week* (May 7, 2008): 20–22.

McRobbie, Angela. "Top Girls?" *Cultural Studies* 21, no. 4–5 (2007): 718–737.

Medina, Jennifer. "Boys and Girls Together, Taught Separately in Public School." *New York Times* (March 11, 2009): http://www.nytimes.com/2009/03/11/education/11gender.html. Accessed: October 8, 2011.

Mortenson, Greg. *Stones into Schools: Promoting Peace through Education in Afghanistan and Pakistan.* New York: Penguin, 2009.

Mortenson, Greg and David Oliver Relin. *Three Cups of Tea: One Man's Mission to Promote Peace...One School at a Time.* New York: Penguin, 2006.

Policy and Program Studies Service of the US Department of Education's Office of Planning, Evaluation, and Policy Development. "Single-Sex versus Coeducational Schooling: A Systematic Review." Washington, DC: US Department of Education, 2005, http://www.ed.gov/about/offices/list/opepd/reports.html.

Pollitt, Katha. "The Bitter Tea of Greg Mortenson." *The Nation* (May 16, 2011): 9.

Ruth, Jennifer. "Between Labor and Capital: Charlotte Brontë's Professional Professor." *Victorian Studies* 45, no. 2 (Winter 2003): 279–303.

Salomone, Rosemary C. *Same, Different, Equal: Rethinking Single-Sex Schooling.* New Haven and London: Yale University Press, 2003.

Saltman, Kenneth J. *Capitalizing on Disaster: Taking and Breaking Public Schools.* Boulder, CO and London: Paradigm Publishers, 2007.

Sax, Leonard. *Why Gender Matters: What Parents and Teachers Need to Know about the Emerging Science of Sex Differences.* New York and London: Doubleday, 2005.

Sayers, Dorothy L. *Gaudy Night.* New York: Harper Paperbacks, 1936.

Tilburg, Patricia A. *Colette's Republic: Work, Gender, and Popular Culture in France, 1870–1914.* New York and Oxford, UK: Berghahn Books, 2009.

2

Educating for Cosmopolitanism: Lessons from Cognitive Science

Mark Bracher

In her 2005 MLA Presidential Address, "On Rooted Cosmopolitanism," Domna Stanton proposed "cosmopolitanism as an educational ideal and a rich literary and cultural mine for our work" (629). She argued that although "we do not typically see ourselves as the heirs of cosmopolitanism,... what we, the teacher-scholars of the MLA, do in our many diverse ways is to exemplify and promote a cosmopolitan education" (629). Specifically,

> when we read "foreign" texts in the original or in translation, we advocate an encounter with people who are markedly different from and at the same time much like ourselves—a complex encounter made in a sympathetic effort to see the world as they see it and, as a consequence, to denaturalize our own views. Those pedagogical practices involve cosmopolitanism by implicitly rejecting parochial, chauvinistic beliefs in the exclusive value of our language, culture, nation or ethnos and by inherently embracing diversity as fundamental to the construction of the self in—and as—its relation to others. (629)

Stanton concluded her speech by calling for a concerted effort on the part of language and literature teacher-scholars to form our students into cosmopolitans: in "teaching the languages and the literatures of the world in the classroom," she declared, "*we must try to form citizens* not only *of* the world but also *for* the world" (638; first emphasis added; other emphases in original).

This is certainly a worthy aim, for the more cosmopolitans we form, the less violence and injustice there is likely to be. This is the case because "cosmopolitanism...require[s] us to acknowledge the humanity of others, [and] to intervene against active and passive injustice" (Lu, 264). "Understood as a fundamental devotion to the interests of humanity as a whole" rather than to more limited groups (Robbins, "Introduction" 1; see also Nussbaum, "Patriotism" 4, 7; Malcomson, 234; Anderson, 274), cosmopolitanism entails "a desire to change the world" (Malcomson, 234) so as "to diminish suffering regardless of colour, class, religion, sex and tribe" (Hollinger, 230). "The cosmopolitan ethical principle of the equal worth of all human beings as world citizens" (Heater, 9) "provides us with a morally compelling view of how our many worlds may meet, as they inevitably will, on terms of humanity, justice, and tolerance, which are the foundations of perpetual peace and friendship, rather than on terms of cruelty, inequity, and violence, the foundations of perpetual war and animosity" (Lu, 265; see also Robbins, "Cosmopolitanism" 49, 51).

What, then, beyond the general parameters noted by Stanton, are the specific learning objectives through which literary study can most effectively pursue the worthy aim of forming cosmopolitans? Contrary to the assumption of many of its proponents, cosmopolitan education must involve much more than the acquisition of knowledge about other peoples. As Derek Heater notes, "Knowledge and understanding about developing countries, which is sometimes almost equated with education for world citizenship..., misses the very heart of the matter" (172). Cosmopolitan education, Heater argues, "should rightly be as much about... *acquiring appropriate attitudes and behaviour patterns* as about acquiring knowledge" (177; emphasis added). But what are the "appropriate attitudes and behaviour patterns" for cosmopolitans? Or, as James Donald puts it, "What...would cosmopolitan...graduates *be* in the second decade of the 21st century? What could we reasonably expect such graduates to be able to *do*? And what knowledge and expertise would enable them to be what they need to be and to do what they need to do?" (296; emphasis in original).

It is thus necessary to begin by determining three things:

1. The specific behaviors that constitute cosmopolitanism (see Heater, 177)
2. The capabilities and habits of mind and heart that enable and motivate these behaviors (see Donald, 296; Skrbnis, 127), and
3. The types of educational practices that foster these cosmopolitan capabilities habits of mind and heart (see Stevenson, 258).

As various discussants of cosmopolitanism have noted, none of these tasks has yet been accomplished (Skrbnis, 127–128; Vertovec and Cohen, 21). Indeed, few proponents of cosmopolitanism explicitly identify the specific behaviors that cosmopolitanism entails, and many appear not even to have recognized that certain psychological changes, and hence also the experiences that produce these changes, are prerequisites for the establishment of cosmopolitanism (see Stevenson, 265). As Vertovec and Cohen have observed, "While the trend towards positively reappropriating notions of cosmopolitanism is to be welcomed for its socially and politically transformative potential, practically all the recent writings on the topic remain in the realm of rhetoric. There is little description or analysis of how contemporary cosmopolitan philosophies, political projects, outlooks or practices can be formed, instilled, or bolstered. In short, there are few recipes for fostering cosmopolitanism" (21; see also Robbins, "Introduction," 3; Beck, 29).

The first question, concerning the types of behavior that constitute cosmopolitanism, is fairly easy to answer: cosmopolitanism entails helping others who are in need, no matter who or where they are. Although commentators disagree on how much one should be expected to sacrifice in order to meet these obligations, there is considerable consensus regarding the existence of an obligation to help others in need, including distant strangers (see Appiah, 143–174). As Appiah puts it, for cosmopolitans, "every human being has obligations to every other" (144). The most general helping behaviors include, as we have already noted in passing, "assist[ing] others in danger or distress" (Heater, 185), "interven[ing] against active and passive injustice" (Lu, 264), and "diminish[ing] suffering regardless of colour, class, religion, sex and tribe" (Hollinger, 230). More specific behaviors include actions such as voting and activism in support of human rights and distributive justice for all individuals everywhere (see Tan).

What are the psychological factors, then, that lead people to act in ways that provide help for others, including distant strangers, who are in need? Here the discussions to date are considerably less helpful, for the psychological traits most commonly ascribed to cosmopolitans are incapable by themselves of producing the helping behavior that constitutes the substance of cosmopolitanism. As Skrbnis, Kendall, and Woodward observe, "commentators commonly suggest that in terms of 'disposition,' cosmopolitanism should be understood principally as an attitude of 'openness' toward others [sic] cultures" (127; see also Donald, 299). But as these authors go on to point out, "the notion of openness...is rather vague and diffuse. How is such openness manifested, and what are the sentiments that are embedded within the general attitudinal category of openness?" (127). Their own suggestions, however—"that 'cultural openness' can be manifested in various ways, including...in both intellectual and aesthetic domains" and that "it must also involve emotional and moral/ethical commitments," including "an empathy for and interest in other cultures" (127-128)—do little to advance our understanding of this issue, and the authors rightly conclude that "more research needs to address the specific elements of a cosmopolitan disposition" (128).

Other commentators have suggested that the key psychological factor in cosmopolitanism is a "larger loyalty" (Rorty) or a sense of global citizenship. Heater, for example, argues that cosmopolitanism depends on "an understanding of the nature and significance of world citizenship to the point where it is not questioned, ignored or derided, but accepted as a normal feature of one's social life" (185). Heater believes that if "more people...think more deeply that they belong to a global community and...accept the moral implications of that membership..., this might lead...to a global community in which 'the obligation to assist others in danger or distress was a powerful imperative'" (185). But since *national* citizenship does not motivate people to aid all other individuals in their own nation, it is hard to see how a sense of *global* citizenship would motivate them to aid distant strangers around the world.

The most significant psychological factor of cosmopolitanism that has been identified is compassion for strangers. As Stanton and others have pointed out, Martha Nussbaum has advocated a form of cosmopolitan education centered on literary study that promotes such compassion in readers (Stanton, 631-632; Donald, 303-304; Heater, 155; Vertovec and Cohen, 21). In *Cultivating Humanity*, Nussbaum claims, following Marcus Aurelius, that "to become world citizens we must not simply amass knowledge; we must also cultivate in ourselves a capacity for sympathetic imagination that will enable us to comprehend the motives and choices of people different from ourselves, seeing them not as forbiddingly alien and other, but as sharing many problems and possibilities with us" (85). Literature, Nussbaum maintains, is particularly crucial for cosmopolitanism because it promotes "an expansion of sympathies that real life cannot cultivate sufficiently" (*Cultivating*, 111). She concludes that "if the literary imagination develops compassion, and if compassion is essential for civic responsibility, then we have good reason to teach works that promote the types of compassionate understanding that we want and need" (*Cultivating*, 99).

As attractive as Nussbaum's argument is, however, it fails to offer evidence in support of the two key assumptions on which it is based: that "the literary imagination develops compassion" for real people (as opposed to fictional characters) and that "compassion is essential for civic responsibility." There is ample evidence to support the second proposition, that compassion for strangers leads people to assume responsibility for their welfare. There is ubiquitous anecdotal evidence that, as Robert Solomon observes, "one can hardly feel compassion without wanting to do something to change the world, to end the suffering" ("Defense," 244; see also Nussbaum, *Upheavals*, 335). And there is also significant empirical evidence supporting this point. As the psychologist Bernard Weiner explains, empirical studies demonstrate that emotions are the primary immediate causes of behavior: "Affects are the more proximal and more important determinants of behavior than thoughts are.... The proximal or immediate causes of conduct are affective reactions. That is, feelings are determined by thoughts, and then the personal actions are based on those feelings rather than on the underlying cognitions" (174, 82). And since the emotion of compassion—"being moved to distress by another person's suffering, and wanting to help" (Lazarus and Lazarus, 125)— "promotes help giving" (Weiner, 82), compassion for all humans, no matter who or where they are, advances the central cosmopolitan goal of "justice without borders" (Tan) by promoting help-giving for all people. There is thus good evidence to support Nussbaum's claim that increasing people's capacity to experience compassion for others who are quite different from them is central to the formation of cosmopolitans.

What, then, of Nussbaum's other assumption, that "the literary imagination develops compassion"? In *Cultivating Humanity*, Nussbaum claims that reading certain types of literature "develops compassion" (*Cultivating*, 99) and "broaden[s] sympathy" (*Cultivating*, 93). But here, too, she offers no substantial evidence to support her claim. Instead, her argument relies upon an equivocation: the compassion that is developed and broadened refers to both the compassion readers feel for characters in a text and the compassion they feel for real people outside the text. Nussbaum appears to assume that by arousing sympathy for characters, literature also automatically heightens and broadens readers' sympathy for real people. But while it is obvious that literature often develops compassion for characters in the text and also broadens readers' sympathy by extending it to characters who are strange and different from readers, it is not at all evident that readers who have their sympathy for characters developed and broadened go on to experience greater compassion for real strangers outside the text. Indeed, there are ample cases of individuals feeling great compassion for suffering characters and yet remaining indifferent or even hostile to real people in need who are right in front of them. Rudolph Hess, for example, is said to have wept for characters in an opera being performed during the Holocaust by condemned Jewish prisoners toward whom he remained impassive, and William James relates the story of a wealthy woman weeping at the plight of characters in a play while her servants waited outside in freezing weather (see Solomon, "Defense," 233). In sum, as Suzanne Keen has observed, there is little evidence to support the notion "that novel reading, by eliciting empathy, encourages prosocial action and good world citizenship" ("Theory," 224): "The [presumed] set of links among novel reading, experiences of narrative empathy, and altruism has not yet been proven to exist" (Keen, *Empathy*, viii). Indeed, Keen wonders "whether the expenditure of shared feeling on fictional characters might not waste what little attention we have for others on nonexistent entities" (*Empathy*, xxv). Noting that "the empirical evidence for causal links between fiction reading and the development of empathy in readers does not yet exist," Keen concludes that "whether novels on their own can actually extend readers' empathic imagination and make prosocial action more likely remains uncertain" (*Empathy*, 124, 116).

If experiencing sympathy for literary characters does not reliably lead to compassion—and thereby to help-giving—for strangers around the world, what, if anything, can literary study do to promote the compassion for real (as opposed to fictional) strangers that constitutes the core of cosmopolitanism? Nussbaum herself points to a more promising possibility in *Upheavals of Thought: The Intelligence of Emotions*, published several years after *Cultivating Humanity*. In the more recent book she recognizes that compassion is produced not only by empathy but also, and more fundamentally, by specific judgments, or appraisals, concerning people in need, and that therefore the most effective way to promote cosmopolitan compassion is to develop the capacity and habit of making these compassion-producing appraisals for all people in need. Following Aristotle and contemporary cognitive appraisal theories of emotion, Nussbaum identifies three judgments that are collectively both necessary and sufficient to produce compassion:

1. that another person has a serious need or is experiencing significant suffering (*Upheavals*, 306–311),
2. that the other is not responsible for this suffering or need (*Upheavals*, 311–315), and
3. that the other's well-being overlaps significantly with one's own (*Upheavals*, 315–321).

When people make these three judgments (explicitly or implicitly), they feel compassion, and when one or more of these judgments is absent, the compassion is either vitiated or absent entirely. Othering involves denying one or more of these three facts about the Other. And cosmopolitan justice requires recognizing each of these three facts about the Other. Thus, while empathy often serves as a path to compassion, it is in and of itself neither necessary nor sufficient to produce compassion (*Upheavals*, 327–335). A series of studies done to test the relative importance of empathy and perceived oneness with others in determining helping behavior found that "decisions to help were influenced by perceptions of oneness [with others] but not by levels of empathic concern" (Cialdini et al., 489). From these studies, the researchers concluded that "empathic concern is not the functional cause of helping but a concomitant of perceived oneness, which is the functional cause.... [I]t is because the self is [perceived to be] implicated in the other that the other's welfare is valued and promoted...; the primary role of empathic concern is to serve as an emotional signal of oneness" (Cialdini et al., 483, 491). It is thus not empathy but rather the three cognitive appraisals that are both necessary and sufficient for producing compassion and helping. This means that even if literature does not increase readers' empathy for peoples around the world, it could still increase compassion for them—and thus promote cosmopolitan "justice without borders"—by increasing their compassion-producing appraisals of Others. And this fact suggests that an education that aims to form students into cosmopolitans needs to develop their ability and inclination to make these three compassion-producing appraisals whenever they are valid—that is, concerning needy strangers everywhere.

Nussbaum recognizes this fact. "If we are persuaded that appropriate compassion is an important ingredient of good citizenship," she states, "then we will want to give public support to procedures by which this ability is taught" (*Upheavals*, 425). But while she acknowledges that this means cultivating the three appropriate judgments (*Upheavals*, 425), when she tries to explain how to do this through literary study, she falls back on the arguments from *Cultivating Humanity* about engaging students in perspective taking and empathy, stating "that empathic imagining is an extremely valuable aid to the formation of appropriate judgments and responses" (*Upheavals*, 432). But again, while it is true that empathy *can* be a path to compassion by leading to the three compassion-producing appraisals, it does not *necessarily* do so, as we have seen, and furthermore, as we have also noted, there is no clear evidence that empathy for characters leads to greater empathy for real people. For these reasons, we cannot expect empathic imagining regarding literary characters to be a reliable means of producing the three compassion-producing appraisals outside of literary texts.

The Cognitive Basis of Cosmopolitanism

We are thus left with the question of how the study of literature might promote the capacity and tendency to make the three compassion-producing judgments when they are warranted by the facts. Studies in social cognition and cognitive therapy provide the resources for answering this question. This research has found that our perceptions and judgments of other people—and hence also our emotions and actions regarding them—are produced by cognitive structures that govern multiple information-processing activities, and that when these structures are faulty, they can be corrected by engaging subjects in certain cognitive activities that, as I will show, literary study is ideally positioned to elicit.

What we need to identify are the cognitive structures that prevent people from arriving at the three compassion-producing judgments about others when these judgments are warranted by the facts. That is, what cognitive structures are responsible for the perception that certain people are not suffering when in fact they are, for the judgment that certain people are responsible for their plight when in fact they are not, and for the conclusion that certain people's being does not overlap with one's own when in fact it does? Here, too, cognitive science provides answers. Research in social cognition (i.e., people's perception and judgment of others) indicates that certain faulty cognitive structures that control our social information processing are largely responsible for the three incorrect, compassion-inhibiting judgments about others. Studies also demonstrate that when these faulty structures are replaced by more adequate ones that produce more accurate and comprehensive perceptions and judgments of others, the result is greater compassion and assistance for the Other.

Cognitive Schemas

The key cognitive structures that lead to the three mistaken judgments concerning the Other are cognitive schemas of particular groups of persons and of persons in general. Cognitive schemas are general knowledge structures that comprise multiple types and forms of knowledge concerning a particular category.[1] The basic types of knowledge include propositional knowledge (based in semantic memory), knowledge of particular instances and events (based in episodic memory), prototypes (generalizations or averages of these particular instances and events), and information-processing scripts (based in procedural memory). Any or all of these four types of knowledge can play a significant role in our perception, judgment, emotion, and action regarding other people, determining what we perceive about them, what we focus our *attention* on, what *inferences* and *suppositions* we make about them, what sort of information about them we *search for* when it is not present, what information about them is *encoded* in our memory (and how it is encoded), what we *recall* about them, what *emotions* we have in response to them, and what *actions* we take in regard to them, including what public policies we support.

Prototypes and Dehumanization

When it comes to perceiving and judging Others—people who belong to an out-group rather than to one of our ingroups—the type of knowledge that often plays the main role in guiding our assessment of them is the stereotype, which is a prototype that is automatically (and usually unconsciously) activated whenever we process information about a particular category of person.[2] Thus historically and even today, when many Westerners think of Africans, their perception, judgment, emotion, and action are governed by their prototype (stereotype) of Africans, which represents Africans as primitive, uncivilized, savage, barbaric, irrational, instinctual, passion-driven creatures. This stereotype biases the processing of information about African individuals and groups in such a way that Westerners perceive them as instances of the stereotype. That is, the stereotype serves as a template that governs each step of information processing. It leads people to *expect* that Africans will be irrational, uncivilized, and so on, to *overlook or discount* evidence to the contrary, to *focus on* and *search for* details that can be *interpreted* as evidence of these qualities, to simply *suppose* these details if they cannot be found, and to *encode* these details in memory.

This perception of Africans as primitive, uncivilized, savage, barbaric, irrational, instinctual, passion-driven creatures renders them subhuman, fundamentally different from, and hence possessing little or no overlap, sameness, or similarity with the Western perceiver, who consequently experiences little or no compassion for them and no motivation to help them. Studies of infrahumanization and dehumanization reveal that these judgments are produced by a contrast between one's prototype of the Other and one's prototype of the Human, and that the prototype of the human generally coincides with one's prototype of one's own group. Psychologists have found that when two groups are members of a superordinate group (e.g., Poles and Germans are both Europeans, and Europeans and Africans are both Human), members of each group tend to generalize the distinctive properties of their own group to the superordinate category (e.g., Human). This generalization leads the ingroup (e.g., Europeans) to appear more prototypical of the superordinate group (e.g., Humans) than the out-group (e.g., Africans). The out-group is thus seen to deviate "from the prototype of the superordinate category" and is devalued as a result (Waldzus and Mummendey, 467). As Waldzus, Mummendey, and Wenzel explain, "If the in-group is more prototypical than the out-group, then the out-group deviates from the prototype of the superordinate category, [and] [t]his deviation justifies negative attitudes towards the out-group" (Waldzus, Mummendey, and Wenzel, 77).

Research has also revealed that, conversely, people who recognize their perceived oneness or overlap with the Other exhibit greater compassion and helping behaviors toward the Other (Cialdini et al., 489–492; Levy, Freitas, and Salovey, 1224–1225). Several different laboratory studies based on various research models have shown that "hostility toward the outgroup is reduced...when the outgroup is perceived as equally prototypical to this superordinate category (Gaunt, 734). And ethnographic studies of people who helped members of out-groups have found that perceived oneness, or common humanity, was a key cause of this behavior. Political scientist Kristen Monroe conducted in-depth interviews with rescuers of Jews during the Holocaust, philanthropists, and Carnegie Hero Commission Award recipients and found that all of these altruists "saw themselves as individuals strongly linked to others through a shared humanity" and that "their cognitive-perceptual frameworks differed consistently and significantly from those of traditional rational actors in this one regard" (Monroe, 109). Monroe explains that while other factors have been put forward as explanations of altruism, they are not the crucial cause but rather mechanisms that trigger the perception of a shared humanity: "It is the perception of a shared humanity with the other that these external mechanisms trigger which remains critical, not the mechanisms themselves (Monroe, 110). She concludes that it is the "perception of themselves as individuals strongly linked to others through a shared humanity...that most successfully explains altruism. It is the only factor that consistently and systematically predicts altruism among all the individuals I interviewed" (Monroe, 110).

More generally, research has revealed that non-prejudiced people tend to operate with cognitive person-schemas that produce a "universalist orientation" to other people, "whereby perceivers selectively attend to, accentuate, and interpret similarities rather than differences between the self and others" (Phillips and Ziller, 420). Stephen Phillips and Robert Ziller assessed the differing degrees to which individuals operate with a universalist orientation by having them indicate how strongly they agreed or disagreed with statements such as, "At one level of thinking we are all of a kind," "I can understand almost anyone because I'm a little like everyone," and "The same spirit dwells in everyone" (Phillips and Ziller, 422). They found that people who scored high on this Universalist Orientation Scale (UOS) "were just as accepting of minority targets as they were of nonminority targets, rating them as equally attractive, equally similar, and equally desirable as a potential work partner," that high-UOS individuals "found minority persons more representative of humankind and more attractive than participants scoring low on the UOS" did, and that such individuals discriminate less on the basis of ethnicity" (Phillips and Ziller, 427, 429). Phillips and Ziller conclude that "orientation to similarity between the self and other... is critical to nonprejudice, whereas a difference orientation between self and other... sets the stage for prejudice" (Phillips and Ziller, 421). This is because

> universal orientation avoids the first treacherous act in interpersonal relations, that is, the separation of self and other, which tends to be followed by an invidious comparison of the self and other, to justify the separation. Through the simple act of orienting toward differences between self and others, the foundation is set for conflict rather than accord.... Nonprejudice [in contrast,] begins with an orientation toward similarities between self and other, followed by an integration, or the perception of unity between the self and other even to the extent of seeing the self reflected in the other. (Phillips and Ziller, 430)

Research has, in addition, revealed two basic forms in which out-groups are perceived to deviate from the category of the Human. The most common form involves denying that the Other possesses uniquely human (UH) qualities that distinguish humans from other animals, such as "cognitive sophistication, culture, refinement, socialization, and internalized moral sensibility," including "industriousness, inhibition, and self-control" (Haslam, 256). The other form of dehumanization denies that the Other possesses certain qualities that are central to human nature (HN), such as interpersonal warmth, drive, and vivacity (Haslam, 257). The first (UH) mode of dehumanization characterizes the Western view of the Other, including Africans. Nick Haslam describes the various ways in which Westerners deny uniquely human attributes to their various Others:

> ethnic and racial others have been represented, both in popular culture and in scholarship, as barbarians who lack culture, self-restraint, moral sensibility, and cognitive capacity. Excesses often accompany these deficiencies: the savage has brutish appetites for violence and sex, is impulsive and prone to criminality, and can tolerate unusual amounts of pain.... A consistent theme in this work is the likening of people to animals. In racist descriptions Africans are compared to apes and sometimes explicitly denied membership of the human species. Other groups are compared to dogs, pigs, rats, parasites, or insects. Visual depictions caricature physical

features to make ethnic others look animal-like. At other times, they are likened to children, their lack of rationality, shame, and sophistication seen patronizingly as innocence rather than bestiality. (Haslam, 252–253)

Haslam notes that that the uniquely human characteristics that are denied to the Other also often include a distinct, individual identity that allows individuals in the out-group to be distinguished from each other: agency, the ability to make choices and take effective action; community, or participation in a web of interpersonal relationships involving mutual care and concern; prosocial values, such as equality, helpfulness, and forgiveness, which demonstrate that the group has transcended animal hedonism; and certain "secondary" emotions, such as compassion, guilt, and shame, which are presumed not to exist among animals (Haslam, 254–255). Haslam reports that when people are perceived to lack any of these uniquely human emotions, values, or modes of being, they "lose the capacity to evoke compassion and moral emotions, and may be treated as means toward vicious ends. People who aggress [against them] are spared self-condemnation and empathic distress if their identification with [them] is blocked" by such dehumanizing perceptions (Haslam, 254).

This form of dehumanization leads to each of the three compassion- and aid-denying perceptions. Obviously, it profoundly reduces, if not eliminates entirely, any perception of sameness or overlap with the out-group. But it also significantly reduces the perception of the out-group's suffering, particularly emotional suffering, since animals are generally assumed not to suffer as intensely, either physically or emotionally, as humans (see Costello and Hodson, 4). And this animalizing dehumanization also blocks the perception that the out-group doesn't deserve its suffering or degraded state, since animals aren't thought to deserve a higher quality of life. As Costello and Hodson note, "Portrayals of outgroups as 'subhumans' who are less capable of experiencing emotions and/or pain render the outgroup less deserving of compassion and respect...in the same way that non-human animals are morally excluded for the purposes of exploitation by humans" (Costello and Hodson, 4). Thus insofar as "animals are already defined as lower-life fated for exploitation and slaughter, the designation of lesser humans as animals pave[s] the way for their subjugation and destruction" (Patterson; quoted in Costello and Hodson, 5).

Changing Faulty Person-Schemas

The key to increasing the defining element of cosmopolitanism—helping distant others who are in need—is thus to increase people's recognition of their sameness and overlap with Others. Changing their habitual distorted—and sometimes dehumanizing—perception of Others, however, requires much more than evidence and logical argument. It requires replacing not just faulty propositional beliefs about Others but also multiple nonpropositional forms of knowledge. These nonpropositional forms of knowledge include prototypes, exemplars, and information-processing routines. Prototypes, the most familiar form of which is the stereotype, are models incorporating what are taken to be the most typical features of members of a given category. Prototypes come in multiple forms, including concepts, prototypic individuals, prototypic body images, episode scripts, life scripts, prototypic emotions, and action scripts. Prototypes (including stereotypes) distort perception by automatically attributing all of the prototypical features to any individual who is perceived as belonging to that particular category. Exemplars are individual instances of a particular category, and they occur in the same multiple forms as prototypes, which in fact are formed out of exemplars when similar exemplars reach a critical mass. Exemplars function in the same way as prototypes, transferring their features to any given individual who is identified as a member of the same category. Information-processing routines direct our expectations, attention, information search, inferences, suppositions, and emotional responses to other people, and any or all of these information-processing steps can be misdirected by these routines

Faulty Prototypes of Africans

Each of these forms of nonpropositional knowledge—prototypes, exemplars, and information-processing routines—can produce the perception that the Other bears no similarity to oneself and thus also facilitate the judgment that the Other is not suffering and/or deserves to suffer. Consider the various forms of the Western prototype of Africans and how they deny Westerners' sameness with Africans. *Concepts* used to describe Africans include negative terms of binary oppositions that have no overlap with their positive counterparts. These binary oppositions include civilized/uncivilized, rational/irrational, cultured/barbaric, adult/childlike, rational/ irrational, and humane/savage. Describing Africans with the infra- and dehumanizing terms of these dichotomous pairs effectively denies their full humanity and obscures any significant sameness or overlap between Africans and Westerners.

Prototypic individual figures of Africans embody or invoke similar dichotomous oppositions between Africans and Westerners. One prime example is the African hunter, who is counterposed to the Western farmer, laborer, and entrepreneur (hunting in the West being no longer an occupation but rather a form of recreation or sport). Another example is the African warrior that invokes, and is sometimes explicitly replaced by, the figure of the head-hunter or "spear-chucker," and which is counterposed to the Western soldier, who operates with sophisticated weaponry and technology. These prototypic individuals are often supplemented by *prototypic body images* that also connote infra- or nonhuman status. Such images include men wearing only a loincloth or a penis sheath and barebreasted women, with the lack of clothing being equated to lack of civilization and instinctual restraint. Other overlap-denying images include non-Western forms of makeup, jewelry, and body piercings, tattoos, scarifications, and distortions, as well as skin color and hair and facial features that contrast with their prototypical Caucasian counterparts.

Overlap between Africans and Westerners is further denied by the prototypical actions and events, or *episode scripts*, attributed to Africans by the Western stereotype. Prototypic episode scripts include hunting and foraging in the jungle with technologically rudimentary tools and implements; warring with other tribes (rather than nations), dressed in war paint and animal parts (rather than camouflage uniforms and night vision goggles), using "primitive" weapons such as spears and blowguns (rather than automatic rifles, armored vehicles, aircraft, smart bombs, and drones), and emitting shrieking war cries while shaking spears and shields (rather than moving silently and professionally toward the enemy); and ceremonies involving midnight dances to the beat of jungle drums in the light of a bonfire while dressed in "primitive" costumes and emitting "eerie" sounds (rather than sitting or marching in a calm, "orderly" fashion). Prototypic episode scripts of Africans notably do not include any farming activities (clearing land, planting crops, cultivating them, irrigating them, harvesting them, storing them, caring for domesticated animals, etc.), fishing, preparing food to eat, caring for children, courting, making tools, implements, and weapons, building and repairing houses, or socializing, or governing.

The *life scripts* attributed to Africans are similarly impoverished and overlap-obscuring. The prototypical African life story as embodied in the Western stereotype involves little planning, long-term projects, or collective projects; rather, the prototypical African life involves living in the moment, largely hand-to-mouth, guided by one's instincts. Pursuing personal ambitions and collective goals, raising children, aspiring and planning for their futures, and taking action to ensure those futures are entirely absent from the African life script embodied in the Western stereotype.

These various prototypes often function in concert, even interwoven with each other. And they are also mutually imbricated with the *prototypic emotions* of Westerners regarding Africans, the emotions both resulting from and helping to produce the faulty judgment that Africans have little or nothing significant in common with Westerners. As we saw with compassion, emotions are products of one's appraisal of one's situation or the object of one's attention: when certain specific appraisals of the Other are made, a certain emotion will follow. The various Western prototypes of Africans produce certain prototypic emotions in Westerners because of the specific appraisals they produce. Thus Westerners feel indifference toward Africans because they perceive them as creatures who are beneath them, and they feel disdain, contempt, and even anger toward them insofar as they see them as not only as beneath them but as potentially infecting Westerners or contaminating them with their inferiority. Westerners feel disgust at the supposed bestial nature of Africans. Westerners feel fear and anger at Africans' supposed inclination, as bestial creatures, to do harm to Westerners. And at best, Westerners feel condescending pity concerning not just Africans' deprived state but also their debased nature.

Such emotions are produced by the various other prototypes just discussed, because these prototypes filter and fabricate information about Africans in such a manner as to produce appraisals of Africans that result in the respective emotions. Conversely, these prototypic emotions themselves produce distorted information processing that leads to the judgment that Africans are a subspecies that has no sameness or overlap with Europeans. That is, these emotions not only result from the respective appraisals mentioned, they also function to guide information processing toward such appraisals (see Oatley et al., 258–287; Clore et al.). Fear, for example, orients one to expect, search for, focus on, infer, and suppose threats in the object of one's appraisal. Anger, similarly, prejudices one toward appraising others' intentions as harmful, and disdain, contempt, and disgust cause one to recoil from the Other, thus precluding the perception of other, more benign attributes that these objects might contain. This mutual production of emotions and appraisals can result in a vicious circle in which faulty cognitive appraisals produce these unjust emotions, which in turn distort information processing in ways that reproduce the faulty appraisals, and so on.

And finally, the Western stereotype of Africans includes *action scripts*, prototypic actions for dealing with Africans. These actions follow naturally from the judgment (produced by the other prototypes we have just discussed) that Africans are subhuman and thus have no sameness or overlap with Westerners, a judgment that itself underlies the prototypic emotions, which serve as a source of the action scripts (insofar as each emotion includes a specific action tendency as one of its essential components) and which also supply most if not all of the motive force behind the prototypic actions. These action scripts include ignoring and neglecting

Africans, as the West has often done in response to famine and genocide there (in contrast to its response to similar events in Europe); outright exploitation, domination, and enslavement of Africa and Africans, of which there is a long and sordid history on the part of the West; and efforts to variously "civilize," convert, and "save" Africans from their debased lives—efforts that are at best ethnocentric and paternalistic and at worst a cover for, and another form of, exploitation and domination. Like emotions, action scripts do not just result from judgments, they also influence judgments, by embodying various forms of tacit knowledge (which can of course be false). They do so by first providing a cover of legitimacy and respectability for the judgments on which they are based. In addition, even when no action is taken, the ready accessibility of specific action scripts biases information processing in the direction of the judgments that underlie the action.

Because of these multiple forms of prototype knowledge contained in the Western stereotype of Africans, even if Westerners subscribe to the *proposition* that Africans are fully human, their perceptions, judgments, emotions, and actions (including public policies) regarding Africans will still be distorted by the implicit belief, based in these various prototypes, that Africans are *not* as fully human as Westerners. That is, the various elements of the prototypical African will continue to operate beneath the threshold of consciousness and will override Westerners' conscious, propositional knowledge to produce distorted, dehumanizing perceptions, judgments, emotions, and actions regarding Africans. This basic process has been documented many times with what is called aversive or modern racism, the often subtle and usually unconscious discrimination that white Americans who hold antiracist values manifest toward African Americans (see Jones, 124–130; 150–160).

Correcting Faulty Information-Processing Structures

Preventing the dehumanizing and overlap-obscuring cognitions of the Other, then, requires more than just getting people to subscribe to correct propositional knowledge concerning the full humanity of the Other. It requires correcting each of the perception- and judgment-distorting prototypes of the Other that individuals hold. With regard to Westerners' cognitions of Africans, this means correcting each of the prototypes just discussed, since these generally have greater power in guiding information processing than propositional knowledge does (see Bracher, "Schema" and *Radical*). Several practices can contribute to correcting faulty prototypes. Most importantly, such correction requires the encoding in memory of powerful exemplars of Africans demonstrating their sameness with Westerners rather than just their differences. If individual exemplars of this sort are sufficiently salient and emotionally powerful, they can interfere with or even substitute for the faulty prototype in guiding information processing. In addition, when a critical mass of such exemplars is encoded in memory, they form into a prototype of their own, which can replace the dehumanizing prototypes as the default templates guiding information processing about Africans.

Developing metacognition can also play a valuable role in correcting faulty prototypes: by becoming aware of their multiple forms of flawed prototypes of the Other and understanding how these prototypes operate automatically and outside their awareness, people can develop automatic cues to apprehend this process, interrupt it, and engage in conscious reappraisal of the Other—actions that can themselves become automatic with sufficient repetition. This metacognition, moreover, can include an awareness of each of the various information-processing steps that a thorough and more adequate assessment of the Other would require and then consciously direct one's performance of each of these steps (see Wells, 120–131).

Literary Texts as Schema-Altering Apparatuses

Literature engages readers in each of these schema-altering processes, and teachers who are aware of them and understand how they work can engage students in reading, interpretive, and other activities in class and at home that reinforce these processes and thus contribute significantly to the correction of the three faulty judgments regarding the Other. One of the most basic and most important things teachers can do to promote these corrective processes is to select texts that provide multiple corrective exemplars for each of the prototype categories (i.e., prototypic individuals, prototypic body images, episode scripts, etc.). Simply having students read such texts, however, will not usually be sufficient to alter their faulty prototypes of the Other. For such a change to take place, students must, in addition to encountering the corrective exemplars in the text, also *recognize these textual elements as corrective exemplars and encode them as such in their memories*. Teachers can promote such recognition and encoding not only by framing the corrective exemplars as such for their students but also by instructing students to expect, search for, and focus on such corrective exemplars as they read the text, and by giving students writing assignments in which they describe these exemplars in detail and explain how they are more valid than the faulty prototypes they are countering. The encoding in memory can be further promoted by requiring students to recall these exemplars on exams—a practice that is enhanced by providing students with study questions before the exam that prompt them to encode these multiple corrective exemplars firmly in their memory so that they are readily accessible at exam time—and, more importantly, after the exam as well.

In addition, teachers can help students develop metacognition and correct their faulty information-processing routines through certain kinds of reading instructions and writing assignments. For reading, teachers can instruct their students to expect, search for, focus on, infer, and suppose the existence of information concerning the Other's full humanity and fundamental sameness with themselves—and also to be alert to their own emotions and action tendencies regarding the Other. Teachers can also have their students write about their actual, faulty information processing while reading a particular text, instructing them to notice, describe, and assess the adequacy of the various information-processing acts they engaged in while reading the text. One of the most effective ways for developing metacognition and correcting faulty information-processing routines is to have students keep a diary recording their cognitive encounters (in memory, in imagination, or in actuality, as well as in reading) with the Other, noting the information-processing routines (expectations, inference, supposition, etc.) that they activate in these encounters and assessing the accuracy and consequences of this processing—that is, identifying how the various information-processing acts they engage in work either to obscure or to apprehend the Other's humanity and sameness with themselves.[3]

When students have acquired a critical mass of corrective exemplars of the Other and have developed a certain degree of metacognition regarding their own information processing, their humanity- and sameness-recognizing information processing of the Other can be developed further by having them read texts that represent the Other in ways that obscure or even deny the Other's humanity and sameness with the reader. The reading and writing instructions for these texts should be to note the text's silences and distortions and to provide—through information search, inference, or supposition—the missing or corrective information concerning the Other's full humanity and overlap with oneself. Thus, for reading *Heart of Darkness*, students can be instructed to search for, infer, and/or suppose information about the Congolese people that demonstrate their full humanity and overlap with themselves. Such assignments can involve various deconstructive, psychoanalytic, Marxian, or historicist analyses, such as searching the text's margins for indications of the Other's humanity, inferring the Other's humanity and sameness with themselves from certain qualities or behaviors that the text attributes to the Other and/or to the protagonist's responses to the Other, or drawing on evidence from outside the text to correct the faulty prototypes promoted by the text. For all of these activities, the key is to look for self-other overlap, similarities, sameness.

Notes

1. The term schema is sometimes defined more narrowly to mean abstract knowledge, in distinction from exemplars, prototypes, and information-processing routines. In adopting a broader, more inclusive definition of the term, I am following the usage of Taylor and Crocker, Moskowitz, and others.
2. For a discussion of when prototypes count as stereotypes and when they do not, see Hogan, *Conformism*, 126.
3. The schema-correcting techniques described here are derived largely from Young et al.; Wells; Griffith; Padesky; Smucker and Niederee; and Sookman and Pinard.

Works Cited

Anderson, Amanda. "Cosmopolitanism, Universalism, and the Divided Legacies." In *Cosmopolitics: Thinking and Feeling beyond the Nation*. Edited by Pheng Cheah and Bruce Robbins. Minneapolis: University of Minnesota Press, 1998, 265–289.
Appiah, Kwame Anthony. *Cosmopolitanism: Ethics in a World of Strangers*. New York: Norton, 2006.
Beck, Ulrich. "The Cosmopolitan Society and its Enemies." *Theory, Culture & Society* 19, no. 1–2 (2002): 17–44.
Bracher, Mark. *Social Symptoms of Identity Needs: Why We Have Failed to Solve Our Social Problems, and What to Do about It*. London: Karnac, 2009.
———. *Radical Cognitive Politics: Protest Novels, Schema Criticism, and the Pursuit of Social Justice*. Austin: University of Texas Press, 2013.
———. "Schema Criticism: Literature, Cognitive Science, and Social Justice." *College Literature*. Forthcoming.
Cialdini, Robert B., Stephanie L. Brown, Brian P. Lewis, Carol Luce, and Steven L. Neuberg. "Reinterpreting the Empathy-Altruism Relationship: When One into One Equals Oneness." *Journal of Personality and Social Psychology* 73, no. 3 (1997): 481–494.
Clore, Gerald L., Karen Gasper, and Erika Garvin. "Affect as Information." In *Affect and Social Cognition*. Edited by Joseph P. Forgas. Mahwah, NJ: Erlbaum, 2001, 121–144.
Costello, Kimberly and Gordon Hodson. "Exploring the Roots of Dehumanization: The Role of Animal-Human Similarity in Promoting Immigrant Humanization." *Group Processes & Intergroup Relations* 13 (2009): 3–22.
Donald, James. "Internationalisation, Diversity and the Humanities Curriculum: Cosmopolitanism and Multiculturalism Revisited." *Journal of Philosophy of Education* 41, no. 3 (2007): 289–308.

Gaunt, Ruth. "Superordinate Categorization as a Moderator of Mutual Infrahumanization." *Group Processes & Intergroup Relations* 12 (2009): 731–746.

Griffith, Lucy F. "Combining Schema-Focused Cognitive and Psychodrama: A Model for Treating Clients with Personality Disorders." *Journal of Group Psychotherapy, Psychodrama, and Sociometry* 55 (2003): 128–140.

Haslam, Nick. "Dehumanization: An Integrative Review." *Personality and Social Psychology Review* 10 (2006): 252–264.

Heater, Derek. *World Citizenship: Cosmopolitan Thinking and its Opponents.* New York: Continuum, 2002.

Hogan, Patrick Colm. *The Culture of Conformism.* Durham, NC: Duke University Press, 2001.

Hollinger, David A. "Not Universalists, Not Pluralists: The New Cosmopolitans Find Their Own Way." In *Conceiving Cosmopolitanism: Theory, Context, and Practice.* Edited by Steven Vertovec and Robin Cohen. New York: Oxford University Press, 2002, 227–239.

Jones, James M. *Prejudice and Racism,* 2nd ed. New York: McGraw-Hill, 1997.

Keen, Suzanne. "A Theory of Narrative Empathy." *Narrative* 14 (October 2006): 207–236.

———. *Empathy and the Novel.* New York: Oxford University Press, 2007.

Lazarus, Richard S. and Bernice N. Lazarus. *Passion and Reason: Making Sense of Our Emotions.* New York: Oxford University Press, 1994.

Levy, Sheri R., Antonio Freitas, and Peter Salovey. "Construing Action Abstractly and Blurring Social Distinctions: Implications for Perceiving Homogeneity among, but Also Empathizing with and Helping Others." *Journal of Personality and Social Psychology* 83, no. 5 (2002): 1224.

Lu, Catherine. "The One and Many Faces of Cosmopolitanism." *The Journal of Political Philosophy* 8, no. 2 (2000): 244–267.

Malcomson, Scott L. "The Varieties of Cosmopolitan Experience." In *Cosmopolitics: Thinking and Feeling beyond the Nation.* Edited by Pheng Cheah and Bruce Robbins. Minneapolis: University of Minnesota Press, 1998, 233–245

Monroe, Kristen Renwick. *The Heart of Altruism: Perceptions of a Common Humanity.* Princeton: Princeton University Press, 1996.

Moskowitz, Gordon B. "On Schemas and Cognitive Misers: Mental Representations as the Building Blocks of Impressions." *Social Cognition: Understanding Self and Others.* New York: Guilford, 2005, 153–192.

Nussbaum, Martha C. "Patriotism and Cosmopolitanism." *For Love of Country: Debating the Limits of Patriotism.* Edited by Joshua Cohen. Boston: Beacon Press, 1996, 2–17.

———. *Cultivating Humanity: A Classical Defense of Reform in Liberal Education.* Cambridge, MA: Harvard University Press, 1997.

Nussbaum, Martha C. *Upheavals of Thought: The Intelligence of Emotions.* New York: Cambridge University Press, 2001.

Oatley, Keith, Dacher Keltner, and Jennifer M. Jenkins. *Understanding Emotions.* 2nd ed. Malden, MA: Blackwell, 2006.

Padesky, Christine A. "Schema Change Processes in Cognitive Therapy." *Clinical Psychology and Psychotherapy* 1 (1994): 267–278.
Phillips, Stephen T. and Robert C. Ziller, "Toward a Theory and a Measure of the Nature of Nonprejudice." *Journal of Personality and Social Psychology* 72 (1997): 420–434.
Robbins, Bruce. "Introduction, Part I: Actually Existing Cosmopolitanisms." In *Cosmopolitics: Thinking and Feeling beyond the Nation*. Edited by Pheng Cheah and Bruce Robbins. Minneapolis: University of Minnesota Press, 1998, 1–19.
Rorty, Richard. "Justice as a Larger Loyalty." *The Rorty Reader*. Edited by Christopher J. Voparil and Richard J. Bernstein. New York: Wiley-Blackwell, 2010.
Skrbis, Zlatko, Gavin Kendall, and Ian Woodward. "Locating Cosmopolitanism: Between Humanist Ideal and Grounded Social Category." *Theory, Culture & Society* 21, no. 6 (2004): 115–136.
Smucker, Mervin R. and Jan Niederee. "Treating Incest-Related PTSD and Pathogenic Schemas through Imaginal Exposure and Rescripting." *Cognitive and Behavioral Practice* 2 (1995): 63–93.
Solomon, Robert C. "In Defense of Sentimentality." In *Emotion and the Arts*. Edited by Mette Hjort and Sue Laver. New York: Oxford University Press, 1997: 225–245.
Sookman Debbie and Gilbert Pinard. "Integrative Cognitive Therapy for Obsessive-Compulsive Disorder: A Focus on Multiple Schemas." *Cognitive and Behavioral Practice* 6 (1999): 351–362.
Stanton, Domna C. "Presidential Address 2005: On Rooted Cosmopolitanism." *PMLA* 121, no. 3 (2006): 627–640.
Stevenson, Nick. "Cosmopolitanism and the Future of Democracy: Politics, Culture and the Self." *New Political Economy* 7, no. 2 (2002): 251–267.
Tan, Kok-Chor. *Justice without Borders: Cosmopolitanism, Nationalism and Patriotism*. New York: Cambridge University Press, 2004.
Taylor, Shelley E. and Jennifer Crocker. "Schematic Bases of Social Information Processing." In *Social Cognition: The Ontario Symposium*. Edited by E. Tory Higgins, C. Peter Herman, and Mark P. Zanna. Hillsdale, NJ: Erlbaum, 1981, 89–134.
Vertovec, Steven and Robin Cohen, eds. "Introduction: Conceiving Cosmopolitanism." *Conceiving Cosmopolitanism: Theory, Context, and Practice*. New York: Oxford University Press, 2002, 1–22.
Waldzus, Sven and Amélie Mummendey. "Inclusion in a Superordinate Category, In-Group Prototypicality, and Attitudes Towards Out-Groups." *Journal of Experimental Social Psychology* 40 (2004): 466–477.
Waldzus, Sven, Amélie Mummendey, and Michael Wenzel. "When 'Different' Means 'Worse': In-Group Prototypicality in Changing Intergroup Contexts." *Journal of Experimental Social Psychology* 41 (2005): 76–83.
Weiner, Bernard. *Judgments of Responsibility: A Foundation for a Theory of Social Conduct*. New York: Guilford Press, 1995.
Wells, Adrian. *Emotional Disorders and Metacognition*. New York: Wiley, 2000.
Young, Jeffrey D., Janet S. Klosko, and Marjorie E. Weishaar. *Schema Therapy: A Practitioner's Guide*. New York: Guilford Press, 2003.

3

Learning to Be a Psychopath: The Pedagogy of the Corporation

Kenneth J. Saltman

In his book and film *The Corporation* (2005), Joel Bakan suggests that since legally the corporation is treated as a human person, we ought to ask: What kind of person is the corporation exactly?[1] His answer: "A psychopath." Bakan points to the key characteristics shared by psychopaths and corporations, including disregard for the well-being of others, lack of conscience, coldly calculated self-interested behavior, and grandiosity. Psychiatry classifies psychopaths as suffering from "anti-social personality disorder." For Bakan, corporations behave in antisocial ways by being legally obligated to maximize shareholder profit in any way possible within the bounds of the law.

An oil corporation makes a calculated decision to squeeze extra profit by risking the destruction of an ocean. An automotive corporation calculates the six dollars per human death saved by not recalling a part that explodes in a crash because the insurance payouts are cheaper than the recall. A news corporation willfully lies on a news program about the proven cancer risks of a growth hormone in milk to please advertisers and maximize advertising revenue. A business machine manufacturer does business with a fascist war enemy. A fruit company uses wealth and influence to overthrow a democratically elected government in favor of a military dictatorship. The examples are endless.[2] As Bakan contends, corporate personhood and limited liability are held in place only by human-made laws that could be changed to give priority to public interest over corporate profit. People who are psychopaths have, according to

Jared DeFife, clinical psychology research scientist and associate director of the Laboratory of Personality and Psychopathology, "a certain set of personality traits that includes emotional shallowness, superficial charm, impulsivity with poor judgment, deceitfulness, unreliability, manipulation, and disregard for the feelings (and well-being) of others."[3] Likewise, corporations externalize the social costs of their profit-motivated activities with little regard for the human consequences.

Corporations invest elaborately in superficially charming consumers with fantastic associations between products and a dreamworld of consumption.[4] Corporate leaders are required to make fast—if not impulsive—egoistic decisions always dictated by an interpretation of what will best serve the bottom line. Corporations keep their financial dealings and intentions and strategies from the public and, when confronted, frequently employ deception to evade responsibility for destructive acts and to compete in the marketplace. Such deception includes the systematic use of corporate spies and contracted disinformation campaigns. Corporations produce an image of themselves as reliable and stable, rational and benevolent, and yet will fire thousands of workers, discontinue a product or parts, aggressively lobby for socially destructive deregulations, or offshore production with no notice at all. Corporations are master manipulators and hire professional manipulators and propagandists from the public relations, advertising, and influence industries to achieve their aims. As Bakan rightly argues, corporate psychopathology is not mitigated by either corporate social responsibility efforts or by virtuous individuals being in their employ. Ultimately, corporations are legally beholden to shareholders to maximize profit by any means necessary. Corporations may do altruistic or "socially responsible" projects but only if they contribute to expanding profit and not if it threatens profits. Hence, corporate codes of social responsibility do not mitigate a systemic tendency for externalizing destruction onto the public. The ineffectiveness of voluntary ethical codes is particularly glaring in the sweatshop, oil, and beverage industries as socially destructive practices return as soon as media attention wanes.[5] Nor can corporate behavior be understood as being reliant upon the virtues and goodwill of particular corporate leaders. The leading scholar on psychopaths, Bob Hare, who created the most widely used diagnostic test for psychopathy (The Psychopath Test) contends that psychopaths are overrepresented four-fold relative to the general population in the ranks of business leadership. Hare's perspective complements Bakan's in that both presume that the traits necessary for success for individuals in the business corporation are the same as the traits that are institutionally valued by it.

While the majority of popular discourse about psychopaths is represented by sensationalist scare stories and true crime tabloid television, the scholarly discourse can be divided into three types:

I. Biological Determinism

Hare's checklist can allegedly identify psychopaths through a survey, and it has come to be widely used in prisons and parole hearings to keep incarcerated those who score highly. Scientific study of psychopathology has tended to focus on brain science and in particular differences in amygdala function in psychopaths and non-psychopaths as a way of explaining the absence of empathy for others felt by psychopaths.[6] MRI studies purport to show that the brains of the two groups respond differently when shown grisly violent images: non-psychopaths fire up with activity for fear and stress while psychopaths register pleasure. The assumption throughout much of the scientific literature is that psychopathology is a function of broken biology that, if understood, could be potentially cured through surgical or pharmacological intervention. This is a view in which behavior can be read off biology—a view consistent with socio-evolutionary biology and conservative strains of biopolitics in US political science.[7] While some researchers claim that cognitive behavioral therapy, a kind of reward-punishment behaviorist conditioning approach, is effective for curbing the violence of psychopathic youth, this treatment largely affirms an assumption of biological determinism.[8]

II. A Location for Psychopaths: The Corporation

The second group of academic literature focuses on how psychopaths gravitate to professions that reward traits such as ruthlessness, egotism, a lack of empathy, grandiosity, and predatory tendencies. Most of this literature is concerned with the disproportionate representation of psychopaths in business and specifically in leadership roles in corporations. Bob Hare himself has contributed to this literature with his book *Snakes in Suits,* coauthored with Paul Babiak, and an Australian scholar Clive R. Boddy has cornered the market in academic journal articles that seek to explain corrupt and unethical business practice through the presence of psychopaths in corporations. Unlike Bakan, these authors do not recognize the psychopathic dimensions of the institution of the corporation. In fact, rooting out psychopaths in the ranks of the corporations becomes a convenient explanatory device consistent with the "bad apples" alibi of neoliberal deregulatory destruction. If only there weren't "bad-apple" corporate leaders such as Ken Lay and scam artists like Bernard Madoff, the system would work ethically.

Of course, deregulation set the stage for the entire finance industry to create rip-off products and tank the system, requiring public bailout for survival. British journalist Jon Ronson's popular book *The Psychopath Test* reached a broader audience through NPR's public radio program "This American Life," which did an episode on psychopaths organized around Ronson's book. Both the book and the radio program focus on a notoriously cutthroat CEO of several companies including Sunbeam, Al Dunlap, whose management success was oriented around cost cutting by firing masses of employees. According to Ronson, Dunlap's home is adorned with statues of predatory animals with whom he identifies, and he recounts the extreme pleasure Dunlap takes in giving employees the axe. The literature on the corporate psychopath shares with the biologically deterministic perspective assumption that psychopaths are born, not made.

III. Culturalism

One article, "Deconstructing the Psychopath: A Critical Discursive Analysis," stands out in suggesting that the identity category of the psychopath is a social and historical construction.[9] This familiar Foucauldian argument suggests that the biological uniquenesses of the psychopath are arbitrary physical traits that are made the basis for cultural norming through the expert discourses of medicine and psychology. In this view, there really are no such people as psychopaths, only deeds attributed to this fictive category. What is more, to be a psychopath is to be spoken as a psychopathic subject.

Pedagogy of the Psychopath
Just as the biologically deterministic perspective leaves no way to link physically distinct traits of the psychopath to historically contingent cultural patterns of behavior and affect, the culturally deterministic approach allows for no capacity to comprehend the biology of psychopathy. Moreover, the biological deterministic, culturally deterministic, and "locational" approaches to the psychopath all miss a key aspect to the psychopath that I seek to redress here: psychopath culture is taught and learned—that is, it is pedagogical. The traits of the psychopath are not merely rewarded by certain institutions such as business schools and corporate headquarters. They are also broadly promoted on, for example, reality television programs which celebrate a social Darwinian ethos, calculated betrayal, exclusionary forms of sociality, and cruelty.[10]

This chapter expands Bakan's question from one of asking what kind of person the corporation is (a psychopath) to asking what sorts of persons the corporation educates flesh and blood persons into becoming— not only inside corporations, but also how corporations are involved in educating the public in a number of ways. Perhaps the greatest force that corporations wield is cultural pedagogical. That is, corporations, and particularly media corporations, produce narratives, ideologies, and identifications that form the basis of identities. The pedagogies of the corporation form an inventory from which individuals draw to interpret, act on, and intervene in the social world. Corporate educational projects can be found in formal schooling in the form of school commercialism initiatives such as BP's involvement with creating California's science curriculum, museum education projects such as Monsanto's sponsorship of a permanent exhibit on earth and agriculture at the Field Museum in Chicago, or ExxonMobil's heavy spending to promote public school privatization.[11] Literature such as detective and crime fiction, television, and film also function as cultural pedagogues.[12] In what follows here, I focus on and contrast two very different pedagogical and political interventions on the psychopath produced in popular culture—Patricia Highsmith's Ripley novels and George Manos' *Dexter* television series. I focus on these texts in part to emphasize the extent to which cultural producers affirm or contest broader public discourses, ethical, and political positions.

While the psychopathic character has long taken shape as a cartoonish villain in innumerable films and television shows, only recently has the psychopath appeared as a popular or heroic protagonist in mass media. Patricia Highsmith's Ripley novels and Jim Thompson's crime fiction provide an (1950s) exploration of social life narrated by psychopathic selves. While offering identification with a violent psychopath protagonist, these novels do not celebrate or endorse the amorality they represent, nor do they suggest the virtue in universalizing psychopathic traits for the society. Detective fiction by Robert B. Parker (Spencer series 1970s–2010) and Walter Mosley (1990s–2000s) both have black psychopathic outlaws who must be relied upon to periodically kill for the heroic detective, breaking the law in order to uphold the detective's pursuit of justice that the law of the state fails to provide.

More recently, television shows ranging from gamecon reality TV to *24* to *Dexter* to numerous action films suggest that psychopathic traits such as remorselessness, brutality, and disregard for the well-being of others are no longer characteristic of the social outsider. Instead, these corporate traits are framed as, at the very least, necessary for survival in a neoliberal Darwinian social shark tank or downright heroic in defending the dominant order and harnessing violence and lawlessness in the service of a conservative morality. These antiheroics of the contemporary psychopath share an affinity with an upwardly redistributive economic policy climate as well as with the political state of exception that has expanded since 9/11 and that is used to justify state murder and other law-breaking outside of international and domestic law typified by targeted assassination, the rejection of habeas corpus, the USA Patriot Act, the appropriation of public properties for private exploitation in the recent transformations to eminent domain, and so on. The crucial issue here is that recent narratives of the psychopath have not merely *responded to* a radically transformed and allegedly ethically ambiguous post-9/11 political, economic, and cultural climate. *Dexter* writer James Manos Jr. (Howard, 19–20) joins *Dexter* creator Shawn Ryan in asking the question, "What would people be willing to accept for their own safety?"(Howard, 23). (In other words, are people willing to accept a publicly unaccountable secret police force of murderers privately enforcing a security agenda?) Recent narratives of the psychopath produced by cultural workers including Manos and Ryan have participated in *reeducating the public* to a revised conception of justice in which the vigilante exceptionalism of the psychopath displaces the law of the state.

Though endless fictional and journalistic television programs since the 1970s have ramped up the specter of the psychopathic killer, as part of a redefinition of public space and community, as dangerous, *Dexter* in particular stands out in popular culture for making the psychopath an agent of justice. As dominant ideology, the threat of the violent monster lurking among us has served as a means to sell advertising through spectacular violence. News coverage of mass killers and mass shooting events overtake both political and economic news events with spectacular narratives where the killers are at first depicted as pinnacles of seeming normalcy to their neighbors, only to take a tragic, terrifying turn, making it seem that anybody could turn a gun on the crowds, even the most seemingly unlikely and soft-spoken suspect. Such programming at the same time promotes a conservative conception of the state in which the primary functions of the state in protecting private property rights and relations through state violence appears instead as protection of individuals from the ever-present threat of violence from deranged killers, child molesters, and so on.

The recent elevation of the violent psychopath to heroic stature coincides with an economic moment in which capitalist reproduction requires fewer workers, greater inequalities in wealth and income, a concentration of wealth at the top, and the expansion of a disposable segment of people at the bottom. As Michele Byers has pointed out, *Dexter* offers identification with a neoliberal subject of capacity achieving justice for the failed public sector.[13] The figure of the heroic psychopath appears at a time when the United States can be easily described, as Charles Ferguson has done, as a predator nation in which deregulation of public controls over finance and the private sector joins with radical upward redistributions in not just wealth and income but also control over public priorities and government. With both political parties thoroughly under the sway of corporate money and committed to neoliberal privatization and deregulation in every area from education to housing to healthcare, politics has been transformed into a matter of the capture of public money and pillage of resources. In such a climate of social exclusion and atrophied opportunity, the promise of success and power appeals to the ordinary American through identification with the ultimate predator.

I identify the rise of the psychopathic character as a recent heroic figure in popular culture and particularly in popular fiction, television, and film perhaps best typified by the television show *Dexter*. Patricia Highsmith's Ripley novels prefigured the themes found in *Dexter*, including a protagonist without a conscience or guilt, a protagonist with a self-consciously performed identity and feelings of emptiness behind the performance. While Highsmith's psychopath suggests a violence and sadism at the core of the empty consumerism that characterizes postwar life, *Dexter* in contrast participates in a circus of cruelty offering antisocial identifications as a promise of negotiating a failed sociality. While Highsmith's work illustrates the impossibility of a social world organized around psychopathic traits and the violence of consumer capitalism and the class system, *Dexter* shares with action films a world view in which the violence of the social can only be adequately met with the private exceptional violence of the psychopath outside of the failed public sphere.

Ripley
Patricia Highsmith's series of Ripley novels spanned the cold war with *The Talented Mr. Ripley* published in 1955 and the last of the five books, *The Boy Who Followed Ripley*, appearing in 1990. Two novels—*The Talented Mr. Ripley* and *Ripley's Game* were made into films. The Ripley novels followed Highsmith's success from her book *Strangers on a Train*, which Hitchcock made into a popular film. Thematically, *Strangers on a Train* shares with the Ripley novels a focus on characters who learn to kill without conscience. In *Strangers on a Train*, however, the characters free themselves from conscience by switching murders—they meet on a train, share their grievances, and agree to perform the killing of the other's adversary. In the Ripley novels, on the other hand, Highsmith puts both the feeling of transgression and the pursuit of reprieve in the character's development, with the narration working through the problem of what a character who kills without remorse looks like. Ultimately, though, the killer in *Strangers on a Train* gives himself away to the police authorities by displaying his guilt. Highsmith's future narratives struggle to resolve this problem of how to get away with murder and perform the "perfect crime" without physically revealing the secret. The answer to this "problem" of conscience lies in performing impersonation so thoroughly that

one becomes the person being impersonated. One can avoid suspicion and detection by projecting a confidence earned through total identification with an other who one has become. Guilt, conscience, and responsibility can be sloughed off or externalized along with the prior personality.

Highsmith illustrates how one dissolves conscience, exculpating responsibility and guilt through identification with a fictional other. Guilt and responsibility for destructively self-interested behavior can be sloughed off or "externalized" like the identity position left behind. The novels cover Thomas Ripley's development from a provincial American, middle class, sexually confused, insecure young man to the role of a confident, bourgeois, cosmopolitan, killer and art forger. One of Ripley's talents is impersonation. In the first novel, he falls in love with and then kills and impersonates Dickie Greenleaf. Dickie's father has hired Ripley to find Dickie in Italy and convince him to return home to his family, their boat building business, and conventional 1950s lifestyle. Instead of convincing Dickie to return, Tom reveals the father's plot and emulates Dickie's lugubrious expat ruling-class lifestyle of leisure: sunbathing, painting, boating, partying, and traveling in Europe. Tom first inserts himself into Dickie's relationship with his girlfriend, Marge. When Dickie tires of Tom's company, refusing to drop Marge and spurning his affection, Tom kills Dickie on a motorboat, takes his fine things, and impersonates him for many months. During this time, he kills Dickie's friend Freddie Miles to avoid discovery. Tom forges a will to capture Dickie's inheritance and reluctantly abandons his assumed identity of Dickie. In the later novels, Tom has added to his income and supported his penchant for the good life by marrying a French heiress of an industrial chemical fortune. Additional income derives from his conspiracy to forge new paintings, supposedly by an artist named Derwatt (who, in fact, is dead), and to create several businesses from the artist's renown. Tom also dabbles in smuggling and exchanges favors with a shadowy connection in Germany named Reeves Minot. In *Ripley Under Ground*, after impersonating Derwatt (who is dead but said to be in Mexico), Tom kills an American businessman named Murchison who is on to the Derwatt forgeries. In *Ripley under Water* and in *Ripley's Game*, Tom's killing follows from complicated schemes in response to his being insulted. In the last novel, *The Boy Who Followed Ripley*, Tom kills to protect a boy killer who admires and emulates him.

Scholarship on Ripley has focused on the performance of identity in the Highsmith novels without historicizing the idea of identity with the problem of conscience that the novels raise.[14] Like a method actor, Ripley becomes those he impersonates, believing that the small details of affect, manner, and clothing "make the person." The literature has largely sidestepped, however, the object-relations dimensions of Ripley. Ripley loves things and can only love other people as things. He must kill—that is, inanimate the loved other such as Dickie Greenleaf—and then incorporate Dickie into himself through impersonation. Tom loves himself as Dickie, luxuriating in his things and carefree cultural capital, but despises himself as anxious, middle-class, poorly dressed Tom Ripley. Ripley is radically alienated, realizing prior to murdering Dickie that he will always be alone and cannot ever truly connect with or love and be loved by others. Through the murder and impersonation of Dickie, Tom achieves class ascension. That is, Ripley's class elevation is effected through crime rather than through aristocratic inheritance (like Dickie, Marge, and Heloise) or meritocratic upward mobility—inclusion into a corporate dominated economy through submission to the rules of the game. Ripley makes his own rules for how to live. He represents desire freed of middle-class mores, self-limitation, and morality that would check his ambition for having things and being free in terms of his time.[15] Ripley embodies Mill's *homo oeconomicus* defined by advancing one's interest through icy calculation. Like the person of the corporation, Ripley has no checks on his desire, no moral code, no deep commitments to anyone beyond himself (all commitments are strategic), no conscience, and no guilt. He is an elevated consumerist survival machine capable of morphing into different forms to achieve the scheme of the moment.

Highsmith asks her reader to identify with the profoundly amoral character of the psychopath's consciousness. She pushes an obvious disjuncture between the reader's sense of right and desire for Ripley's success. Ripley is a tantalizing monster who is enviable to the reader for being cultured, for being free and smart, and for his nice things—his Gucci luggage, his Alfa Romeo, his chateaus, on so on. His lack of convictions or deep passions make him profoundly unheroic and, coupled with his affected ruling-class lugubriousness, even boring. In a sense, Highsmith is an anti–Ayn Rand, illustrating a world in which the radically self-interested and conscienceless behavior performed by Ripley is thoroughly antisocial and could never be universalized. As well, the world of bourgeois privilege is one largely acquired by lucky inheritance and, in Tom's case, by crime. Highsmith shows us a world in which meritocratic ideology is rendered suspect at best. In the context of inherited privilege of his ruling class peers, Tom's class mobility through forgery appears more as a strategy for gaming the class structure than as injustice.

Water plays a recurring role in the Ripley novels as that which swallows up Tom's lost love objects. Tom's parents drowned in Boston Harbor in an accident, leaving him to be raised by an unloving and cruel aunt. He kills Dickie on a motorboat and buries him in the sea. Tom's psychopathology is the result of the loss of the loved objects, his parents. Tom seeks to overcome his extreme aloneness by uniting with Dickie. Dickie's rejection brings Tom to the realization that he will never overcome aloneness. This realization precipitates the murder, as the only solution to Tom's aloneness is for Tom and Dickie to be one person. By killing Dickie, Tom also kills himself off. In *Escape from Freedom*, Erich Fromm describes the sadomasochistic relation. Fromm explains that individuals experience repeated trials of separation from others throughout life. The growth of individual strength separates one from others and how one forges new social relations can be productive (through creative work or love) or destructive (through sadism and masochism). For the sadist, love can only be achieved by having the other, controlling the other. Killing the other is the ultimate act of controlling the other by making the other inanimate. It is the dynamic changing nature of others that defies control. Tom exemplifies the masochistic abandonment of self described by Fromm as well as the sadistic aim for total control of the other. As well, Tom typifies what Fromm describes as the replacement of being with having in consumer capitalism. Unable to feel love for others, Tom passionately loves jewelry, furniture, clothing, and homes. Ripley's consumerism is not the middle-class one of endless acquisition and disposal of consumer goods but rather the acquisition of select things.

> Evenings looking at his clothes—his clothes and Dickie's—and feeling Dickie's rings between his palms, and running his fingers over the antelope suitcase he had bought at Gucci's. He had polished the suitcase with a special English leather dressing, not that it needed polishing because he took such good care of it, but for its protection. He loved possessions, not masses of them, but a select few that he did not part with. They gave a man self-respect. Not ostentation but quality, and the love that cherished the quality. Possessions reminded him that he existed, and made him enjoy his existence. It was as simple as that. And wasn't that worth something? He existed. (Highsmith, *The Talented Mr. Ripley*, 249)

In the 1980s Brett Easton Ellis's *American Psycho* continued this theme, situating the equation of consumerism with violent psychopathology in the Reagan era and its obsession with brands. Ellis's character is a narcissistic monster without a fleshed out motivation. In the 1990s, Chuck Palahniuk's *Fight Club* illustrates, in an unfortunately sexist way, the deadening, maddening, and emasculating experience of life reduced to having. The result in this case is a schizophrenic split in which an out of control alter ego pursues anticapitalist mayhem through a quasi-fascist political movement before being discovered and killed off by the protagonist. In Ripley, Highsmith illustrates a fundamental horror of consumer capitalism by collapsing having and being. Being is only having. It is as simple as that.

Is not the horror of the powerful, predatory, self-aggrandizing person emptied of care for other people, emptied of responsibility to others, emptied of conscience the horror of corporate personhood? Part of the way corporations signify personhood is in how they are able to separate from the actual person, taking the form of a person in the very act of squeezing out the content. Ripley solves the problem of conscience by becoming the other, emptied of content but full of details such as the rings, the clothes, the gait, and the pronunciation. Essence is in the possession of incidentals and in the possession of gestures. As Tom realizes, "Hadn't he learned something from these last months? If you wanted to be cheerful, or melancholic, or wistful, or thoughtful, or courteous, you simply had to act those things with every gesture." (Highsmith, *The Talented Mr. Ripley*, 193) Having killed Dickie, Tom earns confidence finally through having Dickie's things and the things he can have with Dickie's money, "Tom had an ecstatic moment when he thought of all the pleasures that lay before him now with Dickie's money, other beds, tables, seas, ships, suitcases, shirts, years of freedom, years of pleasure. Then he turned the light out and put his head down and almost at once fell asleep, happy content, and utterly confident, as he had never been before in his life." (Highsmith, *The Talented Mr. Ripley*, 112)

The promise of freedom, happiness, and confidence through the possession of the right things and gestures is the promise that the corporation makes to the individual in consumer capitalism. Omnipresent advertising, public relations, product placement, and consumer fantasies work to instantiate an ambivalent consumer identity at the core of the self—lack/desire—you lack this one thing that would install you in the symbolic fantasy space but the act of consumption promises fulfillment. Consumer pedagogies succeed in replacing our consciences with self-definition through having things, enacting the right gestures, and impersonating the elevated fantasy figures of consumption. The survival and flourishing of personhood for corporations depends on the way flesh and blood people identify with the brand of the corporation and its associated fantasy world. Moreover, people learn to assent to corporate power, environmental despoliation, and human exploitation by sharing with the corporation the logic of impersonation and externalization in which *to be* is always a promise of *being someone else* who is defined by having and by always having more.

If the Ripley novels enact the limits of *homo oeconomicus*, the television series *Dexter* provides a very different point of identification with predation.

Dexter

A Showtime original series, *Dexter* has been broadcast since 2006 through 2012 (at this writing) and was inspired by Jeff Lindsay's novel *Darkly Dreaming Dexter*. The serial killing protagonist Dexter witnessed the violent murder of his mother at the age of three and developed the characteristics of a violent psychopath as a child. His adoptive father Harry noticed Dexter's tendencies and taught him a code for living with and concealing his impulses from others. Throughout the series, Dexter lives by "Harry's Code" which allows him to largely limit his serial killing to those who "deserve it." Dexter is a vigilante serial killer who mostly kills only other killers.

Dexter shares with the Ripley novels a focus on a radically isolated protagonist who desperately wants to connect to others but knows that such connection is impossible. Dexter understands his disconnection from others as a function of hiding his secret unquenchable urge to kill, an urge which he refers to as his "dark passenger." Like Ripley, Dexter's identity is a performance. Yet, while Ripley's performance does not have an authentic self behind it (Tom Ripley is a performance), Dexter's killer self is the stable identity that needs to be concealed. *Dexter* largely relies on the biological determinist explanation for Dexter's behavior, suggesting that his predisposition as a psychopath was shaped in a particular direction by his experience of his mother's murder. Dexter's brother, also a serial killer, is represented as also having the biological predisposition, yet, having experienced the mother's murder at a later age, has no capacity to modulate and limit his serial killing impulse the way Dexter does. Dexter's authentic killer persona is intimately shared with the viewer through narrative voiceovers that mostly occur when Dexter is alone driving or disposing of a body on his boat or pursuing a victim. He depressively ruminates over the curse of his dark passenger and over his inability to really connect with others because of his need to keep his killings secret.

Dexter works for the Miami Dade police as a civilian employee specializing in blood spatter patterns for the homicide division. His job allows him access to research of his own future victims, and his own victims frequently intersect with the high profile cases being worked by homicide. The show suggests that the law of the state is largely ineffectual relative to the private code of the killer. Moreover, the means of upholding the law of the state is constituted when private individuals connected to the state break the law in the interests of security. This logic accords with the trend of the federal government since 9/11 to break both domestic and international law in the name of national security. It also accords with the neoliberal tendency to portray the government as failed in order to justify privatization, contracting, outsourcing, and deregulation.

As a figure with which to identify, Dexter shares with countless action hero vigilantes a promise of transgression in the service of conservative morality, of upholding the social order through the enforcement of retribution. Ripley kills to become his loved object, to attain his life of having things, or to conceal his impersonations and forgeries. Dexter has to kill, and so he channels his murderous uncontainable impulse that stems from his broken biology merged with his experience of the violent loss of his mother. Dexter directs his Thanatos to temporarily relieve it before it inevitably builds back up. In *Dexter*, only by breaking the law can the moral law be upheld. The seductiveness of such a promise for the viewer is that it invests exceptional godlike moral authority in each person. For spectators to identify with Dexter is to assume the fantasy space of God. Justice, in this view, cannot be achieved through community deliberation or collectively enacted legislation. Nor does justice require checks and balances and public oversight. In fact, public oversight is an impediment to justice in Dexter. A profoundly antidemocratic view, justice here is the preserve for the few with strong wills and strong enough bodies. *Dexter* asks viewers to accept justice through the assumptions and values of totalitarianism. Justice as it is expressed in *Dexter* is the justice of the secret police. Dexter is an attractive character. He dresses stylishly, is handsome, cares for his family. Most importantly, he inverts the most inhuman brutality by bringing the viewer into intimacy with his ongoing existential crisis and loneliness. He confides in and confesses his true feelings in narrative voice over only to the viewer. If Ripley kills and impersonates the longed for other, *Dexter* positions the viewer as the longed for other who can merge with Dexter through shared secrets, intimate details, and a blood lust that no one else can know. Like Ripley, Dexter desires to inanimate his victims. Dexter treats his victims as disposable consumer goods, like meat in a supermarket ready for consumption—he wraps his victims in plastic wrap on a table and stabs them in the heart. He universally dismembers them, disposing of them in garbage bags, and dumps them in the sea. Yet, unlike Ripley, Dexter's murders are not motivated by a desire to impersonate his victims to abandon himself and unite with them. Rather, Dexter repeatedly kills himself off symbolically in the act of killing other serial killers. Inanimating the other through murder is not a desperate act of loving and masochistically abandoning the self and becoming the other as it is for Ripley. Dexter's killing is sadistic in that it allows for temporary control over the dark passenger. Like consumerism, Dexter's dark passenger is an unquenchable thirst to consume, destroy, dispose. Consuming his victims only briefly assuages his frustrating desire for more. Dexter's victims are bad product, society's spoilage, and he is merely "taking out the trash." The vast majority of Dexter's victims are radically objectified as deviant monsters even before he cuts them into dismembered objects. In a historical moment in which entire populations, the poor, homeless, failed consumers are treated as disposable, unworthy of social investment, and blamed for being positioned as such, *Dexter* encourages a brutal view of the social as populated by unknowable monsters who should be secretly killed.[16]

Dexter as a character exhibits the traits of corporate personhood. *Dexter* not only offers up a predatory character for identification in the aforementioned predatory economic climate, it also suggests as natural and inevitable privatized solutions to a naturalized violence of the social world. The violence of financial capital, the violence of state enforced property interests, and the symbolic violence of racism do not exist. Instead, violence is largely a biological effect. The denial of social causes of violence paired with a privatized solution to naturalized violence produces an understanding of social violence in which public and policy decisions play no part. The only relation to violence in this picture for the viewer becomes one of a spectator who is brought into intimacy with Dexter, the agent of privatized "justice." The pedagogy of *Dexter* affirms alienation as inevitable, promising agency only through a fantasy of being the ultimate predator in the inevitably violent society of exclusion.

Conclusion

In this chapter, I have argued that we ought to build on Joel Bakan's insight that corporate personhood is psychopathic by recognizing the pedagogies of the corporation that educate individuals into psychopathic social relations. I have drawn on the novels of Patricia Highsmith because she illustrates the social limits of psychopathic traits. There can be no society of psychopaths. Moreover, Highsmith highlights the way that identity in consumer capitalism operates through impersonation and externalization of conscience, guilt, and responsibility as individuals are defined through having. She paints a disturbing, horrifying, and prophetic picture of amoral sociality. I have discussed *Dexter* as exemplary of a newly celebrated predatory culture and selfhood at a historical moment of predatory politics and economy. Fromm reminds us that the historical possibility for consciousness and criticality were made possible by the alienation and objectification that capitalist development fostered. In the era organized by pillage and predation, creativity and critical thought are being harnessed in the service of making empty display selves defined by having. The problem of corporate personhood is not just the giving of rights to a fictive entity that removes responsibility from those who control capital and the abdication of social responsibility for the destructive effects. Regulating corporate behavior and repealing the legality of corporate personhood would be socially valuable steps toward the end of limiting the tendencies of corporations to externalize destruction on the public and educate individuals into the values of competitive acquisition, consumerism, and the traits of psychopathy.

Notes

1. Joel Bakan, *The Corporation: the Pathological Pursuit of Profit and Power* (New York: Free Press, 2005). Bakan cowrote the documentary film *The Corporation* directed by Mark Achbar in 2005.
2. These examples are all taken up in detail in both the book and film *The Corporation*.
3. Jared A. DeFife, "Predator on the Prowl," in *The Psychology of Dexter*, ed. Bella Depaulo (Dallas: BenBella Books, 2010), 7.
4. See Jean Baudrillard *The Consumer Society* and the work of Sut Jhally.
5. The film *The Corporation* illustrates this point well through the examples of Kathy Gifford's sweatshop apparel manufacturing practices and BP's pollution. Coca-Cola's water privatization, use of paramilitaries against labor unionists, and other abuses have been documented by the Killer Coke campaign. Self-imposed "social responsibility" codes cannot be relied upon when the demand for profits runs contrary to human interests and the media spotlight turns to other spectacles.
6. See for example, Kent A. Kiehl and Joshua Buckholtz, "Inside the Mind of a Psychopath," *Scientific American Mind* 21, no. 4 (Sep./Oct. 2010): 22–29.
7. See Thomas Lemke, *Biopolitics: An Advanced Introduction* (New York: New York University Press, 2011), 18.
8. Kiehl and Buckholtz, "Inside the Mind of a Psychopath," 22–29.
9. Cary Federman, Dave Holmes, and Jean Daniel Jacob, "Deconstructing the Psychopath: A Critical Discursive Analysis," *Cultural Critique* 72 (Spring 2009): 36–65.
10. See Nick Couldry, "Reality TV, or the Secret Theater of Neoliberalism," *The Review of Education Pedagogy Cultural Studies* 30 (2008): 3–13. For a link to the theater of cruelty and public pedagogy see Henry Giroux, *Youth in a Suspect Society: Democracy or Disposability?* (New York: Palgrave Macmillan, 2010).
11. Robin Truth Goodman and Kenneth Saltman, *Strange Love, or How We Learn to Stop Worrying and Love the Market* (Lanham, MD: Rowman & Littlefield, 2002), discusses these examples at length as cultural pedagogy.
12. See Robin Truth Goodman, *Policing Narratives and the State of Terror.*
13. Michele Byers, "Neoliberal Dexter?" in *Dexter: Investigating Cutting Edge Television*, ed. Douglas Howard (New York: I. B. Tauris), 2010.
14. See for example, Michael Trask, "Patricia Highsmith's Method," *American Literary History*, 22, no.3 (2010): 584–614; and John Dale, "Crossing the Road

to Avoid Your Friends: Engagement, Alienation, and Patricia Highsmith," *Midwest Quarterly.*
15. This insight comes from Robin Truth Goodman's personal communication.
16. For excellent recent discussions of the politics of disposability see Henry Giroux, *Youth in a Suspect Society* (New York: Palgrave Macmillan, 2010); and Zygmunt Bauman, *Wasted Lives* (New York: Polity, 2005).

Works Cited

Babiak, Paul and Robert Hare. *Snakes in Suits: When Psychopaths go to Work.* New York: Harper Collins, 2006.

Bakan, Joel. *The Corporation: the Pathological Pursuit of Profit and Power.* New York: Free Press, 2005.

Baudrillard, Jean. *The Consumer Society: Myths and Structures.* Translated by Chris Turner. London: Sage Publications, 1998.

Bauman, Zygmunt. *Wasted Lives: Modernity and its Outcasts.* New York: Polity, 2005.

Byers, Michelle. "Neoliberal Dexter?" *Dexter: Investigating Cutting Edge Television*, ed. Douglas Howard. New York: I. B. Tauris, 2010. 143-156.

Couldry, Nick. "Reality TV, or the Secret Theater of Neoliberalism." *The Review of Education Pedagogy Cultural Studies* 30 (2008): 3-13.

Dale, John. "Crossing the Road to Avoid Your Friends: Engagement, Alienation, and Patricia Highsmith," *Midwest Quarterly* 51.4.

DeFife, Jared A. "Predator on the Prowl." *The Psychology of Dexter*, ed. Bella Depaulo. Dallas: BenBella Books, 2010. 5-16.

Federman, Cary, Dave Holmes, and Jean Daniel Jacob, "Deconstructing the Psychopath: A Critical Discursive Analysis," *Cultural Critique* 72 (Spring 2009): 36-65.

Ferguson, Charles. *Predator Nation: Corporate Criminals, Political Corruption, and the Hijacking of America.* New York: Crown Business, 2012.

Fromm, Erich. *Escape from Freedom.* New York: Henry Holt, 1941.

Giroux, Henry *Youth in a Suspect Society: Democracy or Disposibility?* New York: Palgrave Macmillan, 2010.

Highsmith, Patricia. *The Talented Mr. Ripley.* New York: W. W. Norton, 1955.

Goodman, Robin Truth and Kenneth Saltman. *Strange Love, or How We Learn to Stop Worrying and Love the Market.* Lanham, MD: Rowman & Littlefield, 2002.

Kiehl, Kent A. and Joshua Buckholtz. "Inside the Mind of a Psychopath." *Scientific American Mind*, 21.4 (2010): 22-29.

Lemke, Thomas. *Biopolitics: An Advanced Introduction.* New York: New York University Press, 2011.

Ronson, Jon. *The Psychopath Test.* New York: Picador, 2011.

Trask, Michael. "Patricia Highsmith's Method." *American Literary History*, 22.3 (2010): 584-614.

4

Corporate World Literature: Neoliberalism and the Fate of the Humanities

Jeffrey R. Di Leo

Higher education in America is undergoing some radical changes. Many within the academy fear that they are changes for the worse—and that the vision of the academy they believe in is on the brink of complete destruction. Whereas twentieth-century American professors enjoyed a high degree of control over university curriculum and the fundamental right to critically inquire into any subject without fear of losing their position within the university, academics in the new millennium are facing increasing degrees of curricular scrutiny, as well as department closures, unreasonable expectations, and job insecurity. This, coupled with the possibility of academic life without tenure and academic freedom, is fundamentally changing the manner in which many approach academe.

One of the major causes of these changes in the academy is the escalating trend to see higher education as a type of business or corporation. In the business world, products are marketed and produced with the aim of growing market-share, and values and processes are determined by their ability to raise sales and profitability. The application of increasingly severe versions of this operational philosophy to the academy has in large part contributed to the move toward contingent faculty appointments, a vocation-based curriculum, and the curtailing of critical freedoms. If this situation is not reversed, there is a strong possibility that the university of the future will be more like a vocational training center staffed by part-time instructors than a nexus of critical inquiry facilitated by full-time faculty.

But the changes do not end here. Students too are getting into the corporate spirit. In their recent book, *Higher Education? How Colleges*

Are Wasting Our Money and Failing Our Kids—and What We Can Do About It, Queens College political science professor Andrew Hacker and New York Times journalist Claudia Dreifus report that "over half of all undergraduates now enroll in vocational *training* programs, which range from standbys like nursing and engineering to new arrivals like resort management and fashion merchandising" (3). With numbers like these, it not surprising that liberal arts faculty find it increasingly difficult to compete with their vocational, technical, and professional colleagues for resources—particularly, during times of economic crisis.

It is under these conditions, namely, the rising dominance of vocational majors and the well-documented ascent of the corporate university that I would like to briefly consider the fate of the humanities. Specifically, I'd like to propose that if we do not change the way we approach literature and the humanities, the corporate university will not only continue to attract larger numbers of majors, and marginalize and remove large chunks of the humanities curriculum, it may also put the humanities on the path to extinction.

The Last Corporate University

If humanities scholars were not interested in the future of their disciplines and simply allowed the forces of the neoliberal university to determine their fate, there is every reason to believe that these disciplines would eventually disappear in academe's vocational haze. However, many humanities faculty are concerned with the future of their disciplines—and have chosen to devote some of their scholarly attention to it. The economic and political dimensions of universities have become a very hot and contested topic of late—especially within scholarly organizations affiliated with the humanities. It is not uncommon now to find, for example, standing room audiences at the MLA (Modern Language Association) or ACLA (American Comparative Literature Association) for presentations about the job market or the fate of tenure, while sessions devoted to subjects such as comparative arts or Chaucer have more empty seats than full ones. Indeed, one of the major contributions of the rise of cultural studies in our profession is the normalization of metaprofessional scholarship, particularly among committed humanities professors. While the profession of literary studies has by far been the loudest and most articulate voice in this discussion (bolstered in part by Cary Nelson, an English professor, who now serves as president of the American Association of University Professors), other humanities disciplines such as philosophy and history have not been far behind.[1]

What is important to recall is that prior to the rise of cultural studies in the late 1980s and 1990s, discussion of the metaprofessional dimensions of the university were nowhere as dominant as they are today. Philosophy professors used to research and write about philosophy, and English professors about literature. These were the hot topics at scholarly meetings, while metaprofessional subjects such as the job market, academic publishing, and tenure were primarily discussed in the lounge over coffee. While students and professors definitely had strong opinions on these subjects and shared many of the same concerns that are in vogue today about the job market, salaries, job security, and publishing, they were not things that were widely regarded as fair game for conference presentation, let alone scholarly publication.

We've come a long way though over the past 20 years—and this is one of the reasons to be hopeful that the humanities can weather education's corporate hurricane. The publication of books like Bruce Wilshire's *The Moral Collapse of the University: Professionalism, Purity, and Alienation* (1990), Stanley Fish's *Professional Correctness: Literary Studies and Political Change* (1995), and David Damrosch's *We Scholars: Changing the Culture of the University* (1995) opened the door for taking these discussions out of the coffee lounge and into the scholarly forum. If major scholars in our field, for example, Wilshire in philosophy, Fish in English, and Damrosch in comparative literature, were publishing scholarly works on the economic and political life of the academy, then the rest of us could—and should—too. The book, however, that kicked the door down—and radically altered the nature of metaprofessional discourse in the humanities—was one by a relatively unknown associate professor of comparative literature at the Université de Montréal.

Bill Reading's *The University in Ruins*, which came out in 1996, turned the discussion of the academy by humanists decidedly more political and economic. And his book, more than any other from this period, established the role of the market in the administration of universities as a central topos in our metaprofessional deliberations. Soon the phrase "corporate university" came to be the central signifier for everything that is wrong with universities in America. Excellent books such as Derek Bok's *Universities in the Marketplace* (2003) and David Kirp's *Shakespeare, Einstein, and the Bottom Line* (2003) continued to hammer home this point over the next 15 years. These and other studies inform us that universities in America have been and continue to be run more like businesses or corporations than—well—universities.[2]

However, in spite of their collective insights on the corporatization of the university, there has not been much consensus within corporate university literature on either how to get out from under this administrative model or how the humanities is going to survive—if not thrive—under this model. Moreover, the majority of the studies published in the past ten years continue this trend. In addition (and somewhat unsurprisingly), most recent studies of university conditions do not even discuss the attacks of September 11, 2001 or the repressive, neoliberal, educational policies established in the wake of these events, both of which play a large role in the challenges currently facing the humanities. A good example is the much discussed and very popular recent study by an Ohio State University English professor.

In *The Last Professors: The Corporate University and the Fate of the University* (2008), Frank Donoghue predicts that while "professors have only been around for the last eighty years,"[3] don't count on them being around for the next 80. In the process, he makes no pretense about having a solution to this situation, and clearly states, "I offer nothing in the way of uplifting solutions to the problems that I describe."[4] Rather, Donohue simply aims to show both how we got into this situation, and why we are not going to be able to get out of it. The future of the faculty and disciplines caught in this downward spiral is not his concern.

While his honesty about this is commendable, the fact that he does not propose any solutions begs the question as to the purpose of the book, particularly when so much had already been written about this subject. The bibliography to Donoghue's book has almost two hundred entries, most of which confirm his point that corporate logic and values provided the foundational and continuing conditions of the university in America. While it is interesting to read, for example, about the ways in which business interests have historically tempered and contained the humanities, it is disappointing to find not even a glimmer of a *defense* of the humanities against corporate interests, or an attempt to help affected faculty resolve this situation. What does one say, for example, to a business person, university regent, or a state legislator who asks why *should* they support the humanities in higher education rather than say provide students with skills to succeed in business? What does one say to a distraught colleague whose work in the humanities is deemed unimportant or inessential? Studies without such insight are, in times of a well-known academic crisis, of limited value.

Moreover, and perhaps more problematic, there is no effort to argue that corporate values such as efficiency, productivity, and usefulness, are in themselves the wrong values for the academy (even though Donoghue finds them to be "oppressive"[5]). Statements like "the very corporate values from which we humanists wish to distance ourselves"[6] pepper the book though it is never demonstrated that values such as "usefulness" are ones that *we humanists* need to distance ourselves from—after all, isn't, for example, "usefulness" the cornerstone of American pragmatism, which is itself a paradigmatic example of American humanism?

As such, Donoghue's book is not a defense of the values that the academy should have, and not an argument against the values that it does have. Nor does it make any effort to contend with the devastating effect of the corporate university on the humanities. In this respect, Donoghue's book is not that different from most of the other recent studies of the corporate university: lots of description of problems with faculty salaries, tenure, adjunct hiring, loss of research support, decrease in publishing opportunities, vocationalization of the curriculum, and so on, though little insight how to get out of this situation or how to at least cope with it.[7]

Unfortunately, studies like Donohue's are far too common. Though their doom and gloom snapshots of academe might make for good summer reading, they must be regarded as missed opportunities to work toward a revaluation of the academy—and the demise of the corporate university. Instead of simply bemoaning long-standing oppressive values underlying academic culture, scholars like Donohue need to build a case for their revaluation, particularly if these values are participating in the demise of the humanities.

Nonetheless, arguments in support of the humanities in the face of the growing corporatization of the university are not easy to make— particularly when so many undergraduates are now enrolled in vocationally grounded education (and particularly if one refuses to instrumentalize the humanities). After all, student demand is a large part of the corporate university's modus operandi. And though Hacker and Dreifus might find some joy in ranting that these programs do not qualify for inclusion in an institution of higher learning, and take some pleasure in saying things like "While we're sure something is imparted in these classes, we're not comfortable calling it *education*" (3), responsible, collegial scholars do not do this. Denigrating and insulting our colleagues and our students is not the way to ensure the future of the humanities. Nor do making trite comments like this one (also by Hacker and Dreifus) help very much: "College should be a cultural journey, an intellectual expedition, a voyage of confronting new ideas and information, together expanding and deepening our understanding of ourselves and the world" (3). Statements like this only make it more difficult for the liberal arts to differentiate their aims from those of say a Carnival cruise ship—with books. Instead of repeating shopworn assessments of the problems facing higher education (a la Donoghue) or insulting our colleagues and students (a la Hacker and Dreifus), we need to look for ways out of the neoliberal abyss.

Death of the Neoliberal Arts

In many ways, the problems facing the humanities have only intensified in the past ten years (that is, since 9/11). Not only has there been an increase in military funding of university research, but there has also been a rise in support for academic programs that support the militarization of higher education.[8] Moreover, during this same period, there has been a decrease in funding for humanities scholarship and research aimed at fundamental social and environmental issues, as well as cutbacks in liberal arts coursework and programs. In this context, the liberal arts and critical studies in American higher education are better labeled the *neo*liberal arts and *un*critical studies. What is even worse is the way in which neoliberal ways of viewing higher education and the liberal arts have trickled down into the views of American youth.

The future of the liberal arts hinges in large part on the ability of people who share a passion for the liberal arts to be able to share their emotional force and communicate their intellectual power with others. Seeing and hearing people who are fully committed to their art is often believed to be the best way of supporting the arts. The poet who intensely and emphatically reads his poetry reveals his commitment to his art; the philosopher who cleverly turns every statement into a question and undermines beliefs demonstrates the perennial and complex nature of philosophy; the novelist who convinces others to believe in her characters and care for their well-being shows the power of mimesis.

However, part of the current problem of the humanities is that these traditional ways of drawing people into the humanities are no longer working. Students facing the prospect of getting into debt to attend college are less interested today in studying things that might be good for the mind, but are potentially hard on their wallets—and career aspirations. A generation or two ago, students were more passionate about things like poetry and history. The current generation though is more committed to pursuing lucrative vocational careers than enjoying the critical and creative wonders of the liberal arts—to relieving their massive student debt than pursuing majors that they believe will only exacerbate their economic woes.

Pollster Daniel Yankelovich has noted that "75 percent of high school seniors and 85 percent of their parents said college is important because it 'prepares students to get a better job and/or increases their earning potential.'"[9] In itself, the situation would not be so dire for the liberal arts if these students and their parents had some knowledge of—if not appreciation for—the liberal arts. After all, corporate employment aspirations (and success) are not mutually exclusive with an appreciation for the liberal arts. However, according to Yankelovich, "44 percent of students and 19 percent of their parents could not answer the question, What does a liberal arts education mean?"[10] In addition, Yankelovich's polling indicated that "the overall impression of liberal arts education among 68 percent of the students and 59 percent of the parents was negative or neutral."[11]

These beliefs about higher education and its value would be challenges for the humanities even in good economic times. However, since the economic meltdown of 2008, they have made the situation in the humanities even worse. The rising cost of higher education and the shrinking job market coupled with prevailing perceptions about the value of a college education have had a decidedly negative impact on the liberal arts.

Some of the more disturbing numbers associated with this negative impact are the decreasing numbers of humanities majors. For example, 40 years ago, 64,286 students received bachelor's degrees in English. However, in 2007 it was reported that the number of bachelor's degrees awarded in English had shrunk to 53,040. This drop would not be so significant if one did not also take into account that during this period, the total number of bachelor's degrees almost doubled. Taking this into account, the 64,286 majors in 1971 equates to approximately 128,500 in 2007, thus bringing the weighted decrease in English majors over this span to around 60 percent.[12]

Perhaps a better gauge of the state of the liberal arts though is the number of students who attended liberal arts colleges, but did not receive degrees in the liberal arts. In 1987, just over 10 percent of all students attending the 225 liberal arts colleges in the United States received degrees in vocational fields, whereas by 2008, that percentage rose to nearly 30 percent. At the lowest tier (or ranked) liberal arts colleges the percentage is well over 50 percent.[13]

Can the liberal arts get a bigger slap in the face than this? Is there no clearer indicator of the decreasing value of a liberal arts education than students attending liberal arts colleges but in increasing numbers *not* majoring in the liberal arts? In the same way that a drastic increase of business majors at colleges dedicated to the arts would not be a good sign for the arts, so too are increasing numbers of vocational majors at colleges dedicated to the liberal arts a bad sign for the liberal arts. One goes to Julliard to study opera—not operations management; one goes to Williams to study philosophy—not finance.

Vocational aspirations and careerism among students are radically altering liberal arts education in America. The liberal arts curriculum is slowly giving way to vocational—or, if you will, *corporate*—instruction. If something is not done about this soon by critically engaged academics, there is every reason to believe that the move toward more vocational courses and majors will accelerate—and that the liberal arts curriculum that remains will more and more be tailored to serve the needs of an increasingly vocational- and corporate-minded student base. How then do we, as educators, meet the demands of vocationally motivated undergraduate students while at the same time resist emptying our liberal arts courses from their historical, political, and critical roots? How do we protect the distinctiveness of the liberal arts, while at the same time convincing students of their difference from vocationally grounded courses and majors? Pursuit of answers to pedagogically complex questions like these will go a longer way toward resolving the problems facing the humanities in the corporate university than merely continuing to heap scorn upon our vocational-minded colleagues and students.

It is my belief that we need not ignore the desires of our vocational-minded students or denigrate them, but rather engage them in a progressive form of dialogue with and through the liberal arts courses that we offer. We need to view the humanities courses that continue to be offered as opportunities to demonstrate to our students—and the advocates of vocational-based curriculum—their multifaceted educational value. Not just *say* what we are teaching is important, but also *show* it. At a time when the humanities is struggling within the corporate university for funding, respect, and its future, we need to view each course that we offer as though the fate of the humanities hinged on its success. While this defensive posture may seem unfair, particularly when courses in "resort management" and "fashion merchandizing" do not have the same pressures put upon them, we must realize that it is not vocational-based education that is under siege within the corporate university. Rather, it is areas of the curriculum such as literature and philosophy that are struggling to prove their value to a growing vocational-, technical-, and professional-minded student base.

All of this is of course no easy task. In many ways, every course and major within the corporate university curriculum should be regarded as a "corporate" course—or thought of as implicitly containing the adjective "corporate." That is to say, "World Literature" is actually "Corporate World Literature" within the corporate university. Why? Because this signifies the way in which the corporate university continuously puts its intellectual value under erasure; makes the course a continual site of contestation and defense; demands that the course always consider itself from the perspective of the neoliberal values that threaten its future. This implicit adjective demarcates the conditions of the possibility of this course within a model of university organization that allows vocational, technical, and professional values to determine curriculum rather than academic freedom, disciplinary constraint, and intellectual history. Academic interests are contingent upon market interests in the neoliberal university—and the implicit adjective "corporate" serves as a grave reminder of this.

Nevertheless, "corporatizing" humanities courses does not mean that we ignore the historical and political dimensions of the works that we are teaching; rather it means that we need to be careful not to assume that students prima facie care about the critical foundations of texts. Teaching corporatized literature or philosophy courses requires a more complex dialogue between the teacher and the students in order to respect their mutual desires. In the end, however, this respect of different desires may be one of the only ways to prevent the eventual extinction of large swaths of the liberal arts curriculum—especially if our corporate liberal arts courses bring about a greater knowledge of and appreciation for the liberal arts.

Academics need to continue to show concern with the crisis in the humanities, but not by simply writing off its problems as intransigent or long-standing. Also, we need to recognize that while we are busy worrying about things like tenure and academic freedom, the very disciplines in which we exercise that tenure and freedom are eroding away beneath us. Tenure and academic freedom are not worth very much to the philosopher whose philosophy department has been closed, or to the foreign languages professor whose language is being phased out of the curriculum. Odd as it may sound, it may be our capacity as teachers and advocates of the humanities that is our best defense against extinction—it surely though is not pedagogical apathy or intellectual arrogance.

While scholarly attention to perennial metaprofessional topics like tenure and academic freedom is important, attention to the demise of the liberal arts curriculum by vocational, technical, and professional pursuits seems more urgent, particularly for affected scholars. However, rather than writing about the erosion of the humanities curriculum by the hand of the corporate university, we need to use our pedagogical prowess to act against it. With micro-level adjustments in pedagogy such as the corporatization of liberal arts courses, academics can work toward altering negative neoliberal perceptions of the value of the liberal arts. While most would probably rather teach their courses as "pure" liberal arts courses, this academic freedom is currently not widely available in the age of the neoliberal arts. So, until the neoliberal arts revert back to being the liberal arts, curricular compromises are an effective way to protect the liberal arts from immediate demise.

Notes

1. The American Association of University Professors (AAUP) is the foremost defender of faculty rights and privileges in America. Nelson, current national president of the AAUP and Jubilee Professor of Liberal Arts and Sciences at the University of Illinois at Urbana-Champaign, recently published *No University is an Island: Saving Academic Freedom* (New York: New York University Press, 2010). In addition, Ellen Schrecker, former editor of the *Academe*, the official magazine of the AAUP, and professor of history

at Yeshiva University, just published *The Lost Soul of Higher Education: Corporatization, the Assault on Academic Freedom, and the End of the American University* (New York and London: The New Press, 2010). Both books are excellent surveys of the assaults on academic freedom.

2. An abbreviated list also includes CUNY sociologist Stanley Aronowitz's *The Knowledge Factory: Dismantling the Corporate University and Creating True Higher Learning* (Boston, MA: Beacon Press, 2001), and freelance journalist and New America Foundation fellow Jennifer Washburn's *University, Inc.: The Corporate Corruption of Higher Education* (New York: Basic Books, 2005).

3. Frank Donoghue. *The Last Professors: The Corporate University and the Fate of the Humanities* (New York: Fordham University Press, 2008), xi.

4. Ibid., xi.

5. Ibid., xv.

6. Ibid., 26.

7. One noteworthy recent exception to this trend in philosophy is Mark Taylor's *Crisis on Campus: A Bold Plan for Reforming our Colleges and Universities* (New York: Alfred A. Knopf, 2010). Taylor's book raised eyebrows with its argument that the university as we know it is outdated and broken, and requires nothing short of radical restructuring. Among Taylor's many suggestions for change are salary increases for productive faculty, and salary decreases for unproductive ones (213); creation of a National Teaching Academy to support teaching excellence around the country (190); and adding a fourth division for schools of arts and science called "Emerging Zones" in addition to the more traditional tripartite division of the natural sciences, social sciences, and arts and humanities (145). His most controversial claim is to do away with tenure: "The only way for American higher education to remain competitive," writes Taylor, "is to abolish tenure and impose mandatory retirement at the age of seventy" (204). Taylor, however, became a lightning rod for public remonstration because of his attacks on things like tenure and traditional disciplinary structures. One Barnard philosopher accused Taylor in the *Times* of "crass anti-intellectualism," while another critic in *The New Republic* called his book "unbelievably misguided," and part of the growing "syndrome" of intellectuals turning incendiary, brief op-ed pieces into reckless books.

8. See Henry Giroux's essay in this volume, "The Post-9/11 Militarization of Higher Education and Neoliberalism's Culture of Depravity: Threats to the Future of American Democracy."

9. Daniel Yankelovich's study is cited in Victor E. Ferrall Jr., *Liberal Arts at the Brink* (Cambridge, MA: Harvard University Press, 2011), 50.

10. Ibid., 50.

11. Ibid., 50.

12. Daniel Born, "What is the Crisis in the Humanities?," *Common Review* (Spring 2010): 5.

13. Ferrall Jr., *Liberal Arts at the Brink*, 55.

Works Cited

Aronowitz, Stanley. *The Knowledge Factory: Dismantling the Corporate University and Creating True Higher Learning.* Boston: Beacon Press, 2001.
Bok, Derek. *Universities in the Marketplace: The Commercialization of Higher Education.* Princeton, NJ: Princeton University Press, 2003.
Born, Daniel. "What is the Crisis in the Humanities?" *Common Review* 9.2 (2010): 5.
Damrosh, David. *We Scholars: Changing the Culture of the University.* Boston, MA: Harvard University Press, 1995.
Donoghue, Frank. *The Last Professors: The Corporate University and the Fate of the Humanities.* New York: Fordham University Press, 2008.
Ferrall, Victor E. *Liberal Arts at the Brink.* Cambridge, MA: Harvard University Press, 2011.
Fish, Stanley. *Professional Correctness: Literary Studies and Political Change.* Boston, MA: Harvard University Press, 1995.
Giroux, Henry. "The Post-9/11 Militarization of Higher Education and Neoliberalism's Culture of Depravity: Threats to the Future of American Democracy." *International Journal of Sociology of Education* 1.1 (2012): 27–53.
Hacker, Andrew and Claudia Dreifus. *Higher Education? How Colleges Are Wasting Our Money and Failing Our Kids—and What We Can Do About It.* New York: St. Martin's Press, 2010.
Kirp, David. *Shakespeare, Einstein, and the Bottom Line: The Marketing of Higher Education.* Boston, MA: Harvard University Press, 2004.
Nelson, Cary. *No University Is an Island: Saving Academic Freedom.* New York: New York University Press, 2010.
Reading, Bill. *The University in Ruins.* Boston, MA: Harvard University Press, 1997.
Schrecker, Ellen. *The Lost Soul of Higher Education: Corporatization, the Assault on Academic Freedom, and the End of the American University.* New York and London: The New Press, 2010.
Taylor, Mark. *Crisis on Campus: A Bold Plan for Reforming our Colleges and Universities.* New York: Alfred A. Knopf, 2010.
Washburn, Jennifer. *University, Inc.: The Corporate Corruption of Higher Education.* New York: Basic Books, 2005.
Wilshire, Bruce. *The Moral Collapse of the University: Professionalism, Purity, and Alienation.* Albany, NY: State University of New York Press, 1990.

5

Reading the "Other" in World Literature: Toward a Discourse of Unfamiliarity

Swaralipi Nandi

A few days ago, we were discussing Achebe's short story, "Dead Men's Path," in my World Literature class. Students summarized the text as the story of a superstitious village in Africa where a modern, educated man tried to make a difference but failed. They unanimously agreed that Mr. Obi, the impudent headmaster of the village school, was right in objecting to the villagers' superstitious desire to keep their sacred path open. However, he should have been a little more cautious in reasoning with the village folks. I asked them what they thought of the young woman dying after the ancestral burial place was desecrated. "Do you think that this might be a curse of the spirits?" I egged on. There was a unanimous denial: they did not think there was any hint of supernatural in the story; it was about protesting against "silly" superstitions of the African villagers; the death was just a coincidence. "But why not?" I persisted. "What if we read it as a supernatural story of the ancestors' wrath bringing disaster to Obi and the village? Suppose the story was set in a small town in Georgia and it tells the tale of an ancient curse? We have so many ghost stories like this." Now the students were visibly uncomfortable and then finally one said, "Do you think that might be a possibility? Maybe the writer is really talking about the supernatural events then...I am not sure...but that would be so *uncanny*."

In an instant, the certitude with which the students had interpreted the story stood dubious. It was easier for them to connect the notion of superstition to a remote African village that had never seen the light of modernity. But to overlook the presumed connection between Africa, superstition, and a messiah of modernity for some other reading that questions these cultural markers was uncomfortable. No longer did they feel confident about dismantling the text through the authority of their own understanding and scientific reasoning. Instead they felt anxious and "*uncanny.*" Significantly, "uncanny" is the precise term that Gayatri Spivak uses in *Death of a Discipline* to propose the new way of approaching World Literature. Though Spivak's "uncanny" was less of the English word "uncanny" and more of Strachey's translation of Freud's word *unheimlich*—which she explains as turning something familiar into something unfamiliar—my students' discomfort at the disruptive elusiveness of the foreign text echoes Spivak's notion of the unfamiliar. This chapter seeks to analyze "World Literature" through the paradigm of this "uncanny" or unfamiliar as a pedagogical approach for American students to read non-Western, marginal, and translated texts. Analyzing the history of Eurocentrism of World Literature in America, as well as the dynamics of its revision to include the non-Western other, I argue for a pedagogy of alterity that is in sync with the trends of critical cosmopolitanism that proposes to open up a new way of conceptualizing the Third World "other" as a part of the global collective.

World Literature and the Question of the Other

The World Literature that I will be discussing here is solely in the context of American academia, the initiation of which can be traced back to the 1920s. John Pizer narrates a comprehensive historical trajectory of the concept of World Literature in the United States, attributing its American origins to the translation of Eckermann's *Gesprache* into English by Margaret Fuller—a member of the transcendentalist group—under the title *Conversation with Goethe in the Last Years of his Life*. A seminal German text by Goethe's young student Eckermann, *Gespräche mit Goethe in den letzten Jahren seines Lebens*, recounts the account of Goethe's idea of *Weltliteratur*, which passed into common currency as "World Literature." The central idea behind Goethe's multifaceted, and often variously interpreted, notion of the *Weltliteratur* was an aspiration for moving beyond national boundaries and encountering literatures from the other parts of the world. Thus, calling national literature a rather "unmeaning term," Goethe rejected the idea of the "national" or "patriotic": "It is to be hoped that people will soon be convinced that there is no such thing as patriotic art or patriotic science. Both belong, like all good things, to the whole world, and can be fostered only by untrammelled intercourse among all contemporaries, continually bearing in mind what we have inherited from the past" (quoted in Strich, 935). For Goethe, the resources of national literature were bound to be exhausted, since "left to itself every literature will exhaust its vitality, if it is not refreshed by the interest and contributions of a foreign one" (quoted in Damrosch, *What is World Literature*, 7). The need was therefore to create an interaction between the various traditions of foreign literatures that not only enrich each other intellectually, but also affect a mutual understanding and tolerance among diverse nations. Goethe's rejection of the insularity of the nation and his desire to engage with the world is certainly an echo of the cosmopolitism ideals of the Enlightenment that was characterized by, as Schelereth defines, "an attitude of mind that attempted to transcend chauvinistic national loyalties or parochial prejudices in its intellectual interests and pursuits. In the ideal, the 'cosmopolite' or 'citizen of the world,' sought to be identified by an interest in, a familiarity with, or appreciation of many parts and peoples of the world" (xi–xii). Goethe too sought to envision a world literature that would transcend the regional and facilitate a global cultural exchange.

Theoretically idealistic, Goethe's notion of world literature is nevertheless essentially Eurocentric in its conception. As Gail Finney has noted: Goethe's world literature, that he uses almost synonymously with European literature, is significantly different from the contemporary discipline of comparative studies (quoted in Pizer, 25). Though Goethe articulates his admiration for the non-Western texts, especially for Chinese literature—for when Eckermann expresses skepticism about the Chinese novels, Goethe exclaims that the Chinese had an older literary history than their European forefathers (quoted in Damrosch, *What is World Literature*, 12)—his primary focus is on Germany and its "Western neighbors" (as he wrote in 1827: "It is pleasant to see that intercourse is now so close between the French, English, and Germans, that we shall be able to correct one another. This is the greatest use of World Literature, which will show itself more and more" [quoted in Stritch 350]). Evidently, Goethe is not aiming at multiculturalism, nor is he apologetic to assert that not all literatures should be imparted the same value:

> But while we thus value what is foreign, we must not bind ourselves to some particular thing, and regard it as a model. We must not give this value to the Chinese, or the Serbian, or Calderon, or the Nibelungen; but, if we really want a pattern, we must always return to the ancient Greeks, in those works the beauty of mankind is constantly represented. All the rest we must look at only historically. (132) (quoted in Damrosch, *What is World Literature*, 12)

While Pizer passionately defends Goethe against criticisms of Eurocentrism, arguing that it merely reflects the logical limitation of "international cultural mediation in his age" (27), World Literature has predominantly stuck to its Eurocentric origins in its conceptualization in the American context.

Coming back to the evolution of World Literature as a discipline in American academia, Pizer chronologically narrates the important historical junctures that shaped world literature. Fuller's translation of Ekermann inspired Thomas Higginson in 1890 to propose courses in the American curriculum that "stress what is universal in literatures" (87). Higginson's emphasis was to search for the "common Western heritage" particularly in the Great Books courses that began to develop between the world wars (88). Significantly, like Goethe, Higginson takes into account only the Western literatures—only those "nations which have brought their product to the highest external perfection" (quoted in Pizer 89)—and as Pizer asserts, Higginson's model for a selective canonicity dominated the World Literature curriculum. Higginson's ideas were soon taken forward by Richard Moulton whose *World Literature and Its Place in General Culture* (1911) situates World Literature essentially in the context of the English-speaking world. As Pizer comments on Moulton's vision: "Moulton's consistently underscored 'English point of view' inspires him to see 'the Hellenic and Hebraic' civilizations as most significant for the historical development of his and his audience's culture...Most other literatures are either entirely extraneous to the English-speaking world or stand in the relation of collateral propinquity to it" (90). Consequently, Moulton divides his anthology into three definite sections of "Literary Pedigree of the English speaking people," "World Literature from the English point of view," and the "Five Literary Bibles" that he argued to be fundamental for the cultural development of the Western world—the Holy Bible, the classical epics and tragedies, Shakespeare, Dante, and Milton and versions of the story of Faust. Moulton's vision of a curriculum based on these seminal works certainly tries to impart a particular model of sociocultural and moral values that define a quintessential Western identity. World Literature for him is, thus, not so much about opening up the "literary, cultural and personal horizons" (Moulton, 437) as he claimed it to be, but rather was a training that would reinforce the essential cultural identity of the Western world. In a similar strain, Philo Buck, the founder of the discipline of Comparative Literature, emphasizes the desired Western focus of World literature courses, asserting a cultural alliance between Europe and America as the center of the world in contrast to the non-Western margins.

The focus on Western literatures remained a defining trait of World Literature courses for decades together. Though subsequent proponents of World Literature in the 1950s like Calvin Brown and Lionel Trilling criticized the contemporary trends of World Literature and called for revisions in the courses, none suggested a revision of the Euro-American centrism of the discipline. Instead, while Bown asserted that comparatists should intervene with their specialization in European languages to include more classics and canonical texts in World Literature courses that were increasingly taken over by the English departments and modern English and American literatures, Trilling lamented the overshadowing of the great English literary traditions by an emerging trend of multiculturalism in World Literature. Trilling's contempt for the diversity of World Literature as a rival for English Literature is caustic, and he commented sarcastically:

> Events are bringing into question the preponderating importance of the Judaic-Hellenic-Christian tradition. For a time, we of the West have dominated the world. But we know that we can no longer dominate it, ought no longer dominate it, should never have dominated it. We thought we could teach and lead others: we have sinned the sin of pride. Now we must listen to new voices too long unheard. There is the voice of China, there is the voice of India, and very likely a good many others when we come to look for them. If we listen to these voices, then the voice of the Judaic-Hellenic-Christian tradition becomes but one in a great chorus. And of course any one national temporal part of that voice comes to seem small and thin indeed, let alone any personal part of it. Can we spend our students' time on Keats when all the Upanishads wait? (374)

Trilling staunchly objected to this apparent democratization of literatures through World Literature, arguing that imparting equal value to all cultures actually leads to "an implied denial of the actuality, of the force and value, of any culture" (379). Simultaneously, Trilling rejected the idea of a World Literature based on translations; for translations being imperfect, the only literature worth considering should be literature in English.

It was not until 1959 that the first objection against the Western concentration of "World" literature was voiced by Werner Friederich in the Comparative Literature Conference organized by the University of Wisconsin. Friederich expresses his dissent from the constricted focus of World Literature, which in effect renders the word "world" in World Literature a misnomer. As Friederich sharply points out, it is almost a "psychological faux pas" to state that World Literature is centered within the geographical limits of Europe:

> Just because our own intelligence is limited, we feel justified in making such atrociously arbitrary decisions—just as our limited religious tolerance

insists on calling a truly virtuous man a fine "Christian" because somehow it seems inconceivable to us that this exalted adjective might be applicable to Mahometans and Buddhists. We all share, collectively, in our frequent failure to acquire the good will of other nations and continents—and for that reason too, the term World Literature, simply should be abolished for academic, political as well as psychological reasons. Sometimes, in flippant moments, I think we should call our programs NATO Literatures—yet even that would be extravagant, for we do not usually deal with more than one fourth of the 15 NATO-Nations. (14–15)

Friederich's impassioned call for a diversification of the courses of World Literature however does not necessarily reject the supremacy of the United States in a post–World War II world. Instead, his plea for exploring the other cultures beyond Europe—which he divides into qualitative categories of "the friendly cultures of Japan and India, the at present aloof culture of the Mahometanism, the at present hostile culture of China" (20)—is specifically a call in the context of the geopolitical realities of the contemporary time when United States was emerging as the global leader after the fall of Europe and thus sought to expand its political and cultural alliance beyond Europe. Nevertheless, Friederich was one of the earliest ones to identify the "Western" problem of World Literature and call for its revision. Similarly in the same 1959 conference of Wisconsin, another speaker, Hazel Alberson, pleaded the case for the inclusion of non-Western literatures in the World Literature curriculum. Her plea was not a radical one that calls for a total overthrowing of the Western canon; rather, she argued for creating a niche for the non-Western literature alongside the Western literary giants. Alberson in a way goes back to Goethe's original idea of World Literature that aimed at an active interaction between diverse cultures and the inculcation of a cosmopolitan world view among men of different nations on the basis of universal humanity. The aim of such a course, Alberson asserts, is "to arouse a respect for the traditions of the East, to erase some of the contempt that stems from ignorance, and promote a larger tolerance" (49).

From this point onwards, courses on World Literature increasingly opened up to include literary traditions from non-Western cultures. From a postmodernist point of view, Frederich Jameson argued for the fragmentation of the Western canon that was preserved as an epithet for the centered subject and the "unified personal identity." Since one increasingly encounters "an unavoidably fragmented society," it is best to honestly face the "fact of fragmentation on a global scale" (67). For Jameson, the otherness of the Third World literature is something that the Western audience needs to experience, leaving their conservatism about their own cultural past and a narrow European canon. Though Jameson made sweeping generalizations about what constitutes Third World texts, and was aptly admonished by Aijaz Ahmad's equally famous essay, he did initiate, as Pizer asserts, a link to cultural studies in World Literature courses. The World Literature course at University of California, Santa Cruz, modeled after Jameson's ideas, served as a pioneer in opening up the discipline from its Euro-American centrism to a non-hierarchical study of diverse cultures. Pizer mentions a list of other thinkers on World Literature who consequently opened up to the inclusion of the non-Western in the discipline, including conservatives like Bennett and Lynne Cheney.

By the 1980s, World Literature had started to change significantly, moving beyond its core concentration on Western canon to diffuse and include literatures from other formerly neglected literary traditions of the world. As David Damrosch (*What is World Literature*) testifies, by the 1990s even the most conservative anthologies like the Norton anthology came out with an expanded edition in 1995, devoting a considerable amount of space to non-Western literatures. The opening up of the canon however came with its own set of problems. There were very few teachers who could actually teach World Literature courses of such a wide breadth. But apart from that, there were more serious pedagogical issues about teaching non-Western texts in an American classroom that keep haunting us today. How do we introduce texts from a plethora of foreign cultures to uninitiated American students so that they end up with a sense of the "world" and not an essence of it? Traditionally, World Literature has approached the non-Western "other" through two broad paradigms of commonality and cultural difference, both of which are also significant concepts in theorizations of contemporary cosmopolitanism. I will be exploring the problems of both these paradigms in the contexts of both world literature and cosmopolitanism in the next section.

Problems of Reading the Other: Reading Sameness and Difference

Needless to say, the issue of Euro-US centrism in World Literature did not end with just the inclusion of the non-Western texts in the curriculum. Instead, the methods of approaching those non-Western texts raised important questions about alternative Western hegemony. The reception of non-Western texts among Western readers has a long trajectory of domesticating the "other" to something familiar. Several postcolonial theorists have contended that domesticating the foreign text through translation, and thereby the foreign culture by extension, has been a consistent practice of cultural appropriation in the colonial period. Tejaswini Niranjana cites William Jones's famous injunction—that translation would serve "to domesticate the Orient and thereby turn it into a province of European learning" and contends that as translator and scholar, Jones's Indian texts were responsible for the most influential introduction of a textualized India to Europe (12). Richard Kearney observes that this trait of cultural reduction is essential to Western thought: "The activity of philosophy, the very task of thinking is the reduction and domestication of otherness... To think philosophically is to comprehend—*compendre, comprehendere, bregeifen*, to comprehend, to include, to seize, to grasp, and thereby master the other, thereby reducing its alterity" (Kearney, 370).

The issue of "domestication"—Lawrence Venuti's term for translating "in which the foreign text is imprinted with values specific to the target language culture" (*Translator's Invisibility*, 49)—has been a central point of critique especially in postcolonial translation theories. Venuti's seminal book *Translator's Invisibility* argues how British and American translation practice since the seventeenth century has been largely focused on the erasing of the foreign, partly through a policy of non-translation, or, where translation does take place, by the selection of more easily assimilated source texts and the use of a "fluent" translation practice that "domesticates" the source to conventional forms in the receiving culture, making the act of translation and the translator's work "invisible." Venuti's next venture, *The Scandals of Translation*, exposes even more blatant instances of domesticating translations inscribing domestic values on foreign texts, almost to the point of distorting the original text. Thus, as Venuti points out, the English translation of Umberto Eco's bestselling *The Name of the Rose* deletes 12 pages of the original to improve smoothness of the text for the English language reader (154). The tales of a village priest and a Communist mayor by Guareschi was manipulated in translation so that they "spoke directly to the American link between the power of male heterosexuality and anti-Communism" (131). Similarly, Venuti examines Japanese literature translated into English, finding that publishers and translators in effect conspired to show only one aspect of Japanese literary culture by translating just a few authors who are not necessarily representative of Japanese literature. Kawabata, Mishima, Tanizaki, and later Abe and Oe were, for a long time, the only representatives of Japanese literature made accessible to English-speaking audiences.

In a different context of postcolonial writing, it is the same protocol of searching for the sameness in the foreign that accounts for the success of what Timothy Brennan terms the "cosmopolitan writer" of the non-western world among the Western reading public. The cosmopolitan writer, according to Brennan, is one who echoes the structures of the West—hybridity instead of fixed national identity, "Western" values of democracy and freedom instead of traditional cultures (142)—and all those paradigms that make literature more appealing to the global audience through the conventions that the West finds easier to grasp. In a similar strain, Masood Ashraf Raja (2009) aptly points out that the reasons for the failure of Rushdie's *Grimus*, though it also incorporates the fusion of Eastern and Western literary traditions like his hugely successful *Midnight's Children*, lies in the fact that the latter had "a voice more amenable to metropolitan tastes, a voice that would fit the horizon of expectations constructed around diasporic fictions, a certain ideal type created by the metropolitan critics" (4).

Foreign texts in the World Literature curriculum have been more than often domesticated to fit into the literary paradigms already at hand, a phenomenon that Vilashini Cooppan evocatively describes as turning "the tenth century Japanese *monogatari* prose narrative into the novel of *avant-la-lettre*, *The Tale of Genji* into *La Princesse de Cleves*, Naguib Mahfouz into Egyptian Marcel Proust, Rushdie into the Indian Gabriel Marquez" (Teaching World Literature, 38). A cursory look at the World Literature course descriptions posted online reveals the astounding tendency of seeking a sense of global solidarity by discovering the similarities or connections between the texts in most course objectives. Sarah Lawall identifies this as the central problem of cross-cultural studies, for the foreignness of a text in an intercultural study, in all probability, is substituted for some version of local experience. Citing Jurij Lotman's argument, Lawall suggests that the non-Western texts in World Literature texts are meant to represent difference and thus fill the role of an oppositional other but their foreignness has also been "domesticated through being channeled by local recognition patterns"(12). It is for the same reasons that Takayuki Yokota-Murakami condemns the practice of "comparativism" in literature altogether because it is inevitably exclusionary (187). Asserting that the search for a universal concept has always been the driving force behind any comparative reading (21), Yokota-Murakami concludes that any "translinguistic/civilizational comprehension cannot be achieved except by a distortion of the object in accordance to the viewer's paradigm.... Comparison, then, is realized through the imposition of the observer's paradigm upon the other" (187–88). For Yokota-Murakami, the only option is to reject comparative study totally, since it inevitably presupposes the "violence" against, and oppression of, "the Other" (187, 189).[1]

The problem with applying Western models to non-Western texts is not only an ethical issue but also practical, precisely because it is not impossible to read an even utterly unrelated foreign text through the paradigm of sameness. Peter Rabinowitz mentions this as a serious problem especially in a reading community where close reading of the text is encouraged. Picking one or two texts from a non-Western foreign context in a World Literature classroom that relies mainly on close reading does not only signify "tokenization" but also an appropriation of the foreign text through the Western culture where the universality is not altogether impossible to establish—"the more closely they read, the more echoes they find, *even if they are not there*" (238, emphasis added).

A potent example of such misreading or imposed reading can be found in David Damrosch's comparative analysis of Sophocles's *Oedipus* and Kalidasa's *Shakuntala* in *How to read World Literature*. Though Damrosch condemns the reductionist trait of "pure universalism" that misses the complexity of the work, he emphatically argues for establishing connections between the diverse texts, especially through an exchange of texts through translations instead of setting them "loose in some deracinated space" (*What is World Literature?* 276). Damrosch's fundamental thesis in his previous book *What is World Literature?* is that texts should circulate beyond their culture of origin—World Literature, according to him, signifies the active circulation of texts in other literary systems beyond that of its original culture (4). However, Damrosch takes this concept of intercultural literary exchange to a different level of reading the foreign text through "the expectations and reading skills shaped by the many works we have read in the past" (46). Damroch makes use of the fund of prior knowledge and attempts a comparative reading of *Oedipus* and *Shakuntala*, justifying his preference for using familiar models to read a foreign text:

> To be effective, a comparison of disparate works need to be grounded in some third term or set of concerns that can provide a common basis for analysis. Without some meaningful ground of comparison, we will be left with a scattershot assortment of unrelated works. Bewildered by their sheer variety we could be reduced to construct the random connections favored by the literary critics in Jorge Louis Borges' story 'Tlön Uqbar Orbis Tertius.' (46)

Interestingly enough, in spite of his own cautionary reminders against reading the foreign text through the paradigm of similarity, Damrosch's interpretative approach is predominantly dictated by the terms of the Sophoclean play rather than Kalidasa's work. Damrosch reads *Oedipus* and *Shakuntala* primarily through the paradigms of character, plot, and the concept of fate—all of which are traditional parameters of literary criticism for classical Greek play.

It is a little confusing why Damrosch chose *Oedipus* to compare with *Shakuntala*. *Shakuntala* has been one of the most popular texts of non-Western origin that has been repeatedly translated, appreciated and interpreted by Western scholars, often with the objective of constructing and appropriating the exotic Orient. Dorothy Figueira's *Translating the Orient. The Reception of Sakuntala in Nineteenth-Century Europe* discusses the immense influence *Shakuntala* had on Western literature and the numerous adaptations it has inspired. Consequently, *Shakuntala* has been read in comparison to several Western texts and legends—with the legend of the birth of Semirami (see Donald McKenzie) on the basis of mythical structures, with Shakespeare's *Tempest* on the basis of *Sringara rasa*[2] and with Jean Giradoux's *Ondine* on the basis of romanticism and Oriental philosophy.[3] While Damrosch himself critiques such comparative reading of the texts based on similarities in themes and world views—calling Goethe's assimilation of *Shakuntala* into his literary categories "as if the play were a straightforward middle-class European romance" (Anthology)—he explains his own comparative choice as based on their similarity of being different. As he explains, "Reading *Shakuntala* along with *Oedipus* can help us see how both playwrights held very different assumptions from most of their modern successors" (52). While this paradigm of difference that supposedly ties these two distinctly different genres of classical plays is left ambiguous throughout the chapter, Damrosch ends up imposing the structural and thematic characteristics of Oedipus on Shakuntala through a close reading of the texts. Thus, the plot progression of *Shakuntala* is argued to mirror the plot of *Oedipus*, both Oedipus and King Dushyanta share similarities in their character and Damrosch lays a significant emphasis on the concept of fate that is an important structural characteristic in Greek classical drama in both the plays.

Reading both the plays through the paradigm of fate or tragic flaw presupposes a misleading conflation of the two distinctly different notions of fate present in each play. The fate predicted by Delphi's oracle in *Oedipus* is more relatable to the modern notion of predestination of Western philosophy that invokes an entirely different philosophical reference to the notions of fatalism, predeterminism and free will. Durvasa's curse in *Shakuntala*, on the other hand, is essentially a penalty for a sin, an atonement for one's own *karma* in the classical Hindu scheme of things and hence one's own doing. Thus the damnation of Oedipus and the damnation of Shakuntala are not only totally unrelated concepts, but imposing one on the other amounts to an epistemic violence. Moreover, Damrosch's attempt to relate the characters in the two plays and interpret them through their royal stature, an analysis of their Freudian subconscious and the paradigm of tragic flaw moves the focus of *Shakuntala* from the female character to the male lead, Dushyanta, as the central agency of the narrative. With Dushyanta taking up the central space as the main protagonist of the play on a comparative scale with Oedipus in Damrosch's reading, Shakuntala is pushed to a similar state of marginality as that of Jocasta. Ironically, while Shakuntala becomes an interesting study of Indian womanhood for many critics, including Romila Thapar's informed analysis of the changing notions of Indian womanhood that could be tracked through various versions of the story of Shakuntala, Damrosch displaces the centrality of the female character altogether. Damrosch's comparative reading of *Shakuntala* fails to even mention the *rasa* theory of classical Sanskrit drama or place the text in the literary and cultural contexts of classical India. Damrosch virtually reinterprets the text completely as a sister text to *Oedipus*. Though he does discuss the stylistic and syntactical uniqueness of Sanskrit poetry as modes of difference, his larger models of familiar interpretive protocols are enough to domesticate the text on several levels. Thus, what Damrosch justifies as method of avoiding the "bewilderment" of the "other" ends up being a hegemonic imposition of the familiar.

This practice of comparing two completely unrelated texts, by taking into consideration the cultural and literary modes of only the Western one can be perilous, more so perhaps in a World Literature class than in a Comparative Literature class. Here we need to make a conscious distinction between World Literature and Comparative Literature as academic disciplines. World Literature courses in American academia are targeted mostly as introductory courses for undergraduate students who have minimal or no exposure to a foreign language. These survey courses attempt to teach students what Pizer calls the "*breadth* of the world's cultural diversity" (108) in contrast to the objectives of *in-depth* engagement with foreign literature and culture of the Comparative Literature and the Cultural Studies programs. As John Pizer points out, "Comparative Literature has traditionally been, and should remain, the preserve of those already proficient in different languages, already attuned to movement towards the Other of discrete cultures" (113). World Literature courses can only initiate that interest for exploring the other cultures early in the student's college career, which she can pursue later through graduate courses of Comparative Literature. However, World Literature cannot practically teach students cultural nuances and in-depth reading of foreign texts nor can it be expected to inculcate the critical sensibilities that a Comparative Literature course aims to do. Approaching a non-Western, foreign text through the model of finding its similarities with a familiar Western text can be self-defeating for an undergraduate student with no training in foreign cultures or languages outside the Euro-American context. Not only do the students miss out on the cultural nuances of the text that would have stood out if at least read autonomously, the "world" in World

Literature ends up looking like an inferior version of the "home" with no uncertainty of encountering difference. Moreover, students start expecting Western comparative texts for every foreign text they encounter and texts that do not fit any Western counterpart appear as aberrations.

If the trope of familiarizing the foreign is problematic, the trope of "difference" in World Literature does not come without its set of problems. More than often, the inclusion of the non-Western foreign in a predominantly Western system or culture signifies an act of tokenism and exoticization. As Graham Huggan aptly points out, "cultural difference also has an aesthetic value, a value often measured explicitly or implicitly in terms of the exotic.... it seems quite clear that the value of the latest multicultural anthology or ethnic autobiography has something to do with the exotic appeal of these culturally different products" (13). The value of cultural difference is thus a byproduct of the culture of commodification, where the cultural other is packaged and offered in a superficial and simplified form for its readymade consumption by the West. In a similar strain, through an in-depth analysis of contemporary World Literature anthologies, Wail Hassan argues that the inclusion of the Western sections in the anthologies overtly show a tendency to showcase the non-Western foreign as a token of difference in a predominantly Eurocentric World Literature course. Analyzing the subsequent editions of the *Norton Anthology of World Masterpieces*—one of the most widely used anthologies for World Literature survey courses—Hassan observes that while the first four editions of the anthology concentrated solely on Euro-American masterpieces, making world literature coterminous with Western literature, the fifth edition of 1985 that included works from the non-Western world also reveals a hidden Eurocentric agenda. Only R. K. Narayan, Mishima Yukio and Wole Soyinka, quite inexplicably, gained entry in the main anthology as "Contemporary Explorations," and the 1992 edition, again without any explanation, dropped these three to include Chinua Achebe and Naquib Mahfouz. Such random inclusions and exclusions, Hassan suggests, offer a quick sampling of the non-Western texts rather than any serious engagement with them:

> The experience of reading becomes truly a contemporary exploration for the reader-tourist consumer with a short attention span and thirst for the exotic commodities. Reading and teaching World Literature has become a leisurely stroll in a global literary mall that is structured at once to satisfy and reinforce Western modes of consumption and interpretation (8).

Not only that, excerpts from the Quran, as Hassan notes, was strategically put under the rubric of the "Middle Ages"—an age which invokes the connotations of the "Dark Ages" in European history. Moreover, the 1995 edition added the non-Western section as an "expansion" to the Western canon, which carries the connotations of annexation, globalization and colonization (9). Hassan thus concludes that the inclusion of the non-Western foreign in the anthology does not signify a subversion of the Western hegemony, nor does it suggest the "fundamental structural changes reflecting a new vision of global reality"; rather, such changes end up asserting the non-Western foreign as just an appendix and a token presence in the Western literary system.

This "packaging of alterity" (Figueira) in most disciplines that include the non-Western other, whether be it in world literature, multicultural or postcolonial studies, can provide an easy access to the elements of foreign that does not require the trouble of foreign-language learning. Thus, such pedagogies, as Dorothy Figueira argues, also "feed American isolationism, for in the Internet age, when the globalization of English has contributed to diminishing the need to learn languages, the Other can in these formats be consumed 'on the cheap'" ("Comparative Literature versus World Literature," 30). Figueira also points out a more serious concern with such disciplinary tokenism of difference, arguing that such celebrations of alterity within the academic curriculum tend to substitute the actual need for cultural tolerance in and outside the American academia:

> The institutionalization of World Literature, like other pedagogies of alterity, claims to redistribute rights and radically rethink issues of recognition. My fear is that these efforts create a smokescreen for societal and institutional unwillingness to change the academic situation of *real* Others, namely minorities in American academe. With such theories and pedagogies, institutions can avoid grappling with race and difference under the pretense of doing something progressive. (35)

Figueira's critique echoes the argument John Guillory makes in his famous *Cultural Capital* where he argues, on the same lines, of the dissociation between institutional radical practices and the actual actions of social justice. He critiques the gesture of literary canon revision in universities that assume that such representation is "standing in for representation in the political sphere," thus suggesting that "socially defined minorities cannot be redressed by the same strategy of representation" (11). As Guillory argues, the inclusion of the non-Western other in the literary canon will be assimilated as a cultural capital and will not affect any actual subversion of power unless there is actual demographic change in the university and more members from the marginal communities enter the university.

The conflation of the writer's identity with that of the social group or culture he/she represents gives rise to another serious problem of misinterpreting the foreign in reductionist terms. When a foreign writer's text is read as an authentic documentary about his/her culture, instead of the writer's own creative response to that cultural context, the text is seen less as a creative work and more as a repository of extracted cultural information. Searching for the authentic foreign experience in a foreign text can end up creating more stereotypes for students about their global others. Rob Burton's comment on *Midnight's Children* indicates the problematic consumption of the global text as the authentic voice of the marginal: "The narrator, like Rushdie is a subaltern: a voice from the Empire, one who is writing back to the Mother country in order for their story to be heard" (104). Not only is the non-Western writer assumed to be the authentic speaker for his culture, he/she is also inextricably equated with the narrator, and thereby the presence in novel becomes a voice of cultural authenticity.

Assuming that the non-Western writer is a native informant who can "speak for" the marginal experience with insider's knowledge, is not only fallacious but also reinforces the same hegemonic norms of appropriating otherness. Spivak's critique of Foucault and Deleuze's dialogue in "Can the Subaltern Speak" specifically addresses the problem of this conflation. Positing a close reading of the double meaning of representation in Marx, as it appears in the *Eighteenth Brumaire of Louis Bonaparte*, Spivak argues the limits of "representationalist realism" (69). As Marx speaks of representation as *vertretung* (that is, political representation, or "speaking for") and representation as *darstellung* (as in re-presentation or staging), Spivak critiques a conflation of these two: the "position that valorizes the concrete experience of the oppressed" while being "uncritical about the historical role of the intellectual" (69). While Spivak goes on to argue the inextricability of the Other voice, her warning about the intellectual endeavor that attempts to usurp marginal agency by claiming "what actually happens" is significant:

> It has helped positivist empiricism—the justifying foundation of the advanced capitalistic neocolonialism—to define its own arena as 'concrete experience,' 'what actually happens.' Indeed, the concrete experience that is the guarantor of the political appeal of prisoners, soldiers and school children is disclosed through the concrete experience of the intellectual, the one who diagnoses the episteme. (6)

Often, texts from the non-Western margins come to be consumed and appreciated for the testimonial value they supposedly carry. A quick skimming through of the Amazon book reviews for the internationally acclaimed non-Western novels is enough to reveal how Khaled Hosseini's *Kite Runner* is admired for its "authentic picture" of Afghanistan and how the recent Booker sensation, *White Tiger* by Arvind Adiga, is applauded for bringing out the "real India." One of the most important lessons that we need to impart to our World Literature students is that a text does not necessarily stand as a testimony for a whole culture. A text grounded in a local cultural paradigm is still a writer's own creative response to his specific cultural and literary contexts, which he can represent, highlight and even subvert, but can never claim to "authentically" report.

Toward an Ethics of Difference

Approaching the non-Western foreign text through the paradigms of familiarity and difference both entail their own respective problems. Yet I would argue for the paradigm of difference over the paradigm of familiarity, precisely because a training in respecting and identifying "difference"—no matter how problematic the definition of that alterity might be—is still an important lesson for non-hegemonic global coexistence. Embracing universalism just because multiculturalism is problematic cannot be a solution; instead we need to be more critically aware of the problems of alterity and consciously circumvent the easy consumption of the global other.

But can a sense of belonging to the world, which exposure to world literature aims to do, be gained by rejecting familiarity? Can cosmopolitanism be built on difference? Cosmopolitanism, in its diverse forms, has mostly been theorized on the paradigm of shared sameness. Kant's version of Enlightenment cosmopolitanism, articulated in his influential works like "Idea for a Universal History from Cosmopolitan perspective" and "Perpetual Peace," builds on the notion of a universal law of morality based on universal reason. Similarly, Martha Nussbaum emphasizes recognizing "common aims, aspirations, and values, and enough about these common ends to see how variously they are instantiated in the many cultures and many histories" as an essential precondition for a cosmopolitan consciousness. Even contemporary cosmopolitan theorists like Kwame Anthony Appiah, in spite of his informed discussion on multiculturalism and Eurocentric cosmopolitanism, still insists on the quintessential human values we share universally (29). However, with the trope of universalism in cosmopolitan thought being critiqued as a Eurocentric vision,[4] we need to look at more critical cosmopolitanisms of Paul Gilroy and Walter Mignolo who rethink cosmopolitanism from a postcolonial position.

Gilroy suggests that cosmopolitan solidarity can be built on differences more than on shared commonality. As he emphatically asserts in *Postcolonial Melancholia*, "the methodical cultivation of a degree of estrangement from one's own culture and history…might qualify as essential to a cosmopolitan commitment" (67). This cosmopolitan vision finds "civic and ethical value" in the encounter with otherness. For Gilroy, it is not just about gaining self-knowledge through the encounter with the other. Rather, "we might consider how to cultivate the capacity to act morally and justly not just in the face of otherness—imploring or hostile—but in response to the xenophobia and violence that threaten to engulf it, purify or erase it" (67). In the same strain, rethinking cosmopolitanism outside the narrative of European modernity, Walter Mignolo appeals for a cosmopolitan solidarity based on the epistemic diversality that "shall be the ground for political and ethical cosmopolitan projects. In other words, diversity as a universal project (that is, diversality) shall be the aim instead of longing for a new abstract universal and rehearsing a new universality grounded in the 'true' Greek or Enlightenment legacy" (15). Mignolo's version of cosmopolitanism thus does not seek to build solidarity on the basis of quintessential human commonality but rather builds a consensus for difference. It is a cosmopolitanism where "diversity" itself is a "universal project."

A World Literature course imparts important lessons of making sense of the world on a microcosmic level. Thus, a training in encountering difference and stepping out of one's familiar space is of utmost importance for American students in the contemporary culture of homogenizing globalization.[5] As John Pizer points out:

> When American students consider the contemporary world outside their borders, or even when they venture into this external world through travel or surfing through foreign Websites, it is only a slight exaggeration to say that what the inattentive among them see, hear, and experience is: America. The perception is generally interrupted only when acts of terror committed by foreigners take place. When such events occur, the Other emerges as a figure indeed marked by radical alterity, but precisely thereby as evocative of violence and malevolence, someone to be dreaded, despised and feared. Such perceptions are still widespread in the wake of the atrocities committed on September 11, 2001. Otherwise, American values, American business, the English/American language, American popular culture, and American architecture have become so predominant, at least superficially, across most of the globe that even the American eager to experience and

appreciate cultural diversity, to know the "Other" as other, generally must make substantial efforts... This of course is not to say that American students have more inherent difficulty than students in other countries in comprehending cultures other than their own. (5)

World Literature thus has a crucial role to play in American education. Encountering the bizarreness of the "Other" through World Literature can be unsettling and yet a learning experience for an American student who is regularly fed on the rhetoric of American superiority as world leaders. At a time when American intervention has increased in every part of the globe, whether be it through political intervention and fighting against terror in the Middle East, Afghanistan, and Pakistan, or be it through the economic globalization of the multinational companies in the remotest part of the world (as shown by a famous Indian advertisement of Coca-Cola where a tourist traveling to a remote village in Ladakh vainly searches for water, only to get Coca-Cola instead), the unsettling of the American attitude of being the center of the world is the first step toward a humbling experience of being part of the globe as just one among the others.

We should also remember that teaching cultural difference in the contemporary age of electronic media is a more daunting task than ever before, precisely because students have more access to information, including misinformation, than ever before. Students signing up for World Literature courses are not *tabula rasas* on whom we can inscribe our lessons of alterity. With easy access to information through the Internet, personal encounters with a variety of foreign cultures in their increasingly diversifying society, and the constant bombardment of images and global news through journalistic media, contemporary students are more likely to have already heard and encountered the cultural contexts that they encounter in their World Literature courses and are, consequently, more likely to come to class with their own authority of knowledge, including their own sets of stereotypes, presumptions, and ideas about those cultures. Teaching them how to read against the grain of their own "familiar" presumptions, or what Spivak calls "the arrogance of the cartographic reading of World lit" (*Death*, 73) is the task at hand.

Spivak invokes the concept of "uncanny" as the gateway to a more critical form of alterity. She refers to the word uncanny in Freud's sense of the *unheimlich*, denoting "the turning of what is homey into something *unheimlich*"—or, *uncanny* in this German-substitute sense. To consider the word this way is in itself a disciplinary exercise in Comparative Literature: "In what circumstances the familiar can become uncanny and frightening, I shall show in what follows... What is heimlich thus comes to be unheimlich" (74). Spivak appeals for the "defamiliarization of the familiar space" (76) through what she calls forcing a reading—a reading that turns "identitarian monuments into documents for reconstellation" (91). Ingrained to Spivak's concept of the "unfamiliar" is her concept of "planetarity," which she proposes as planet-thought that can overwrite the globe:

> Globalization is the imposition of the same system of exchange everywhere... To talk planet talk by way of an unexamined environmentalism, referring to an undivided natural space rather than a differentiated political space, can work in the interest of this globalization in the mode of the abstract as such. I have been insisting that to transmute the literatures of the Global South to an undifferentiated space of English rather than a differentiated space is a related move. (72)

Spivak's proposal thus emphasizes on the indecisiveness of a planetary identity to overwrite the existing available political and cultural identities. Displaced from all available parameters of definition, the Other will as be transmutable as the self, the cartographic boundaries being dissolved, just like what Spivak describes through a vivid metaphor, a planetary surface that looks politically undeterminable from the window of a plane. While Spivak's vision of planetarity maybe too abstract to apply for World Literature survey courses (Spivak proposes this specifically for in-depth musings in Cultural Studies and mentions that language training is crucial for this) we can certainly borrow Spivak's idea in moderation and visualize a World Literature course that teaches the students to confront and be humbled by "unfamiliarity" and question their own centrality in the globe.[6]

As Vilashini Cooppan tellingly asserts: "I prefer to imagine my students' surprise at discovering another Mosul and Baghdad than the one flashing forth in fire and smoke on CNN as the mark of a moment of incommensurable knowledge. Who are 'they' and what is 'their culture'? These unspoken questions of the classroom that read one Baghdad in the shadow of another were in the end unanswered by the *Nights*" (37). As long as our students' faith in the CNN version of Baghdad is shaken by *Arabian Nights*, I think we are doing fine.

Notes

1. Also see Rey Chow who asserts that the trope of the universal represents the perpetuation of existing power relationships: "I would therefore offer the hypothesis that the current and rather euphoric talk about globalization is more of the same old ongoing Western modernist narrative in which the

enlightened belief in universals (inclusionism being one such universal) proceeds hand in hand with, or is the mere flip side of, the perpetuation and enforcement of cultural boundaries (that is, practices of exclusion)" (69). Rey Chow, "How (the) Inscrutable Chinese Led to Globalized Theory," *PMLA* 116, no. 1, Special Topic: Globalizing Literary Studies (Jan., 2001): 69–74.
2. See Sheela Rani Khare, "Multiple Facets of Love in the Plays of Kalidasa and Last Plays of Shakespeare," in *Studies in Literature in English*, vol. XIII, ed. Mohit Kr. Ray, (New Delhi: Atlantic Publishers, 2007), 10–38.
3. See Arthur C Buck, *Jean Giraudoux and Oriental Thought: A Study of Affinities*. American University Studies: Series III, Comparative Literature, vol. 6. (New York: Peter Lang, 1984).
4. For a critique of Kant's cosmopolitanism, see Walter Mignolo, "The Many Faces of Cosmo-polis: Border Thinking and Critical Cosmopolitanism," *Public Culture* 12, no. 3 (Fall 2000): 721–748; for a critique of Martha Nussbaum see Judith Butler, "Universality in Culture," in *Martha C. Nussbaum with Respondents*, ed. Joshua Cohen. *For Love of Country: Debating the Limits of Patriotisms*, Boston: Beacon Press, 1996. 45–53; for a critique of Appiah see Mohammad R. Salama, *Islam, Orientalism, and Intellectual History: Modernity and the Politics of Exclusion since Ibn Khaldun*. London and New York: I.B. Tauris, 2011.
5. Vilashini Cooppan makes a similar claim about the potential of world literature to change the hegemony of globalization: "In this fact lies the intriguing possibility that literary studies may be *the* vantage point from which to begin to interrogate and remake globalization theory, and to endow it with a more nuanced, 'connective and disruptive' vocabulary with which to describe cultural processes and cultural productions" (23). See Vilashini Cooppan, "Ghosts in the Disciplinary Machine: The Uncanny Life of World Literature," *Comparative Literature Studies* 41, no. 1 (2004): 10–36.
6. Robert Wininger articulates world literature creating a similar effect of self-questioning: "The toughest lesson for me, then, is that world literature forces me to forego, at least as regards those languages that I do not command, all that I normally hold dear, namely close formal-aesthetic and historical analysis of texts. Lone scholars that we often are in a professional field that remains quintessentially individualistic, we can no longer judge for ourselves. Our categories become suspect the moment we sense, if we sense, a lack of applicable coordinates." See Robert Wininger, "Lost in Terra-Cognita or What is and to What End Do We Study World Literature," *Comparative Literature* 62, no. 4 (2010): 315–335.

Works Cited

Alberson, Hazel S. "Non-Western Literature in the World Literature Program." *The Teaching of World Literature: Proceedings of the Conference at the University of Wisconsin April 24–25, 1959*. Edited by Haskell M. Block. Chapel Hill: University of North Carolina Press, 1960, 45–52.

Appiah, Kwame Anthony. *Cosmopolitanism: Ethics in a World of Strangers.* New York: Norton, 2007.
Brennan, Timothy. *Salman Rushdie and the Third World: Myths of the Nation.* New York: Macmillan / St.Martin's, 1989.
Burton, Robert. *Artists of the Floating World: Contemporary Writings Between Cultures.* New York: University Press of America, 2007.
Cooppan, Vilashini. "The Ethics of World Literature: Reading Others, Reading Otherwise." In *Teaching World Literature.* Edited by David Damrosch. New York: The Modern Language Association of America, 2009, 34–43.
Damrosch, David. *What is World Literature?* Princeton, NJ: Princeton University Press, 2003.
———, ed. *Teaching World Literature.* New York: The Modern Language Association of America, 2009.
———. *How to Read World Literature.* Oxford: Wiley-Blackwell, 2009.
Figueira, Dorothy. *Translating the Orient: The Reception of Sakuntala in Nineteenth-century Europe.* Albany: State University of New York Press, 1991.
———. "Comparative Literature versus World Literature" *The Comparatist* 34 (May 2010): 29–36.
Friederich, Werner P. "On the Integrity of Our Planning." In *The Teaching of World Literature: Proceedings of the Conference at the University of Wisconsin April 24-25, 1959.* Edited by Haskell M. Block. Chapel Hill: University of North Carolina Press, 1960, 9–22.
Gilroy, Paul. *Postcolonial Melancholia.* New York: Columbia University Press, 2005.
Guillory, John. *Cultural Capital: The Problem of Literary Canon Formation.* Chicago: The University of Chicago Press, 1993.
Hassan, Wail S. "World Literature in the Age of Globalization: Reflections on an Anthology." In *Aspects of Contemporary World Literature.* Edited by P. Bayapa Reddy. New Delhi: Atlantic, 2008, 3–17.
Huggan, Graham. *The Postcolonial Exotic: Marketing the Margins.* London: Routledge, 2001.
Jameson, Fredric. "Third-World Literature in the Era of Multinational Capitalism." *Social Text* 15 (Fall 1986): 65–88.
Kearney, Richard. *Twentieth Century Continental Philosophy.* New York: Routledge, 1994.
Lawall, Sarah. "Introduction: Reading World Literature." In *Reading World Literature: Theory, History, Practice.* Edited by Sarah Lawall. Austin, TX: University of Texas Press, 1994, 1–64.
Mignolo, Walter. "The Many Faces of Cosmo-polis: Border Thinking and Critical Cosmopolitanism." *Public Culture* 12, no. 3 (Fall 2000): 721–748.
Moulton, Richard G. *World Literature and Its Place in General Culture.* New York: Macmillan, 1911.
Nussbaum, Martha. "Patriotism and Cosmopolitanism." *Boston Review.* 19, no. 5 (October–November 1994). http://bostonreview.net/BR19.5/nussbaum.php>

Pizer, John. *The Idea of World Literature. History and Pedagogical Practice*. Baton Rouge, LA: Louisiana State University Press, 2006.

Rabinowitz, Peter J. "Against Close Reading." In *Pedagogy is Politics*. Edited by Maria-Regina Kecht. Urbana, IL: University of Illinois Press, 1992, 230–244.

Raja, Masood A. "Salman Rushdie: Reading the Postcolonial Texts in the Era of Empire." *Postcolonial Text*. 5, no. 2 (2009). postcolonial.org/index.php/pct/article/download/1073/948; p1–14.

Schlereth, Thomas. *The Cosmopolitan Ideal in Enlightenment Thought: Its Form and Function in the Ideas of Franklin, Hume, and Voltaire, 1694–1790*. Notre Dame, IN: University of Notre Dame Press, 1977.

Spivak, Gayatri Chakravorty. "Can the Subaltern Speak?" In *Marxism and the Interpretation of Culture*. Edited by C. Nelson and L. Grossberg. Urbana, IL: University of Illinois Press, 1988. 271–316.

———. *Death of a Discipline*. New York: Columbia, 2003.

Strich, Fritz. *Goethe and World Literature*. Translated by C. A. M. Sym. London: Routledge, 1949.

Tejaswini Niranjana. *Siting Translation: History, Post-structuralism and the Colonial Context*. Berkeley: University of California. Press, 1992.

Trilling, Lionel. "English Literature and American Education." *The Sewanee Review* 66, no. 3. The University of the South 1858–1958: The Centennial Symposia (Summer, 1958): 364–381.

Venuti, Lawrence. *The Translator's Invisibility: A History of Translation*. New York and London: Routledge, 1995.

———. *The Scandals of Translation: Towards an Ethics of Difference*. London and New York: Routledge, 1998.

Yokota-Murakami Takayuki. *Don Juan East/West: On the Problematics of Comparative Literature*. Albany: State University of New York Press, 1998.

6

Pedagogy for Healing and Justice through Cambodian American Literature

Jonathan H. X. Lee and Mary Thi Pham

Introduction

Literature, when written or performed correctly, can yield what Faulkner refers to as the "pillars to help [us] endure and prevail." It is this type of literature that we seek to excavate from a haunted Cambodian past and to illuminate an American society that has long misunderstood, misrepresented, and mishandled the Cambodian American communities into the margins of humanity. Through explorations of Cambodian American "healing narratives," we attempt to undo the internal colonization, "the patterns of exploitation and domination of disenfranchised groups *within* the United States" that have been a part of Cambodian American narratives (Spivak, 792; emphasis original). We invite Cambodian and non-Cambodians to retire the Cambodian American "victim narratives" by spotlighting narratives that heal and empower. Jonathan H. X. Lee notes that

> For many Cambodian Americans, first generation refugees, 1.5 and second generation Cambodian Americans, comfort and ease are often far from their lives. Seen—if they are seen at all—as perpetual victims, as refugees, their social and economic struggles with gang activities and welfare dependency dominate the discourse about them, pointing out and blaming their recent history as the origins of their "plight." But they have survived, and even with scars, they thrive, and in so doing, have brought their wealth of culture, their wealth of community, and their tremendous strength that was gained through their struggle to survive. (2010, xiv)

Since Cambodian American literature[1] is growing, the scope and breadth of this chapter is limited to Anida Yoeu Ali's poem, "Absence, Part 2: Crying," Chath pierSath's poem, "Reunion," and Peauladd Huy's poem, "I am here."

This chapter shifts our focus from the Cambodian American "victim narratives" to the production, promotion, and distribution of "healing narratives." First, the cultural and social terrain of Cambodian American history is laid out. We argue that Cambodian Americans are "socially dead" and therefore unable to connect to their traditions, cultural lifeways, histories, and social institutions because of the legacy of the Khmer Rouge's genocidal campaign. Having experienced "social death," Cambodians and Cambodian Americans are hindered in their attempts to seek justice and to heal from the evils of the Khmer Rouge regime. However, shifting the narrative and popular imagination of Cambodian Americans from being "victims" is a central step toward becoming "socially undead." This part requires that we focus on the production and transmission of "healing narratives." Before articulating the differences between victim narratives and healing narratives, we explore, albeit briefly, the interconnection between this narrative shift in discourse with what we term a pedagogy for healing and justice. One central question that we invite readers to explore is: "What's at stake in the continual production and perpetuation of Cambodian American 'victim narratives' in society?" We juxtapose this question with a delineation of "healing narratives" through an examination and explication of several Cambodian American literary texts that fall under this category. This chapter expands the concepts of language as a healing agent and its functions to raise awareness, seek justice, and transmit hope to the next generations. Lastly, the relationship between literature and society is explored, proposing the integration of Cambodian American literature into the US classrooms and literary spheres.

Cultural Historical Background

The Cambodian autogenocide, which lasted for three years, eight months, and twenty days, between 1975 and 1979, when the Khmer Rouge (KR) held power in Cambodia, has been described as one of the most radical and brutal periods in world history. It was a time of mass starvation, torture, slavery, and killing. Imagine children separated from their families, trained as soldiers, and ordered to kill not just strangers, but also their own parents. Imagine being held guilty of crimes that you have not committed and being forced to admit guilt, then sent to reeducation camps and labor camps as punishment for the said criminal activities, or sentenced to death. The KR, under the leadership of Pol Pot, attempted to copy Mao Zedong's Great Leap Forward in China, and create an agrarian utopia based on rice agriculture. This would create the "cleanest, most fair society ever known in our history," as stated in a propaganda radio broadcast (Hinton, 8). However, the message failed to mention that creating this "cleanest" and "most fair" society required the destruction of families, social support systems, and cultures.

Invoking the concept of "social death" defined by Claudia Card as "central to the evil of genocide... [the] loss of social vitality is loss of identity and thereby of meaning in one's existence. Seeing social death at the center of genocide takes our focus off body counts and loss of individual talents, directing us instead to mourn losses of relationships that create community and give meaning to the development of talents" (63). For Cambodian Americans, social death was compounded by mass migration of refugees seeking safety. This resulted in culture shock, survivor's guilt, and the challenges of adapting to a new, modern society. Fleeing one's homeland does not simply represent leaving a physical space, but also a disconnect that occurs from losing one's sense of self, culture, and history. The loss is physical, somatic, cultural, and symbolic. The number of Cambodians who died under the Khmer Rouge remains a topic of debate; Vietnamese sources say three million, while others estimate 1.7–2 million deaths. More than three decades later, Cambodians worldwide are still haunted by this grim chapter in their history—collectively and individually. Traumas among Cambodian Americans are transmitted across multiple generations silently and unconsciously. First generation refugee-survivors remain quiet about their experiences and transmit social death—the inability to sustain and maintain connections to traditions, community, and history—to their Cambodian American children. The birth of subsequent generations to a community that has been destroyed and ties to past generations that have been severed through separation and death is termed natal alienation (Card, 74). Card states, "Those who are *natally* alienated are *born* already socially dead" (74; emphasis original). Children who experience natal alienation grow up with a superficial understanding of their heritage, family histories, parents' culture, and roots because access to cultural resources is limited. While this may not be the case for all, or to the same degree, for some refugees of the Cambodian genocide who immigrated to the United States, social death and natal alienation are applicable concepts that highlight the link among psychological, social, and cultural traumas. How can Cambodian Americans employ literature to become "socially undead" and hence to reengage with society, community, and self? Cambodian American literary expressions provide one path toward becoming "socially alive" that is part and parcel of the complex process of healing and the search for justice.

Pedagogy for Healing and Justice

Among Cambodians living in Cambodia and the diaspora, *peace* is elusive, since *justice* may never be achieved. "How is justice possible if Pol Pot is already dead?" many survivors asked after 1998. In 2003, The Extraordinary Chambers in the Courts of Cambodia (ECCC) was established between Cambodia's government and the United Nations, with a mandate to prosecute senior members of the Khmer Rouge for war crimes and crimes against humanity. Today, many of the surviving victims and their descendants fear that the majority of the Khmer Rouge leaders and low-level personnel will go unpunished because the judicial process is being manipulated by the current prime minister Hun Sen, himself a known former Khmer Rouge leader. In fact, Prime Minister Hun Sen declared in October 2010 to UN Secretary General Ban Ki-moon that no new cases would be investigated.

On June 27, 2011, Case 002 opened and is currently proceeding, with no planned successor. The four defendants are: Nuon Chea, 84, Pol Pot's second in command; Khieu Samphan, 79, the regime's head of state; Ieng Thirith, 79, former minister of social affairs; and her husband Ieng Sary, 85, who was the foreign minister. All four reject the charges against them and maintain their innocence. Khieu Samphan has also refused to cooperate with the court.

The taste of injustice affects the lives of Cambodians at home and in the diaspora. Ou Virak, president of the Cambodian Center for Human Rights, acknowledged that even though the Khmer Rouge crimes were committed more than 30 years ago, "they remain ingrained in Cambodia's collective psyche." Virak hypothesizes that the collective psyche of Cambodian subjects is suspended in an in-between state of ambivalence and fear, which exemplifies the victim narrative. However accurate Virak's statement may be, Cambodians and non-Cambodians can shift their focus from the impossibility of justice to the possibility of transformation, and by extension, to the possibility of other forms of justice.

Although judicial justice may be impossible to achieve in post-conflict Cambodian and Cambodian American communities, small but meaningful progress toward achieving other forms of social justice and healing is possible through literary expressions. Teri Yamada documents how Cambodian American writers employ memoirs as a way to not only record history and tell their story, but also to transform trauma from pain and terror to socially engaged efforts to demand justice for survivors of the Killing Fields (Yamada 2005, 2010). Similarly, Cathy Schlund-Vials writes about praCh Ly, a Cambodian American hip-hop artist who employs Khmer musical styles and techniques, with voice clips from movies about the Killing Fields, and family narratives to construct an identity *as* Cambodian American and a transnational subjectivity that situates the self in a vexing position between two worlds: America and Cambodia (Schlund-Vials). Lee argues that the 1.5 generation and second generation Cambodian Americans will creatively employ the works of Cambodian Americans coupled with their own family narratives to (re)create, (re)discover their history and construct a self that is consciously Cambodian and American. These creative expressions are central to the healing and becoming socially undead that lies beyond judicial justice (2010, 343–353).

We, therefore, envision a pedagogy of healing and justice that is inspired by bell hooks's conception of "liberatory pedagogy" (9) and Paulo Freire's concept of "humanizing pedagogy" (68). Healing and justice pedagogy is achieved when Cambodians and non-Cambodians are exposed to Cambodian American literary expressions. Analysis of this genre of literature authenticates Cambodian Americans as humans as opposed to "victims" that, invoking Freire, requires "action and reflection" as a praxis that is capable of transforming the world (125). In regards to the case at hand, this praxis of action and reflection can alter Cambodian Americans from "victims" to human beings who transform their past and dictate their own futures. As Freire suggests, "The important thing, from the point of view of libertarian education, is for the people to come to feel like masters of their thinking" (124). For Cambodian Americans, this means the possibility of piecing together the fragments of an identity that was shattered under the Khmer Rouge. Rebuilding Cambodians' lost sense of identity is a starting point for tackling individual, community, and national healing.

Cambodian American Victim Narratives

It's useful to examine a "victim narrative" and inspect how its features differ from a "healing narrative." There are no clear markings that determine whether a text is a "victim narrative" or a "healing narrative" and each reader experiences a text differently. We evaluate whether a text is a "victim narrative" or a "healing narrative" based on the way the text lifts or squashes the human heart.

One example of a "victim narrative" is Sharon May's interview with Soth Polin. Throughout the interview, Polin shares his love for literature and his writing career, but even within these narratives, they are clouded by despair and lingering visceral haunting(s) of the Khmer Rouge. Polin explains to May the crippling effects the Khmer Rouge has on the imagination and states:

> Even if we had more writers of my generation, we could not succeed if we continued writing as we did. There is something that we cannot get past.

> It just kills the imagination. It is the atrocity of the Khmer Rouge. Even if you are reaching in your imagination for a new destination, you cannot get past their cruelty. When you try to write something without mentioning the Khmer Rouge, you can't. The next generation will forgive that, they will forget, but for us, we cannot forgive it. (16–17)

Polin's answer speaks to his generation's creative energies being stymied by the memory and trauma of the Khmer Rouge regime. He also distinguishes between the experiences of his own generation and that of future generations who may still be affected through intergenerational trauma. However, unlike his generation, they may still be able to transcend the loss through literary production.

This hopelessness is further reflected when May asks Polin: "What advice do you have for young writers?" He replies with a hopeless question, "That is difficult to answer. I cannot give advice to myself. How can I advise other people?" (16). Although Polin's answer is honest, it also reflects a person who is unable to lead others. He lacks personal agency. When May probes Polin to disclose how the Khmer Rouge affected him, he concludes by saying:

> As I said before about the Khmer Rouge: you cannot get past it. You resuscitate a painful past, and you have to talk about it. You cannot pass over it. That is a lesson for humanity: not to let it happen again—that atrocity and that cruelty. Maybe this is why I cannot finish my writing: because of this story. Because of this, I lost my inspiration. Because the reality surpasses the imagination. (20)

Polin has admitted defeat as a writer and cultural producer. The personal and collective pain has incapacitated Polin's imaginative and narrative power. He can only share his story and depend on May's benevolence to take up the healing work. This text engulfs the reader's optimism and deflates the spirit, indicating a "victim narrative."

What purpose lies in making distinctions between a "victim" and a "healing" narrative? Kelly McKinney raises challenging questions for psychotherapists who use the "testimony method" [2] to heal political violence survivors and critiques the reframing of the trauma story in the way it attempts to portray "historical truth" by casting patients as "innocent victims, paradoxically denying a sense of their full moral and psychological agency rather than restoring it" (Haaken in McKinney, 267). Victims are painted in a one-dimensional lens untainted by vengeful thoughts. The creation of this "false, pure victim identity" that some clinics practice in their healing sessions are detrimental because the patients lose their "authentic selves" and must suppress their desire for revenge; this suppression retards the patients from tapping into their personal agency (McKinney, 267). McKinney's findings challenge popular beliefs that the simple retelling of a "victim narrative" elicits liberation and results in fewer victims burdening society. We caution against this false liberation. The (re)creation of these "victim narratives" perpetuates a cycle of helplessness in which the patients cannot access their agency.

In addition to perpetuating victimization, the (re)production of Cambodian American "victim narratives" uses Cambodia's historical past as a scapegoat and legitimates that the United States is based on meritocratic values, denying the existence of racial inequality. For example, in *The New York Times*, Patricia Brown reports on sex trafficking of Southeast Asian American minors. However, she does not explicitly show that there's a direct correlation between high crimes and poverty. Instead, she links the vulnerability of Cambodian American girls to being raised by emotionally distant parents affected by the Khmer Rouge. While this is not to understate the post-traumatic stress disorder of those who have been affected by the Khmer Rouge's reign of terror, we are showing how the framing of this reporting is misleading. She not only briefly mentions poverty, but Brown also relays that "the Polaris Project, a national advocacy organization, estimates that a stable of four girls earns over $600,000 a year in tax-free income for the pimp. Drug dealers here are increasingly switching to prostitution, inspired by the bottom line and fewer risks" (2011). This huge figure gears readers' mind frames toward profit rather than poverty. This kind of reporting elides the real issues that many Cambodian American communities are facing: high poverty, crime, and low funding. Furthermore, Brown cites organizations like Asian Health Services and Banteay Srei, suggesting that the girls are already receiving social help, therefore no further resources are required for under resourced and unprivileged Cambodian American communities.

The Khmer Rouge regime is still being blamed for all social unrest within Cambodian American communities. This tendency to use the Khmer Rouge regime as a scapegoat is disproportionate to the actual Cambodian refugee experience in the United States and must be reexamined critically to aid Cambodian American communities in effective ways. Ownership of our social problems ensures a society based on democratic values. Since we are all interconnected, this benefits all communities and society as a whole. More empowered Cambodian Americans result in a lesser presence of victimization in our society and a healthier nation-state. This is an invitation to retire "victim narratives" and to counterbalance them with the cultural production of "healing narratives."

Cambodian American Healing Narratives

Does literature have the capacity to incite social change? David Morris posits that suffering exists beyond language (27), but that literature is a safe, alternate space that's more distant from the writer and reader, and hence, suffering becomes more accessible (31). According to his assessment of literature's functions, it can be used to tap into suffering in ways that are inaccessible through the "transmission model."[3] If suffering can be accessed it allows for the opportunity of healing. Morris concludes that:

> the content of the utterance while crucial to its writer or speaker, matters less in suggesting what literature can tell us about suffering than the sheer act of speech itself: affliction has at last broken through into language. We are finally in the presence of words that cross over from the other side of torment. (30)

Voice is a portal for the suffering to finally be released. Morris's assessments of literature coupled with Faulkner's assertions regarding the poet's role are good measures for recognizing "healing narratives." Morris claims that studying certain elements of literature can aid us in the way we think about suffering. We deviate from Morris in the elements that he examines. Instead of studying voice, genre, and moral community, we examine the interplay among history, literature, subjectivity, cultural production, and social suffering, justice, healing, and empowerment for self and community.

Poetry: Writing for Self, Writing for Others

"The world changes the poetry, and the poetry changes the world," says U Sam Oeur during an interview with Sharon May (189). Oeur's statement is reflective of the "victim narratives" that were produced after the atrocities of the Khmer Rouge regime. Before war broke out in Cambodia, poets celebrated beautiful things. After the war, the poems were bathed in the aftermath of genocide (189). The second half of Oeur's quote that "poetry changes the world" articulates the potency of poetry to transform. Although Cambodian American poetry still addresses feelings of hopelessness, some of the poems' tones are gradually shifting toward healing, empowerment, and justice.

Poet: Anida Yoeu Ali[4]

An example of a "healing narrative" is Anida Ali's poem "Absence, Part 2: Crying." Ali begins by capturing the essence of "absence" through various metaphors. Absence is leaving, separation, shadows, silence, mourning deaths, witnessing tears, remembering home, sacrifice, and so on (1–20). Taking on multiple meanings, "absence" doesn't merely connote a state of being away or a state of deficiency; "absence" is also the consequences of the Khmer Rouge's destructive regime. This poem serves as documentation of these absences and the crimes against humanity.

The poem may seem like a "victim narrative" because of the endless depiction of tragedies, but there is hope. Partway through the poem, Ali asserts that absence is "the heart's unrecorded ache," but as this is uttered, the poem becomes self-reflexive and creates a space for the heart's unrecorded ache (21). In the process of telling, Ali uses her poem as a means to record these losses; her use of form reinforces and echoes the contents of her message by giving legitimacy to grief and by acknowledging the suffering of the victims of the Khmer Rouge. By revealing the absence that is felt when the suffering of millions continue to go unacknowledged and newborns, who are born natally alienated, are embedded in a "dying generation / of living memories," the poem becomes a space for healing and seeking social justice for all generations (42–43). Ali also addresses the suffering of her parents. This poem is reflective of the promising "healing narratives" that are emerging from 1.5 and second generation Cambodian American artists.

According to Lee's "ethics of identity formation," 1.5 and second generation Cambodian Americans are better candidates than the first generation to "lead the way to inter-generational recovery, since they did not directly face the horrors of the Khmer Rouge like their parents did, and can therefore more easily confront the past and move through it" (2010, 351). Ali's poem employs this by preventing future generations from experiencing historical amnesia. Thus, her poem fits Morris's valuations of literature by addressing and healing personal and cultural wounds, and Faulkner's criteria for being a voice that lifts humanity's heart and serves as a pillar to "help [us] endure and prevail."

Poet: Chath pierSath

Another "healing narrative" is Chath pierSath's poem, "Reunion" in which a poet imagines his own death in order to reunite with his mother. The beginning shows serene images of the way he remembers Cambodia before the atrocities of war and autogenocide. As he leads us further into the poem, there are various images: demonstrations against the massacre of their innocence, a celebratory dance in the monsoon for all the loved ones who died, his mother's embrace, and a reunion. The poem closes with a solo line declaring: "Having known her is my sorrow and my inheritance" (14). This is also the last line of his book of poems.

pierSath's poem lends complexity to the "healing narrative" because it occupies both joy and pain. The title "Reunion" conjures both happiness and sorrow because while it speaks of the possibility of a reunion, it simultaneously connotes separation: the absence of his mother through her death and his survival. Unlike a "victim narrative," the poet acknowledges the suffering, but ultimately takes ownership of his inheritance and chooses to celebrate life. Despite the morbidity of imagining his own death, pierSath uses poetry as a vehicle to imagine a happy reunion with his mother by expanding our familiar notions of "death."

Death appears four times in the poem, yielding multiple meanings and positive connotations. The first death refers to the speaker's mother. However, rather than depicting her death, he breathes life into his mother through his poetry and through the afterlife. He memorializes her. Rather than endanger her safety, the speaker conjures his own death. pierSath's second allusion to death engages in poetic license in the way his death embodies agency through its purpose to reunite him with his mother. Death doesn't take on the traditional meaning of dejection and surrendering; instead, it represents a means to "eternal peace" (3).

The third reference to death occurs in juxtaposition with the "thatched-roof house full of strong women / raising their fists against the massacre of their innocence" (8–9). The "massacre of their innocence" alludes to the Khmer Rouge's autogenocide, but the speaker does not depict helpless victims in submission. The powerful activist imagery reimagines the tragedy by transforming suffering into demanding justice; thus creating a path towards self-empowerment. These images are displays of anger (not despair) which have not been appeased because of the lack of justice. As Frank Stewart explains, the function of writing is a means by which "individuals are able to maintain their humanity and resist evil—and, therefore, why the freedom to write is always a threat to authoritarian regimes" (xi). Lastly, the poet alludes to death once more when he dedicates a dance in the monsoon for all of his "loved ones [he] never got to know" (11–12). pierSath's remembrance of these deaths through his writing rehumanizes the dehumanized by paying homage to the innocent lives that were lost. Moreover, he memorializes the death of the innocent who were not provided a proper burial. This "funeral" releases the souls of the dead and allows them the possibility of rebirth. As Buddhists, the dead who are not properly buried are doomed to suffer in the hell realm as "hungry ghosts." Through literary expression, pierSath reunites social bonds and allows for souls to be reincarnated.

Literature Performs "Socially Undead" Ceremonies

In addition to setting the souls of the dead free, the act of telling history is a claiming of public space (Tonkin in Sugiman, 384). Elizabeth Tonkin's research (1992) suggests that testimonial discourse not only involves using language to orient oneself to the topic and audience, but also places a claim that one should be listened to (Tonkin in Sugiman, 384). The poets in this chapter locate themselves in history and assert their testimonial discourse into a public narrative. Pamela Sugiman hypothesizes that the "literacization of memories is always a political act" ("Abstract"). These acts claim and create their own subjectivity. Similarly, the act of resurrecting these personal/national memories/histories has the power to move the Cambodian American communities forward psychologically, socially, and politically.

Through reading these reconstructed accounts, we challenge the "socially dead" effects of the Khmer Rouge regime. Literary production has the ability to perform "socially undead" ceremonies within Cambodian American communities in the way it revives these social connections that the Khmer Rouge regime demolished. This act of defiance is also an act toward liberation. As Paulo Freire states, "Freedom is acquired by conquest, not by gift. It must be pursued constantly and responsibly" (47). Writers and readers of literature are not merely appreciating and adding to the collection of art; we can make a conscious decision to use "healing narratives" as an agent to heal, seek justice, and transmit hope. With each act of reading, we are staying informed, reconnecting with history, and claiming our freedom.

Poet: Peauladd Huy

Huy's poem, "I am here," demonstrates poetry's ability to raise the dead in order to speak about the crimes against humanity that the Khmer Rouge inflicted upon the once-living. The poem is split into three sections with the same speaker using different tones in each section. The speaker states that breaking silences and seeking justice are the main objectives. However, each section uses different devices to achieve this affect.

The tone in section one reminds readers that this is not a matter of "what's already done" (5). The speaker was once alive, a functioning human being like us. Due to the Khmer Rouge take over, s/he experienced an unnatural death. The crimes against humanity committed by the Khmer Rouge are reinforced at the end of the first section when the speaker poses a rhetorical question to the perpetrators: "What more can you do? / Piss on my bones again?" (14–15). The "piss" informs the reader of the cruel conditions under which the speaker lived and died. Moreover, since the opening of the poem is in present tense, the surprised ending jolts the reader into the realization that the speaker has come back from the dead in order to speak. This is an instance of literature performing a "social undead" ceremony by reconstructing relationships between the dead and living.

Section two begins with a direct address to the reader: *"Don't be alarmed, Reader"* (16; emphasis original). The speaker's interpellation creates an unnerving response from the reader and makes the text self-reflexive. The reader is reminded that s/he is reading and something more is at stake; the writer's political act becomes the reader's. The speaker declares: "I am here to speak / because they are too afraid / to remember, still too stunned to speak out" (17–19). By confiding in the reader, the speaker breaks down the wall between the printed words and the reader. Reading is no longer an act of enjoyment and complacency, but a conscious attempt to evoke compassion and to witness this speaker's testimony. To read is to attest to the writer's truth.

The third section begins with a bold warning: *"Reader discretion is advised"* (30; emphasis original). The warning gives readers a choice to either back away from the poem or to continue reading at their own risk. Carrying the same message as the last section, the speaker reminds us that reading is not passive and not for the faint-hearted. This section divulges the gruesome details as to why victims are still traumatized and unable to speak. Unthinkable horrors such as cannibalism lurk in the subconscious of these victims. The speaker asks: "What do you make me of?.../...a ewe / to be gutted-up for your experimental / eating pleasure" (31–34). This section arraigned the culprits to answer to their indictment, and the speaker and readers serve as the judge and jurors. What the judicial system has failed to achieve, poetry may still avail. These unfathomable cruel acts consume and erode the life sources of these victims. They have become numb and socially dead, but poetry addresses and heals cultural wounds.

The tone in this section is more urgent and forceful. It effectively uses interpellation to put the perpetrators on trial: "You, you, and you over there / in council chair" (34–35). The speaker fearlessly identifies the culprits responsible for the horrors these victims were subjected to. S/he asks these murderers, "do you think I don't know / how many gall bladders it took to dye your eyes a permanent yellow?" (35–37). Lee notes that among the Cambodian and Cambodian American communities, it is known that some former Khmer Rouge personnel ate the gall bladders of their victims. Thus, an urban legend circulated among Cambodian American communities that those who have yellow eyes may be former

Khmer Rouge personnel who practiced cannibalism (217–219). Similarly, this poem alludes to these inhumane practices, forcing readers to confront the ethical question: "What are our responsibilities as readers, as witnesses, and as citizens of the human race?"

Cambodian American Literature in US Classrooms

There are ways that we can help heal, seek justice, and transmit hope to future Cambodian American generations; the solution begins in our classrooms. The complaint for a more inclusive literary canon is an ongoing debate in the US educational system. Spivak critiques the United States' English Literature classrooms and pedagogical styles by proposing the creation of a new canon that includes literature that is representative of a transnational cultural. Cambodian American literature is tokenized as "ethnic literature" and marginalized in US English Literature courses and departments. Improvement must not only be made toward erasing the "victim narratives" from 1.5 and second generation Cambodian Americans' psyche, but also by encouraging the study and creation of literary criticism for Cambodian American literature in the United States' curriculum and classrooms.

The study of literature is the study of social forces, and therefore, the remedy to healing social suffering is through mapping the various discourses that have been muted by the hegemonic forces of the dominant group. It is possible to honor "victim narratives" as historical documentation without having to transmit and prorogate the victimization mentality. By using "victim narratives" as a pedagogical tool to terminate its crippling effect, a portal is paved for empowerment. However, society must take responsibility for social suffering, commit to an anti-complicity campaign, and engage in activist work that improves the communities that have been disadvantaged by social/historical/political policies and historical formations. We must begin by promoting and producing "healing narratives." We invite all to create an inclusive conversation within a literary sphere which includes Cambodian American literature not as a subgroup, but as an equally fascinating, thrilling contribution to our existing human narratives.

Notes

1. Our definition of Cambodian American literature is broad because any publication related to Cambodian American experiences has an effect on the reception and perception of their communities.

2. The "testimony method" requires "coaxing" the patient to disclose his/her trauma story.
3. The "transmission model" exchanges information (Spano, 6).
4. Anida Yoeu Ali went by the name of Anida Yoeu Esguerra during publication.

Works Cited

Brown, Patricia Leigh. "In Oakland, Redefining Sex Trade Workers as Abuse Victims." *The New York Times* May 23, 2011. <http://www.nytimes.com/2011/05/24/us/24oakland.html>. Accessed Aug. 23, 2011.

Card, Claudia. "Genocide and Social Death." *Hypatia* 18, no. 1 (Winter, 2003): 63–79.

Esguerra, Anida Yoeu. "[RE]Visions." Bloomington, IN: The Collective Press, 2004.

Freire, Paulo. *Pedagogy of the Oppressed*. New York: Continuum, 2010.

Hinton, Alexander L. *Why Did They Kill?: Cambodia in the Shadow of Genocide*. Berkeley: University of California Press, 2005.

hooks, bell. *Yearning: Race, Gender, and Cultural Politics*. Boston: South End Press, 1990.

Huy, Peauladd. "I am here." *Connotation Press.com* 12, no. 2 (August 2011):. http://connotationpress.com/poetry/829-peauladd-huy-poetry. Accessed Aug. 14, 2011.

Lee, Jonathan H. X. ed. *Cambodian American Experiences: Histories, Communities, Cultures, and Identities*. Dubuque: Kendall Hunt, 2010.

McKinney, Kelly. "'Breaking the Conspiracy of Silence': Testimony, Traumatic Memory, and Psychotherapy with Survivors of Political Violence." *ETHOS* 35, no.3 (2007): 265–299.

Morris, David B. "About Suffering: Voice, Genre, and Moral Community." *Daedalus* 125, no.1: (Winter, 1996): 25–45, Social Suffering.

pierSath, Chath. "After: Poems." New York: Abingdon Square Publishing, 2009.

Schlund-Vials, Cathy J. "A Transnational Hip Hop Nation: praCh, Cambodia, and Memorialising the Killing Fields." *Life Writing*. 5, no.1 (April 2008), 11–27.

Spivak, Gayatri Chakravorty. "The Making of Americans, the Teaching of English, and the Future of Culture Studies." *New Literary History* 21, no. 4 (Autumn, 1990): 781–798. Commonwealth Center for Literary and Cultural Change.

Stewart, Frank and Sharon May, eds. *In the Shadow of Angkor: Contemporary Writings from Cambodia*. Manoa 16, no.1 (Summer, 2004): xi–220.

Sugiman, Pamela. "Memories of Internment: Narrating Japanese Canadian Women's Life Stories." *The Canadian Journal of Sociology* 29, no.3 (Summer, 2004): 359–388.

Van Schaack, Beth, Daryn Recherter, Youk Chhang, Autumn Talbott. *Cambodia's Hidden Scars. Trauma Psychology in the Wake of the Khmer Rouge. An Edited*

Volume on Cambodia's Mental Health Documentation Center of Cambodia, Phnom Penh. 2011. Print.

"William Faulkner—Banquet Speech." *Nobelprize.org.* <http://nobelprize.org/nobel_prizes/literature/laureates/1949/faulkner-speech.html>. Accessed Aug. 14, 2011.

Yamada, Teri Shaffer. "Trauma and Transformation: The Autobiographies of Cambodian Americans (1980–2010)." In *Cambodian American Experiences: Histories, Communities, Cultures, and Identities*, ed. Jonathan H. X. Lee.,. Dubuque: Kendall/Hunt, 2010.

———. "Cambodian American Autobiography: Testimonial Discourse." In *Form and Transformation in Asian American Literature*, ed. Xiaojing Zhou and Samina Najmi. Seattle: University of Washington Press, 2005.

7

A Moving Pedagogy: Teaching Global Literature through Translation

Kyle Wanberg

The study of global literature is in a precarious situation today. It faces a host of different problems and difficulties that stem from the expertise of its advocates, the locus of study and its concentrations, and its circumscription as much as from its purported openness. Its pedagogy bristles with obstacles of self-definition, since it has to contend with exceedingly complex and changing networks of circulation, flows of speculation and interest, the definition of borders, and our efforts to think through and beyond them.[1]

David Damrosch's 2009 volume *Teaching World Literature* aims to demarcate this field by addressing the challenge of pedagogy's coverage. Drawing on his attention to the importance of translation,[2] my own contribution is to bring critical pedagogy into conversation with processes of translation. By "translation," I wish to invoke a complex set of concerns, with a number of related, often overlapping, but distinct connotations. Traditionally, translation refers to the transference of a single text from one language to another. First of all, in this everyday definition of translation, there is already an act of literary creation conditioned by the inspiration of the translator. The final product of this interlinguistic process is collectively received and read in the classroom. Second, translation describes the process of the work's reception and interpretation. This can take place on one's own or it can occur in the classroom. Either way, this form of translation is affected by our experiences and limitations. When it occurs in the classroom, it may become a complex dialogical process, shared among students and teachers. Third, translation is used to describe a process of "worlding" that either facilitates or forestalls communication or understanding across cultures. The term "cultural translation," which designates this form of translation, frequently signals an overestimation of one's mastery over other cultures through a reduction of cultural differences. Finally, translation encompasses relations of power and ideology. Translation is inextricably entangled in prevailing networks of distribution and publication. Not all works are translated equally. Rather, certain works are translated into a select number of languages, and these chosen works reflect a range of geopolitical interests that deem them valuable.

In this study, I argue that a moving pedagogy[3] that draws on each of these four aspects of translation can provide a critical, egalitarian model for understanding the dynamics both within the classroom and in regard to what constitutes global literature. In order to approach the shifting networks of global exchange in which literature is entangled today, the enlightenment vision of the world as a thing that should be instrumentalized and exploited for greater knowledge can no longer hold dominion over the study of literatures of the world. In this sense, the movement within global literature pedagogy must also adapt to contemporary issues within literature and bring the process of translation into practice and awareness in the classroom. By speaking of "moving pedagogy," I mean to suggest a method of teaching that is mobile, but also one that is affective, facilitating transformations and new experiences through literature, as well as reimagining authority and the exercise of power in the classroom. Such a moving pedagogy jettisons the hierarchical nature of what Ngũgĩ wa Thiong'o has called the "aesthetic feudalism"[4] involved in the study of literature. To this end, I will explore the teaching of orature as one model for how global literature can be taught with translation at its center.

Pedagogical efforts to unmask or reveal the world once and for all through literature may be flawed not only because they assume an impossible authority over material that is constantly in flux, but also because the very mode of representation within literature tends to unravel sovereign certainties. Instead, readings that take place outside of traditional power dynamics can engage readers in creative reworkings, or translations, of the world. Taking a translational approach to teaching global literature emphasizes its process rather than the final outcome, since ultimately there are no perfect, authoritative translations. Therefore, this approach also draws attention to a continual need for new forms of adaptation and critique. Calling attention to "the inequality of languages,"[5] my intervention in this study is meant to bring these insights about translation into conversation with critical pedagogy. Just as the schoolmaster's complete authority over the classroom is a fiction, so too are ideas about the translator's sovereignty within the text.

Translation is itself a vital form of literary production that changes, shapes, and sometimes also falsifies representation. It is always already underway in the classroom as much as it is within texts. A moving pedagogy of global literature must consider translation as a selective process that regulates access to works and the worlds they depict just as it influences interpretation. Teaching global literature in a moving way involves considering questions of access, availability, and distribution of translations as well as readers' responsiveness to them. This encourages not only critical, but also existential thought.

A Passage Without Mirrors

First conceptualized by Goethe in January 1827, *weltliteratur* fundamentally shifted the study of literature. This made for the reception of greater diversity, including what Deleuze and Guattari have called "minor literatures."[6] Yet in spite of his liberalism, Goethe was compelled to limit the emergent ethic of *weltliteratur*, holding literary works up to a standard of "civilization" and its "development" that privileged imperialism.[7] While the study of literature expanded to become more inclusive, even today its ethos is tied to notions of progress and development that define a model of literature as being formed within and on the basis of so-called great civilizations. In other words, even as world literature disentangled literary production from the ideology of "national character," it also created cultural and national hierarchies within its international scope. Meanwhile, it tacitly excluded certain forms of literary and cultural production, such as orature. A moving pedagogy of global literature must begin to apprehend the complex networks that connect local interests, geopolitics, and translation.

If world literature was, in a sense, a deconstruction of national literature, I want to argue that global literature must embark on the deconstruction of world literature. In this sense, my study is an invitation to depart from discourses about the world and its literatures, toward a process-oriented, moving pedagogy. A moving pedagogy of global literature calls for a skeptical view of the hierarchies established by "civilizing" discourses and pedagogies of literature. Rather than a force of progress and refinement, civilization, when ascribed to an exclusive and privileged seat of culture, must be recognized as an instrument of domination. A model that exalts the centers of cultural production has too often turned a deaf ear to the deafening silence of unspoken worlds.

The tradition of studying literary works as the product of a single great tradition or civilization is harmful, since it supports an erroneous narrative of cultural disparities within literary productivity and value across different parts of the world. For example, discourses that rely on a notion of the "West" as a privileged seat of culture and civilization often ignore peripheral as well as indigenous cultural productions. By paying tribute to these long-established, cosmopolitan centers while shifting attention away from non-Western literatures, such discourses also set up a politics of "us versus them." Appraising the cultural capital of these exclusive centers, they imply the cultural dependency of the so-called Third World on the first, contributing to perceptions about the disparities between them, including feelings of superiority and inferiority.

Rather than simply revising definitions of what constitutes literature, a revitalization of global literature pedagogy can only come from a new way of translating the vast diversity of literature and orature from across the globe. Within the grand narrative paradigm of world literatures, other cultures have too often been exoticized and fetishized as a radical "other" to the construction of the civilized, cosmopolitan self as a privileged reader of culture. Such an interested readership can also lead to the formation of lacunae around literatures that do not lend themselves to its desires. For example, Abdelfattah Kilito remarks on the disregard for translating Arabic literature that does not echo or resonate with works of European literature. As he writes, "Woe to writers for whom we find no European counterparts: we simply turn away from them, leaving them in a dark, abandoned isthmus, a passage without mirrors to reflect their shadow or save them from loss and deathlike abandon."[8]

"Global literature" calls attention not only to the contingency of the form of the literary product, but also to the interests that facilitate particular translations. The memorialization of certain writers in the canons of global literature is an effect of thousands of other voices that have been lost or forgotten, that fell out of the archive, were left unpublished, or did not find their way into translation for one reason or another. This forgetting or lacuna actually makes translation possible. As Walter Benjamin elucidates, these cultural treasures "owe their existence not only to the efforts of the great minds who have created them, but also to the anonymous toil of their contemporaries."[9] For this reason, discussing literature and cultures which are untranslated is as much a part of global literature as the study of works in translation.

The illusion of knowing cultural others through an experience of literature is dangerous. This essentialism expands the literary world into an imaginary one, to which the real world may be made to conform. It reduces forms of life and ways of being of others to whatever is represented and consumed through literature. This way of reading serves the interests of social forms of domination, providing the reader with a narrative of her own mastery or superiority over cultural forms of difference deemed inferior. This reduces critical differences and excludes the foreigner from the student's experience on a fundamental level.

By foregrounding the complex geopolitical interests that authorized and produced a translation, as well as processes of reception and response, global literature pedagogy can reduce the danger that students will read for an "authentic" experience of the identity of cultural others. Étienne Balibar has argued that *"there is no* identity which is 'self-identical'; that *all identity is fundamentally ambiguous."*[10] Following this insight, I argue that translation presents a critical process for raising questions in the classroom about the discourses that frame these identities, opening our minds and making us vulnerable to worlds of representation and experience.

Worlds in a Word

Contemporary translation theorists have stressed the need to bring relations of power and dominance into conversation with practices of translation. Therefore, it has become essential to interrogate the one who participates in the address of a translation,[11] as well as to parse out the relations between linguistic communities that play a vital role in what gets translated, how, and to whom.[12] Rather than viewing culture as a static entity, critical scholars in Translation Studies have begun to reimagine cultures as highly contested networks of exchange that are often as transforming as transformative.[13]

When people talk about teaching global literature, there is usually some form of translation involved. Yet matters of translation, such as why certain works are translated while others are not, tend to suffer neglect and are often overlooked in literary study, suppressed by what Aziz Al-Azmeh has called a "cross-cultural etiquette."[14] It has been my experience that focusing acts of translation[15] can reduce the danger that students will see the world presented in the work as offering an "authentic" experience of cultural others. A set of questions can be raised not just about the complex geopolitical interests that authorized and produced a translation, but also about processes of reception and response. As Al-Azmeh argues, "cultural systems are ideologies,"[16] and students can be encouraged to critically read such systems as well as the implications of their own reading experiences. Since literary encounters may also be made to conform to long-held prejudices and narratives of cultural, national, or ethnic superiority, a critical response to the interpellation of cultural others and the ambiguity of identity is needed.

Translation takes place as a complex network of negotiations and exchanges that, on the level of the individual, are entangled with unconscious processes, and on a collective level, are imbued with interpretive illations. Because global literature is traversed by complex geopolitical interests, the task of teachers and critics is not to exert control over these ties, but to strive to understand and reveal them. Positive efforts to embrace multiculturalism and diversity in global literature have often given prominence to literature from regions of the Global South or the "Third World." Yet such efforts can sometimes occlude other literary traditions within the colonized world. For example, postcolonial scholarship is prone to forget that multiculturalism can come from within one's own national borders, such as the oral literary heritage of many Native American groups. Confronting these challenges by placing emphasis on the process by which the literary production came into our hands, translation can be used in the classroom to draw attention to the influence and dissemination of these oral traditions across diverse contexts. Integrating works of minor literatures, orature, and the conditions and problems of translation in the classroom represents a major critical prospect for the revitalization of the study of global literature.

Critical Pedagogy

While studying translation as literature can help reduce the likeliness that students will read literary representations unambiguously, classroom dynamics can deeply affect the way students understand complex ideas about texts. Critical approaches to pedagogy can also affect the way students apprehend literary representations. For example, critical pedagogy can help unravel the very psychic structures that institutional forms of education keep in place.

In *The Pedagogy of the Oppressed*,[17] Paulo Freire distinguishes between an oppressive "banking" model of public pedagogy and the liberating practices of critical pedagogy. Whereas in the former, students are pictured as passive receptacles into whom knowledge is deposited by a teacher, in the latter these relations of oppression[18] are dissolved in favor of relations of mutual, dialogical learning. Rather than bestowing knowledge on passive and empty vessels of learning, Freire argues that critical pedagogy must confront and dismantle practices of domination and the maintenance of an unjust status quo through dialogue in the classroom. Yet it is possible for students educated under the oppressive, banking model of education to be liberated through their own experience of becoming conscious of their oppression.

Often enough, pedagogy concerns relations that do not neatly fit the mold of outright subjugation. Consequently, it is essential to develop a critical language that can contend with real-world ambiguities as they arise in the practice of pedagogy. This requires translation to take place on several different registers in the classroom where world literatures are taught, emphasizing its relevance to critical pedagogies of global literature.

Critical pedagogy offers teachers ways to think about forces in the classroom that are often occluded, such as gender, race, and class. For example, bell hooks argues for an "engaged pedagogy," stressing the importance of enjoyment in the classroom. Arguing that the notion of pleasure is essential to the liberating possibilities in the classroom, she notices that when students are enjoying themselves and feel part of a community, they are much more likely to learn.[19] This focus on student engagement facilitates the translation of ideas and interpretations between individuals in the classroom, making it a potential site not only of "fun," but also of transformation.

On the other hand, critical pedagogy attempts to give students the critical tools to navigate the often conflicting messages we receive through the media. In "Education after Abu Ghraib," Henry Giroux argues that the photographs that emerged from the brutal and illegal acts at Abu Ghraib prison not only raise issues concerning the social consciousness of the American public, but also the role of translation within pedagogy. Giroux argues that the photographs are not transparent cultural documents, but rather constitute overdetermined material, formed and reformed by the ideologies of its readers. To this end, he shows the diverse conclusions that talking heads and political spokespersons have arrived at with regard to the acts of torture depicted in the photographs. Against readers' passive absorption into the exegeses offered by these public reactions, Giroux signals a critical need to actively *translate* how we interpret this moment. As he writes, "understood as social and historical constructs, photographic images entail acts of translation necessary to mobilize compassion instead of indifference, witnessing rather than consuming, and critical engagement rather than *aesthetic appreciation or crude repudiation.*"[20]

Framing the photographs as historical productions that reflect brutal, unjust activities, this pedagogical mode of translation emphasizes their contingency, and encourages us, as critical readers, to deconstruct the conditions that make these activities possible. Rather than denying us the legitimacy of our affects, it presses us to emote about them in a socially conscious way and to work toward greater social justice. Giroux argues that the pedagogical dimension of critically analyzing acts of torture and other political atrocities aims to develop forms of ethical translation and interpretation empowered to resist the force of discourses that serve to frame and justify these acts. Rather than passively surrendering to the contradictory ways such discourses frame these acts, Giroux sees critical pedagogy as raising critique and situating the meaning of the photographs in the context of relations of power, their investments in texts, and their collective reception. For example, he asks:

> What pedagogical conditions need to be in place to enable people to view the images of abuse at Abu Ghraib prison not as part of a voyeuristic, even pornographic, reception but through a variety of discourses that enable them to ask critical and probing questions that get at the heart of how people learn to participate in sadistic acts of abuse and torture, internalize racist assumptions that make it easier to dehumanize people different from themselves, accept commands that violate basic human rights, become indifferent to the suffering and hardships of others, and view dissent as basically unpatriotic.[21]

While Giroux is concerned with pedagogy as an urgent means of raising critical consciousness, as a task of translation as well as civic engagement, he also considers the limits of education, seeing its role more in preventing situations of intractable violence from arising than in resolving them once and for all. Drawing on Adorno's "Education after Auschwitz,"[22] Giroux sees critical pedagogy as a way to cultivate modes of critique and social responsibility in order to curb future situations of brutality and inhumanity. Giroux's strong appeal for a pedagogy aimed at social justice against domination accentuates the importance of translation for critical pedagogy as a way to critically understand social exchange framed by multiple, competing discourses and feelings without being trapped within a single ideological framework. This promotes a notion of moving pedagogy, involving a shifting framework of discourses meant to inspire students to read complexities critically, ethically, and with feeling.

Mind over Master

If the classroom offers a space to explore ideas about the world as in a microcosm, then the question for a pedagogy proper to global literature would be: How can we understand this world while maximizing the dynamism of the approach and minimizing the reduction of difference? Critical pedagogy offers valuable insights into failed practices of teaching that exercise domination in the classroom. Yet even as it aims to articulate problems of social injustice and the dynamics of power within the classroom, critical pedagogy sometimes constructs a relatively stable notion of power against which it is directed, a discourse that must explain these workings in order to undo them.

No one is fully in control of situations that arise in the classroom. Rather, each class member brings different sets of experience into play. In his book *The Ignorant Schoolmaster*, French thinker Jacques Rancière tells a story about translation that provides a strong argument for understanding the complex interface of the classroom.[23] He argues that the dominant form of education justifies itself through the principle of inequality (the inferiority of ignorant intelligences and the superiority of the schoolmaster's depths of knowledge). But this same justification is an effect of the very educational systems through which inequality is perpetuated. As he demonstrates, "progress is the pedagogical fiction built into the fiction of the society as a whole."[24] Education has to convince the student of her own inferiority in order to uphold this greater fiction.

Rancière focuses on a French enlightenment thinker, Joseph Jacotot, who documents his discovery that he could successfully teach students without having knowledge of the material to be taught. This revelation originated from finding himself in the predicament of having to teach French to a group of Flemish students whose language he did not speak. In spite of his ignorance of Flemish, he succeeded in getting his students to write, surprisingly adeptly, in French. Having given his students access to a bilingual text, they were able, on his prompting, to train themselves in French letters. Of course, Jacotot's extrapolations are necessarily limited by the close relation of these two European languages, whose correspondences may have been of great help to his struggling students.

Taking Jacotot's lesson as a fundamental paradigm shift for pedagogy, Rancière argues for a basic "equality of intelligences."[25] He argues against what he sees as a stultifying system of learning that prescribes explanation for the ignorant by the schoolmaster whose job is to dispense knowledge from on high. What he calls emancipatory education necessitates a mutual and reciprocal recognition of equality. This is opposed to a social system that assumes the inequality that is established through a form of education that mutilates students by impressing them with their basic inferiority.

I would like to stress that it is no coincidence that the practices of translation in his classroom open Jacotot's eyes to the mechanisms behind teaching. The literal practice of translation facilitated Jacotot's translational pedagogy. By having to translate their own responses into the idiom of their schoolmaster, who could not otherwise understand them, his students were also reconfiguring the dynamics of power in the classroom, since the locus of knowledge was with them rather than with the schoolmaster. Reversing the dominant paradigm of learning, the students taught the schoolmaster that he was not the center of the classroom, or even the ultimate source of their knowledge. Rather, the acts of translation on the part of the students represented the center of the classroom dynamics.

In many ways, Rancière's story complements Freire's critical pedagogy. On the one hand, Freire's work represents a dialectical analysis of pedagogical oppression, and even within his dynamic and egalitarian classroom, there is still an understanding that discourse leads the way to freedom. For example, Freire believes Mao Tse-Tung when he says, "we must teach the masses clearly what we have received from them confusedly."[26] On the other hand, Rancière's analysis offers a democratic hermeneutic of the individual as something quite apart from discourse. In fact, discourse, particularly in the form of explanation, leads to the stultification of students by creating the illusion of their dependency.

On the one hand, Freire's model sets consciousnesses in opposition to one another (as in the relation between the oppressor and the oppressed) rather than examining the self-sustaining social order as being itself a mechanism of inequality. On the other hand, Rancière questions the very discourse of inequality that perpetuates the pedagogical, and hence the social, order. According to Bingham and Biesta, Friere resorts to the very exercise of explanation in order to combat its effects.[27] The dangerous point here is the suggestion that the narrative of injustice itself contains the kernel of liberation. Since this discovery originates from the liberator's discourse, rather than the students', it threatens to become stultifying. Rather, providing students access to their personal modes of interpreting, exchanging information, and producing knowledge, an awareness of translation is necessary for critical pedagogy to prevent its practice from stifling the experience of liberation through its own well-intentioned forms of explanation.

Rancière offers critical pedagogy the insight that it has always been in the business of translating, and when it resorts to explanations, it tends towards stultification rather than emancipation. As he writes, "learning and understanding are two ways of expressing the same act of translation. There is nothing beyond texts except the will to express, that is, to translate."[28] Only by relinquishing sovereign authority, thus doing away with the notion that the teacher is essentially superior to the inferior student, is emancipatory teaching possible.

The effacement of the equality of intelligences goes hand in hand with the promotion of an ideology of language inequality. Thus Rancière argues for the "arbitrariness of languages" that opens communication between human beings, in spite of linguistic differences.[29]

De-ghettoization

A pedagogy that shifts away from an exclusive focus on highly established, canonized works to incorporate indigenous works of orature not only offers new inspiration to the study of global literature, but also raises several important challenges. It requires a shift in the imaginary topography of what constitutes the "global," both in terms of the universal sense ("the world" as singular entity) as well as the networks of exchange that traverse it. As a counterpoint[30] to the fundamental inequality of languages[31] and the disparity of literary capital across cultures, such a shift in focus would be a compelling way to redress the multiform exclusions of underrepresented literatures.

Just as thinking about translation in the classroom necessitates an expanded notion of translation, so too does the study of orature. In orature, translation includes not only the passage of material from one language to another, but will usually also entail the transformation from a performative idiom into graphic representation, often in a language rather distally related to the source language. These processes often involve a wider margin of "intercultural transference,"[32] or interpretive errors, than most literal acts of translation. However, rather than understanding these interpretive errors as forms of loss, we should recognize them as opportunities to expand the notion of global literature to embrace the traditions of literary production that have been widely excluded from the "Western" pedagogical canon.

The term "orature" was originally coined by Pio Zirimu, and taken up as a critical call for the mobilization of decolonizing forces in Anglophone African universities where English literature remained a cornerstone for the exportation of colonial literature in newly postcolonial states.[33] Ngũgĩ wa Thiong'o argues that Eurocentric literary perspectives represent a continuing form of colonialism that disempower or ignore the voices of rural, indigenous producers of local culture, while privileging prose written in European tongues. He suggests that orature is a mobile concept that works against spaces of neglect, while reimagining the geopolitical as traversed by previously forgotten centers of inspiration. In this sense, orature "is against the ghetto and the margin."[34]

Explored mostly in the context of African and African diasporic cultural productions,[35] orature should be recognized as a call for the pedagogical incorporation of indigenous cultural and literary productions that still tend to be marginalized and neglected. The idea put forward in the 1950s by Benjamin Lee Whorf that "the picture of the universe shifts from tongue to tongue"[36] challenges, with reference to translation, dominant and basic assumptions about the way our perspectives about the cosmos itself are conditioned by the languages we know. Arguing that language fundamentally changes our way of being in the world,[37] Whorf demonstrates the essential role played by translation in our understanding not only of the physical, but also literary worlds.

A revitalization of global literature may take place through the incorporation of orature. To facilitate this, a moving pedagogy makes a radical shift away from the progress-centered orientation of world literature toward a more process-oriented heterological conception of global literature. The contemporary model of literature must fit the complex "global" system of today, with its constantly shifting networks of exchange. Because translation is so greatly involved in so many of its forms (as outlined above), a critical approach to orature illustrates how translation can be taught as literature, even if works of orature exceed their translations. Until recently, orature has been widely neglected as a major contribution to the diverse forms of representation within literature, and even today discussion of the concept remains largely limited to African and African diaspora literary studies. I contend that global literature pedagogy must embrace a wider conception of orature as an expression of global indigenous cultural production. This idea requires a major paradigm shift, away from the institutions that hierarchize forms of knowledge and languages, toward a more egalitarian, moving pedagogy with built-in faculties of self-critique.

Translation as Literature

The study of world literature has never entailed a neutral or transparent ideology. Rather, its ambivalent history is aligned with the expansion of empire through an attendant model of culture as an organically growing whole. The opacity of the borders within and between literatures may serve as a cover for geopolitical interests. Counter-narratives to occidental domination that subscribe to the nebulous topography of the "West" and the "East" fall into the trap of constructing monolithic and stable entities that conceal the complex, shifting, adaptive systems of power and its networks of exchange. Such narratives can be turned to support sinister, exclusive imaginaries of two meta-cultures in opposition that ignore diversity and cultural interaction.[38] Because it is a counterpoint to the Eurocentric literary canon, it is important that orature not accede to singular or essentialized definitions. As an inclusive template for reimagining the study of global literature, orature involves works from oral traditions in languages that have traditionally been excluded in the study of literature, including a diverse range of works inspired by creolization, folklore, performance, and song.

For example, Donald Bahr's translation of the Pima Ant Songs in his book *Ants and Orioles: Showing the Art of Pima Poetry* could offer an illuminating addition to a course on global literature.[39] Although they have been largely ignored as a literary text, if the Ant Songs were brought into a global literature classroom, they would raise important issues about genre, authorship, and the process of translation. As a work of orature, the songs are inseparable from their performance and ritual recitation in Pima culture. Yet Bahr's rendering offers an effort at translating the songs' dynamic performativity into both transcribed Pima and written English. Their translation is the result of a collaboration between himself, Lloyd Paul, and Andy Stepp. Yet Bahr and Stepp never met each other. Furthermore, since songs are orally passed on in Pima, transmitted from generation to generation, the Ant Songs represent a collaboration of many more voices. Yet their reception in English marks a fundamental transformation in their medium and form. Hearing the Pima alongside the English can give students some sense of the musicality of the original, but as text the song's performance has been fundamentally altered. While the translation of Pima works of orature tends to preserve their art in written form, it raises interesting questions about the transformation of this art in the process. Furthermore, Bahr's translation is not lacking in problematic adaptations of the original that can be explored in detail. This process can lead to a close reading of translation itself as a form of literature, not only as a creative, interpretive act, but also as a process of cultural engagement. The songs' translation also raise questions concerning the relations of power that have delayed or forestalled translations of this sort, as well as those that facilitated the translation at the particular moment in the mid-1990s when the translation appeared. Finally bringing this kind of work into the classroom gives students the opportunity to hear and engage with orature from an endangered language, and to learn about a culture whose prolonged neglect, even within the nation that encompasses it, is disquieting.

Bringing translation into the study of global literature through orature and through collective, egalitarian interpretive practices in the classroom also means transforming our basic ways of understanding the objects of literary study. Global literature is traversed by translation, and calls upon us as educators and students to critique the conceits of authority that inhere in both the perfectly understood "original" as well as the perfectly formed, authoritative translation. Rather, translational ethics requires that we emphasize the processes of translation: in the translation of the work, its interpretations, and in the ways we translate ourselves. Hence, just as we must find non-hierarchical ways to communicate our ideas in the classroom, we must also develop non-hierarchical models for approaching different works from across the globe. An ongoing process, perennially unfinished, translation undermines the very idea of a stratification of cultures and ideas, and offers, on a global scale, an egalitarian intercourse of interpretation and tongues.

Notes

1. See, for example, Albert Guérard, "Comparative Literature?" *Yearbook of Comparative and General Literature 7* (1958): 1–6.
2. David Damrosch, 2009: 288–97. More specifically, Damrosch argues that "world literature is writing that gains in translation" (288). By this he is referring to gains in readership.
3. A moving pedagogy owes less to Martin Heidegger's famous reading of worlding as unconcealment than to the existential humanism of Edward Said, whose complex notion of the world is not only tied to one's being-in-it in an existential sense, but also to ethical commitments the critic inevitably forms in relation to texts and the worlds they contain (see Martin Heidegger, "The Origin of the Work of Art" *Martin Heidegger: The Basic Writings*. (New York: Harper Collins, 1993). I borrow the concept of worlding from this essay, but employ it here without the specific meaning of a work hermeneutically unearthed and properly exposed. Instead I temper this concept with Edward Said's theory of the World as a vital social process animated by the transformative influence of texts and the ethical and life-serving intentionality of critics and readers (see Edward Said, *The World, the Text, and the Critic* (Cambridge: Harvard University Press, 1983)).
4. Ngũgĩ wa Thiong'o, *Globalectics: Theory and the Politics of Knowing*, (New York: Columbia University Press, 2012), p. 63.
5. Talal Asad, *Genealogies of Religion* (Baltimore: Johns Hopkins Press, 1993), 156.
6. Gilles Deleuze and Felix Guattari, *Kafka: Toward a Minor Literature*, tr. Dana Polan (Minneapolis: University of Minnesota Press, 1986).
7. See Johann Wolfgang von Goethe, *Conversations of Goethe with Johann Peter Eckermann*, tr. John Oxenford (Da Capo, 1998), 160–68.
8. Abdelfattah Kilito, *Thou Shalt Not Speak My Language*, tr. Waïl S. Hassan (Syracuse University Press, 2008), 20.
9. Walter Benjamin, "Theses on the Philosophy of History" from Benjamin, *Illuminations* (1968): 256.
10. Étienne Balibar, *Politics and the Other Scene* (New York: Verso, 2002), 57.
11. Naoki Sakai, *Translation and Subjectivity* (Minneapolis: University of Minnesota, 2008).
12. Talal Asad, *Genealogies of Religion* (Baltimore: Johns Hopkins Press, 1993).
13. Gayatri Spivak, *In Other Worlds* (NewYork: Routledge, 1988).
14. See Aziz Al-Azmeh, *Islams and Modernities*, 2nd edition (London: Verso, 1996), 36. Al-Azmeh argues that the etiquette of representation,

or "multiculturalism as a form of conservative etiquette," often relies on assumptions about the fixity and irreducibility of the cultures represented and exoticized (p. 17).
15. To clarify, I am talking about translation as a complex set of concerns that affect our ways of reading texts as outlined above.
16. Al-Azmeh. *Islams and Modernities*, 33.
17. Paulo Freire, *Pedagogy of the Oppressed*, tr. Myra Bergman Ramos (New York: Continuum, 2009).
18. The relation of teacher and students, modeled on a dialectical system, are misapprehended as a master-slave and a subject-object formation.
19. bell hooks, *Teaching to Transgress: Education as the Practice of Freedom* (New York: Routledge, 1994), 7.
20. Henry Giroux, *Border Crossings: Cultural Workers and the Politics of Education* (New York: Routledge, 2005), 230.
21. Giroux, *Border Crossings*, 232.
22. See Theodor Adorno, "Education after Auschwitz," in *Critical Models: Interventions and Catchwords,* ed. Theodor Adorno,. tr. Henry W. Pickford (New York: Columbia University Press, 1998), 191–204. Elsewhere, Adorno argues that history is usually something that happens to individuals "who are thereby condemned to fall under the wheels" of history. Theodor Adorno, *History and Freedom: Lectures 1964–1965* (Malden, MA: Polity Press, 2006), 12. For this reason he strongly warns against unconscious identifications with the way of the world and the course of history. Expressing a kind of cautionary pedagogy, Adorno asks, "have you capitulated in favour of worshipping whatever happens to be the case?" (Ibid., 57). Furthermore, when he claims that "most people today kick with the pricks instead of against them" (Ibid., 73–74). Adorno is criticizing our susceptibility to assent to the way things are going rather than to think against the grain. As against this mode of thinking, he suggests the subversion of the world through thought. Although he argues that "ideas are being controlled by the socially dominant groups in power at any given time," (Ibid., 32) he suggests that there are limits to this control, and so further opens the door to translation as a pedagogical tool for change.
23. Jacques Rancière, *The Ignorant Schoolmaster: Five Lessons in Intellectual Emancipation*, tr. Kristin Ross (Stanford, CA: Stanford University Press, 1991.
24. Ibid., 119.
25. Jacques Rancière, "On Ignorant Schoolmasters," in *Jacques Rancière: Education Truth, Emancipation*, ed. Biesta, Gert et.al. (New York: Continuum, 2010), 5.
26. Mao Tse-Tung. qtd. in Freire, *Pedagogy of the Oppressed*. 2009; p. 93 (qtd. from Malraux, André. *Anti-Memoirs*. New York, 1968; pp. 361–62).
27. Biesta, et.al. *Jacques Rancière*, 115–6.
28. Rancière, *The Ignorant Schoolmaster*, 10.
29. Ibid., 60–5
30. See Edward Said's musical-theoretical use of this term in Edward W. Said, *On Late Style: Music and Literature Against the Grain* (New York: Vintage,

2007), p. 126. Borrowing a passage from Adrono, Said defines counterpoint as "the decomposition of the given thematic material through subjective reflection on the motivic work contained therein" (Theodor W. Adorno, "Bach Defended Against His Devotees," in *Prisms*, tr. Samuel and Shierry Weber (Cambridge, MA: MIT Press, 1982), 139; qtd. in Said, Edward W. *On Late Style: Music and Literature Against the Grain*. New York: Vintage, 2007; p. 126).
31. See Asad, *Genealogies of Religion*, 156.
32. See Gabriele Schwab, *Imaginary Ethnographies* (New York: Columbia Universitry Press), unpublished manuscript.
33. See Thiong'o wa Ngũgĩ, *Penpoints, Gunpoints, and Dreams: Towards a Critical Theory of the Arts and the State in Africa* (Oxford: Clarendon Press, 1998), 105–28.
34. Ibid., 115.
35. See Micere Mugo, *African Orature and Human Rights* (Lethoso: National University of Lethoso, Institute of Southern African Studies, 1995). Yet even in scholarship in African studies, orature is too often ignored. See for example, the recent collection, *Translation Studies in Africa*. Only one of the essays in the collection, Paul Bandia's "Translation Matters: Linguistic and Cultural Representation," explicitly deals with oral culture, and even this essay does not speak of "orature." Orality and orature seem to be largely hidden behind concepts like "cultural translation" and "verbal art." (Inggs, Judith and Libby Meintjes. *Translation Studies in Africa*. [New York: Continuum, 2009]).
36. Carroll, John B. "Introduction" in *Language, Thought, and Reality*, Whorf, Benjamin Lee. (Cambridge, MA: MIT Press, 1956), vi.
37. See Whorf, *Language, Thought, and Reality*.
38. See for example the panegyrics to imperialism in the guise of "civilization" within reactionary works by Niall Ferguson or Samuel P. Huntington.
39. Bahr, Donald et.al. *Ants and Orioles: Showing the Art of Pima Poetry* (Salt Lake City: The University of Utah Press, 1997).

Works Cited

Adorno, Theodor W. "Bach Defended Against His Devotees." In *Prisms*. Translated by Samuel and Shierry Weber. Cambridge, MA: MIT Press, 1982, 139.

———. "Education after Auschwitz." In *Critical Models: Interventions and Catchwords*. Edited by Adorno, Theodor, translated by Henry W. Pickford. New York: Columbia University Press, 1998.

———. *History and Freedom: Lectures 1964–1965*. Malden, MA: Polity Press, 2006.

Al-Azmeh, Aziz. *Islams and Modernities* (2nd edition). London: Verso, 1996.

Asad, Talal. *Genealogies of Religion*. Baltimore: Johns Hopkins Press, 1993.

Bahr, Donald et.al. *Ants and Orioles: Showing the Art of Pima Poetry*. Salt Lake City: The University of Utah Press, 1997.

Balibar, Étienne. *Politics and the Other Scene.* New York: Verso, 2002.
Benjamin, Walter. "Theses on the Philosophy of History." from Benjamin. *Illuminations.* New York: Shocken Books, 1968.
Biesta, Gert et.al. *Jacques Rancière: Education Truth, Emancipation.* New York: Continuum, 2010.
Damrosch, David, ed. *Teaching World Literature.* New York: The Modern Language Association of America, 2009.
Deleuze, Gilles and Felix Guattari. *Kafka: Toward a Minor Literature.* Translated by Dana Polan. Minneapolis: University of Minnesota Press, 1986.
Freire, Paulo. *Pedagogy of the Oppressed.* Translated by Myra Bergman Ramos. New York: Continuum, 2009.
Giroux, Henry. *Border Crossings: Cultural Workers and the Politics of Education.* New York: Routledge, 2005.
Goethe, Johann Wolfgang von. *Conversations of Goethe with Johann Peter Eckermann.* Translated by John Oxenford. Boston, MA: Da Capo, 1998.
Guérard, Albert. "Comparative Literature?" *Yearbook of Comparative and General Literature* 7 (1958), 1–6.
Heidegger, Martin. "The Origin of the Work of Art." *Martin Heidegger: The Basic Writings.* New York: Harper Collins, 1993.
hooks, bell. *Teaching to Transgress: Education as the Practice of Freedom.* New York: Routledge, 1994.
Inggs, Judith and Libby Meintjes. *Translation Studies in Africa.* New York: Continuum, 2009.
Kilito, Abdelfattah. *Thou Shalt Not Speak My Language.* Translated by Waïl S. Hassan. Syracuse University Press, 2008.
Kraus, Karl. *Dicta and Contradicta.* Translated by Jonathan McVity. Chicago: University of Illinois Press, 2001.
Malraux, André. *Anti-Memoirs.* New York: Henry Holt, 1968.
Mugo, Micere. *African Orature and Human Rights.* Lethoso: National University of Lethoso, Institute of Southern African Studies, 1995.
Mugo, Micere . *African Orature and Human Rights.* Lethoso: National University of Lethoso, Institute of Southern African Studies, 1995.
Ngũgĩ, wa Thiong'o. *Globalectics: Theory and the Politics of Knowing.* New York: Columbia University Press, 2012.
———. *Penpoints, Gunpoints, and Dreams: Towards a Critical Theory of the Arts and the State in Africa.* Oxford: Clarendon Press, 1998.
———. *Decolonizing the Mind: the Politics of Language in African Literature.* Portsmouth, NH: Heinemann, 1986.
Rancière, Jacques. *The Ignorant Schoolmaster: Five Lessons in Intellectual Emancipation.* Translated by Kristin Ross. Stanford University Press, 1991.
———. "On Ignorant Schoolmasters." In *Jacques Rancière: Education Truth, Emancipation.* Edited by Biesta, Gert et.al. New York: Continuum, 2010.
Said, Edward W. *On Late Style: Music and Literature Against the Grain.* New York: Vintage, 2007.
———. *The World, the Text, and the Critic.* Cambridge: Harvard University Press, 1983.

Sakai, Naoki. *Translation and Subjectivity*. Minneapolis: University of Minnesota, 2008.
Schwab, Gabriele. *Imaginary Ethnographies*. New York: Columbia University Press, (unpublished manuscript).
Spivak, Gayatri. *In Other Worlds*. NewYork: Routledge, 1988.
Whorf, Benjamin Lee. *Language, Thought, and Reality*. Cambridge, MA: MIT Press, 1956.
——. *Penpoints, Gunpoints, and Dreams: Towards a Critical Theory of the Arts and the State in Africa*. Oxford: Clarendon Press, 1998.
Niranjana, Tejaswini. *Siting Translation*. Berkeley: University of California Press, 1992.
Rancière, Jacques. *The Ignorant Schoolmaster: Five Lessons in Intellectual Emancipation*. Translated by Kristin Ross. Stanford University Press, 1991.
——. "On Ignorant Schoolmasters." In *Jacques Rancière: Education Truth, Emancipation*. Edited by Gert Biesta, et.al. New York: Continuum, 2010.
Robbins, Bruce. "Comparative Cosmopolitanisms." In *Cosmopolitics: Thinking and Feeling beyond the Nation*. Edited by Cheah, Pheng and Bruce Robbins.. Minneapolis: The University of Minnesota, 1998.
Said, Edward W. *On Late Style: Music and Literature Against the Grain*. New York: Vintage, 2007.
——. *The World, the Text, and the Critic*. Cambridge: Harvard University Press, 1983.
Sakai, Naoki. *Translation and Subjectivity*. Minneapolis: University of Minnesota, 2008.
——. and Jon Solomon, eds. *Translation, Biopolitics, Colonial Difference*. Hong Kong University Press, 2006.
Schwab, Gabriele. *Imaginary Ethnographies*. New York: Columbia University Press, (unpublished manuscript).
Spivak, Gayatri. *In Other Worlds*. NewYork: Routledge, 1988.
——. "More Thoughts on Cultural Translation." *Translate.eipcp.net,* 2008.
Trouillot, Michel-Rolph. *Silencing the Past*. Boston: Beacon Press, 2003.
Walser, Robert. *Jakob von Gunten*. New York: New York Review of Books, 1999.
Whorf, Benjamin Lee. *Language, Thought, and Reality*. Cambridge, MA: MIT Press, 1956.

8

"Re-worlding" in Tsitsi Dangaremba's *Nervous Conditions*

Linda Daley

"Worlding"

Gayatri Spivak's (1985) critique of the "cult text of feminism," *Jane Eyre* (1847), argues that it is impossible to read any nineteenth-century English classic without considering it as something of an aide-de-camp for Britain's imperialist project in its former colonies (1985: 244). She argues that the individualism of that Victorian novel represented by Jane's progression from her poor, orphaned, and alone marginality to her arrival as financially independent, bourgeois heroine, expresses a first world ideology that reflects and perpetuates British imperialism (Spivak, 1985: 246). Conversely, since Spivak's paradigm-forming critique, one that contributes to an analytic history of how European culture "worlds" the Third World or Global South, it should be equally impossible to read any *Bildungsroman* (novel of formation, of education) by an indigenous woman author from a former British colony without invoking *Jane Eyre*. Tsitsi Dangaremba's first novel, *Nervous Conditions* (1988), invokes such a comparison.

Spivak's term "worlding" is a modified borrowing from philosopher Martin Heidegger, which she adapts to account for the cultural, and specifically literary, processes of colonizing nations in their transformation of territories into a sign of inferiority and dependency on the first world or Global North (Spivak, 1985, 1999; Heidegger, 1971). In being rendered as a sign, Spivak argues the effects of these practices of power become naturalized: invisible to those who benefit from them and internalized by those who do not. Spivak's adaptation of Heidegger's concept of "worlding" to the social mission of literature resonates with the discussion by Jean-Paul Sartre from which the epigram preceding Dangaremba's novel gives the work its title.

In his preface to Franz Fanon's *The Wretched of the Earth* (1967), Sartre claims "The status of 'native' is a nervous condition introduced and maintained by the settler among colonized people *with their consent*" (Sartre, 1967: 17). Sartre's preface summarizes Fanon's account of the processes of colonization that includes the forming of a black, colonial elite that mimics the colonizer to perform the violence directed at the sister or brother of the colonized (1967: 15–17). This level of violence precedes the violence between the colonized and the colonizer in the war of independence from which the process of decolonization begins and which Dangaremba alludes to on the novel's last page: "This story is how it all began" (1988: 204). Dangaremba's novel gathers the key moments in the narrator's girlhood to dramatize the violent scenario of consent to colonial oppression at the individual and familial level, and it does so through the dimension of patriarchal domination, for which Fanon's writings do not give specific analysis.

Nervous Conditions also adopts a form of dramatization and narrativization from the colonial elite's library, *Jane Eyre*, a classic work of female rebellion within the confines of Victorian discourses of social progression. Postcolonial literary critics commenting on the novel since Spivak's essay endorse her analysis for the ways in which its form as a *Bildungsroman* imagines Jane as an ideal figure of Victorian female subjectivity that can be aligned to an ideal woman figure of empire (David, 1995: 77). Other commentators note the ways in which race functions in the novel to configure perspectives and voices of female insurrection against male domination in British society; that is, how racial oppression is pressed into service as an analogy for sexual oppression that "reveals a conflict between sympathy for the oppressed and a hostile sense of racial supremacy" (Meyer, 1996: 63). There is a formal similarity between the classic Victorian novel and the postindependence Zimbabwean novel through a similar mode of narration and the common theme of rebellion as a means to self-autonomy. However, whereas the English classic achieves a form of self-identity for its heroine based on her overcoming of difference—and largely, though not exclusively, that difference is represented but unacknowledged in the novel through the trope of race—the late twentieth-century Zimbabwean novel fully acknowledges the importance of difference to identity formation for its female protagonist, and suggests a collectivist form of female culture rather than an individualist one.

This chapter explores the ways in which *Nervous Conditions* works with and against the dominant discourses of British colonialism and British and Shona patriarchy to give voice and representation to the identity of girls and women at the transitional time of Rhodesian nationhood and its imminent decolonization and re-formation as Zimbabwe. I argue that *Nervous Conditions* negotiates the "worlding" phenomenon that Spivak, among other commentators, analyses through what I call a form of "re-worlding" to produce a gripping story of the journey to maturity for its heroine while also incorporating a sophisticated critique of the cost to that identity formation as it occurs under the double ideological forces of patriarchy (British and Shona) and colonialism.

I further argue that through the novel's occasional references to Tambudzai's grandmother, Myubu, Dangaremba has proffered a model of an indigenous feminine identity who negotiates a pathway—fraught as it is—between the English "worlding" and the Shona "earth." That pathway is open-ended and vaguely defined in the novel, but is nonetheless generative rather than destructive of woman-defined social relations. In this fictional universe, Myubu represents what philosopher Luce Irigaray would identify as a figure contributing to the construction of a female imaginary for the narrator-heroine, which is a necessary condition of a women-defined culture. In the next section, I outline the key instances of female rebellion in the novel and apply Irigaray's interpretation of hysteria as a form of female rebellion rather than a form of submission or surrender to patriarchal forces. In the final section, I examine the consequences of patriarchy on the network of woman-to-woman relations in the novel that conform with Irigaray's diagnosis of the rivalry among women that patriarchy establishes, and also the potential within these relations for relating otherwise. While there is a risk in applying the concepts and framework of Western feminists to a non-Western context, and Dangaremba herself has noted the danger, I argue that *Nervous Conditions* adopts a sophisticated negotiation of Western (literary) forms and of (feminist) theory, each of which have benefited Western women's self-representation culturally and politically. In a 1993 interview, Dangaremba endorses the view that *Jane Eyre* was an inspiration to her writing career in newly independent Zimbabwe and that her own first novel is performing a similar role, albeit for a culturally, geographically, and historically different readership. The interviewer(s) asks the author whether *Nervous Conditions* "could serve for young Zimbabwean girls the function that was until then (inadequately) performed by a novel like, say *Jane Eyre*— as a means of inserting themselves into fiction?" Dangaremba replies: "Definitely. It is a very interesting process, this question of identity...all the things you read, with everything that you're taught, you construct a kind of cognitive map for yourself that is comfortable. I feel that for the people who grew up during my parents' time and my own time this was something that was denied to us, absolutely and completely...And I do think *Nervous Conditions* is serving this purpose for young girls in Zimbabwe" (Dangaremba, 1993: 312).

Dangaremba's comments in that interview can be viewed as her account of the "worlding" of Shona territory through the impost of writing on what was a largely oral culture, and yet part of that impost included the very colonial literary forms that she herself acknowledges as formative influences on herself as a reader and also as a writer, which have enabled her to amend the absence of female perspectives and voices in postindependent Rhodesia. For similar reasons she expresses her concerns about the "Western or foreign" feminist theories in arguing that they can be "dangerous because they block the development of indigenous feminist theory" (1993: 316). In this chapter, I extend Dangaremba's own logic regarding literacy and literary forms of the colonizer as both bestowing and dispossessing the indigenous culture and language, to make a similar claim for reading her novel alongside Western feminist theory as a lens through which non-Western patriarchal formations can be interpreted. When Dangaremba states that "the accept/reject continuum [of progressive Western theories] is irrelevant. It's rather a question of interrogating and 'fixing' theories," I take her to be suggesting by "fixing" the idea of adaptation for a specific or local context (1993: 316). Potentially, Western feminist theories offer powerful concepts and strategies for previously unintended (but perhaps nonetheless assumed) contexts in the Global South. More so, I take her remark to be a challenge to the view that "theory" adopts the totalizing critique that is often attributed to it.

Female Rebellion against Patriarchy

Narrated in the first person by the adolescent Tambudzai, the novel recollects the story of her attempts to escape the impoverishment of the homestead for an education and the better life it will bring her and her family. In the last lines of the novel, Tambu states that "the story I have told here, is my own story, the story of four women whom I loved, and our men" (Dangaremba, 204). The heroine-narrator of *Jane Eyre* commences her recollection of the momentous incidents in her educational journey soon after the climactic achievement of marriage, the discovery of the Rivers siblings as relatives, and the creation of her own family. The Victorian novel's narration, then, begins from the perspective of bourgeois triumph of socioeconomic inclusion for its heroine, one that has been secured over the dead body of the first Mrs. Rochester—the Caribbean-born Bertha Mason. *Nervous Conditions* begins with its narrator-heroine noting the death of her brother, the first-born and only son, Nhamo, a situation about which Tambu "was not sorry" because it means that she will no longer be subject to his violence, and will now assume the mantle of the educated one who must provide for her family. Unlike its Victorian precursor, the narrator-heroine of *Nervous Conditions*, by the close of the novel, conveys a more guarded sense of certainty about her progress in spite of having excelled at the mission school, and won a scholarship to undertake higher learning at the white boarding school—the necessary steps toward inclusion in the black colonial elite. In her journey from "female, poor, uneducated and black," Tambu gains the opportunity to "read everything from Enid Blyton to the Bronte sisters" so that she could be "educated" (Dangaremba, 93). However, by the novel's close, she gains a self-awareness that such an education was not the "limitless horizon" that she had previously thought (Dangaremba, 58). The climactic moment in Tambu's journey of education comes through recognition of the cost that membership of the colonial elite had extracted from her extended family and her Shona culture to remark: "Something in my mind began to assert itself, to question things and refuse to be brainwashed, bringing me to this time when I can set down this story" (Dangaremba, 204).

Tambu's questioning comes through her relation with her Anglicized cousin Nyasha after she arrives at the mission to attend school there, lives with her uncle and aunt, and shares a bedroom with her cousin, where the girls swap stories and anxieties about their respective families. "Nyasha was perceptive...I was flattered by everything she said and did," but initially Nyasha's worries and rebellions baffle Tambu (Dangaremba, 89–91). Nyasha embodies or possesses everything that Tambu aspires to for herself—schooling, books, fluency in the English language, an abundance of food, a home with all the mod cons—and she gradually comes to realize that Nyasha's acts of defiance are other than mere outbursts of adolescent selfishness. Nyasha's rebellion starts from secret acts of smoking cigarettes and wearing revealing clothing to vomiting the meals she has just eaten and staying out late talking to a white boy, unaccompanied by her brother. These acts are directed against the authority of her father, Babamukuru. It is when Nyasha's conflict with her father reaches physical violence, provoking an acute mental and physical descent to her near death, that Tambu's awakening to the ideological forces working on Nyasha, and by implication herself, starts to occur: "You know how it is when something that has been the cornerstone of your security begins to crumble. You start worrying about yourself" (Dangaremba, 199). Slowly, and through Nyasha,

Tambu realizes a shift in her own perceptions of the complex web of colonial and patriarchal power relations within the extended family home. Ultimately, she comes to give more respect to her mother's assessment that she had previously dismissed: "It's the Englishness...It'll kill them all if they aren't careful" (Dangaremba, 202).

What motivates Tambu away from the homestead to the mission is the unceasing labor, the grinding poverty—the "primitiveness"—of the homestead that is represented as "dirt." When she starts her schooling at the mission, she does so as a "peasant" with "broad-toed feet that had grown thick-skinned through daily contact with the ground in all weathers" and skin that had "hardened and cracked so that the dirt ground its way in but could not be washed out" (Dangaremba, 58). She hopes to find another self at the mission, "a clean, well-groomed, genteel self" (Dangaremba, 59). The dirt of the homestead contrasts with the "absence of dirt," the order and the bounty available at the mission: "Every corner of Babamukuru's house—every shiny surface, every soft contour and fold—whispered its own insistent message of comfort and ease and rest" (Dangaremba, 70). The most significant expression of her rejection of the dirt, and thereby of the homestead, occurs when Tambu returns after some weeks away at school and the mission house, and complains to her mother: "Why don't you clean the toilet any more?" (Dangaremba, 123). The reproach resurfaces later as a rejection of the mother and the homestead Mainini is less able to manage since the death of Nhamo while he was at the mission being educated: "You think I am dirt now, me, your mother... 'It disgusts me.' that's what you said" (Dangaremba, 140). Having lost not only Nhamo, but also the status that the mother-of-the-son brings to a woman under patriarchy, particularly in Shona culture, and now losing her eldest daughter to Englishness, Mainini loses the will to manage the domestic chores of the homestead, and the will to keep quiet about her sense of shame and fear that her daughter's education represents for her.

What Tambu sees as the antidote to "dirt" is the progress that education achieves, and its clearest and strongest embodiment is her uncle. As the eldest son of Tambu's grandmother, Myubu, Babamukuru was taken to the "good wizards" at the mission for an education. He worked hard by day in the fields, and by night learned his lessons well. The "good wizards" recognized his promise to eventually undertake tertiary studies in South Africa and England, from where he and his wife, Maiguru, return after five years (along with their children), and each with a master's degree. Babamukuru assumes the post as headmaster and academic director of the Church's Manicaland Region, and resumes his duties as patriarch of the homestead and its extended family that includes Tambudzai and her immediate family. Babaukuru is feted upon his return and is viewed not only by Tambu as a god, who holds counsel and judgment over family and homestead problems, he is also the symbol of hard work that Tambu notes had "made himself plenty of power" (Dangaremba, 50). His authority as the family head is reinforced by the adulation and subservience of various family members. Tambu reflects:

> He was a rigid, imposing perfectionist, steely enough in character to function in the puritanical way that he expected, or rather insisted, that the rest of the world should function. Luckily, or may be unluckily for him, throughout his life Babamukuru had found himself—as eldest child and son, as an early educated African, as headmaster, as husband and father, as provider to many—in positions that enabled him to organize his immediate world and its contents as he wished. Even when this was not the case, as when he went to the mission as a young boy, the end result of such periods of submission was greater power than before. Thus he had been insulated from the necessity of considering alternatives unless they were his own. Stoically he accepted his divinity. Filled with awe, we accepted it too. (Dangaremba, 87)

Within the wider, colonial system, it is, however, a precarious sense of power. The burden of his position necessitates unquestioning investment in the colonial discourses of progress, education, and Christianity to make him, as Nyasha says sneeringly to Tambu, a "good boy, a good munt. A bloody good kaffir" (Dangaremba, 200). The burden of raising his extended family out of their "primitive" existence means that since his return from England his "nerves were bad" (Dangaremba, 102). Unable to relax or enjoy his status, there is little laughter or merriment in the home. Babamukuru's burden as the family patriarch rests uneasily on him, alienated as he is from the culture into which he was born, and unaccepted fully into the culture in which he has found material wealth and professional success.

Maiguru adopts a submissive role as wife and mother to support Babamukuru's position of power through various forms of self-effacement: playing down her own educational achievements and hard work to keep her husband's extended family provided for; an excessive show of care for husband and children displayed through baby-talk: "Daddy-dear" and "Daddy-Sweet" to her husband, and "Nyasha-wash, my lovey-dove" to her daughter; and by acting as gatekeeper to her husband's puritanical ideals of womanhood with her daughter and niece in confiscating Nyasha's risqué choice of reading (*Lady Chatterley's Lover*) and protesting her use of tampons. Maiguru's self-effacement, submission, and obedience break down when Babamukuru physically punishes Tambu for not attending her parents' wedding, an event that was a source of embarrassment to her, and a reaction that she could not express. Maiguru leaves her family in protest at the punishment. In response to her mother's act of defiance, Nyasha says: "Now she's broken out, I know it's possible, so I can wait" (Dangaremba, 174). Maiguru's return to the home five days later is viewed by Nyasha as a defeat, but both Nyasha and Tambu note that her sickly baby-talk had disappeared and she "smiled more often and less mechanically" (Dangaremba, 175).

It is the patriarch's own daughter, against whom his moralism is most strongly directed and the most intensely affected by the nervous condition, who, like her father, is caught between two cultures: the school girls think of her as a snob and do not talk to her, while every attempt to assert her English ways result in her father's disapproval. From Tambu's perspective, having had the best education in England, Nyasha has nothing to worry about at home. However, she returns to Africa a stranger in her own homeland where her presumed educational, intellectual, and cultural superiority becomes her psychological and physical undoing. Returning to Africa with English middle-class respectability, her role within that respectability becomes culturally heightened because it is translated through the missionary context of being the daughter of the African headmaster. Along with other women and girls in the family, it is Nyasha in particular who must demonstrate the necessary submissiveness to the authority of the family's head so that the respectability of and respect for Babamukuru's authority can be reasserted more widely in the community. When Nyasha stays out talking to a white boy unaccompanied by her brother, she is beaten by her father and called a "whore," but she retaliates by punching him in the face. She says to Tambu, "I was comfortable in England, but now I am a 'whore' with dirty habits" (Dangaremba, 117). Tambu's awakening to her own predicament as a girl/woman has begun through her proximity to her cousin's vulnerability. She has come to recognize Nyasha as her other self: the other that she aspires to be. Tambu reflects on the violence:

> The victimization I saw was universal. It didn't depend on poverty, on lack of education or on tradition. It didn't depend on any of the things I had thought it depended on. Men took it everywhere with them. Even heroes like Babamukuru did it...all conflicts came back to this question of femaleness. Femaleness as opposed and inferior to maleness (115–116).

Part of Babamukuru's identity rests on an excessive identification with the discourse of Christianity, the very institution that has provided him with the means of securing his family's continued survival, and his investment in it must be demonstrated by the moral probity of the women in the family of which he is the head. Beyond his immediate family, this is shown in his tidying-up of the sexual relations of the unmarried members of the family. Babamukuru insists that the sister of his sister-in-law, Lucia, must marry. As an unmarried, and now pregnant woman on his homestead, Lucia is out of place: technically still belonging to her father's land, but frequently visiting and raising the interest of men on Babamukuru's homestead. Lucia is little interested in either the men, or the marital status that Babamukuru demands; it is to care for her ailing sister Mainini, whom she comes back and forth to look after in order to lift her out of her depressive illness. When Lucia asserts her defiance against a marriage to a man she is not interested in, Babamukuru responds by insisting on a marriage between his brother Jeremiah and Mainini, which does go ahead, to the embarrassment and humiliation of the bride and her daughter. Lucia's rebellion reminds Tambu that women have a relation to each other that need not be structured by their relation to the patriarch.

Nyasha understands her father's complicity with colonialism more clearly than Tambu, but that understanding does not prevent her from becoming a victim to its force. After Tambu wins her scholarship to the white boarding school, Nyasha's sense of self-worth descends further, and in her letters to Tambu she reports that she has developed a "new, svelte" figure. When Tambu returns during school holidays, she is aware that Nyasha has become very thin and applies herself excessively to studying through the middle of the night to pass her exams even though she is unable to concentrate and get her homework right. Nyasha's demise results in hospitalization and is the most extreme example in the novel of the native's nervous condition. The first psychiatrist insists that anorexia nervosa is a condition that an African girl is unable to suffer; the second psychiatrist by contrast does understand its cultural etiology. As a form of hysteria, anorexia nervosa is conventionally thought of as a disease of femininity, of a diet that has gone out of control. However, we can also view Babamukuru's "bad nerves" as his own form of hysteria that, as Elizabeth Grosz tells us, is the experience of the body speaking what the hysteric cannot say (1989, 134). When the hysteric is male, he is attempting to cope with the demands of his investment in the discourses of masculinity that he is unable to express. Babamukuru's hysteria is an attempt to cope with the demands and expectations of membership of the black colonial elite that is predicated on an English culture of empire that has dispossessed his Shona culture and land, and continues to dominate the black population through colonial control to which his authority as father, headmaster, and patriarch gives consent. When the hysteric is a woman, she attempts to cope with the demands and expectations of a male-dominated culture that "relies on women's renunciation of their relations to other women, and of their unmediated relations to their own bodies and pleasures by summoning up an apparently incapacitating 'illness' which prevents her from giving satisfaction to men while satisfying herself in a compromise or symptomatic form" (Grosz, 1989: 135).

While Nyasha remarks that she wants to conform to a Western rather than a Shona ideal of body shape, her anorexia is the "symptomatic acting out of a proposition the hysteric cannot articulate" (Grosz, 1989: 134). The proposition for Nyasha, like that of her father, would be about her alienation from her culture of origin alongside her exclusion from aspects of the dominant culture to which she has been granted partial access. However, her proposition is also explicitly not that of her father because it would express her sexuality as conflicted between that of a Shona woman who must be submissive in her femininity with the dictates of the family patriarch (the most conspicuous display of passive femininity in the novel is when women kneel in deference before the patriarch and all of the family members in closest proximity to him) and that of a Western woman whose education is based on a reasoning that rejects (in principle at least) subjugation to the patriarchal law. Instead of articulating the proposition, the "hysteric 'articulates' a corporeal discourse; her symptoms speak on her behalf" (Grosz, 1989: 135).

Whereas Babamukuru's hysteria is expressed violently toward, particularly, his daughter and niece, the violence of Nyasha's hysteria is directed at her own body in punishing it through an excessive effort to be both the good girl according to patriarchal expectations, and also precisely by exceeding those expectations to the extent that she is thought of by her father and the first of the two psychiatrists she sees as simply a bad girl who is just "making a scene" (Dangaremba, 200). How can we view the nervous condition of Nyasha's hysteria, the most violent and intense within the novel, as a form of female rebellion when it would seem to be the very exemplar of feminine self-destruction?

Philosopher and psychoanalyst Luce Irigaray views hysteria as form of mimicry of the expectations of the dominant cultural norms upon the subject. As a practicing psychoanalyst, she analyses these norms as they are expressed through discourses, as well as in their manifestation in her women clients. According to Grosz (1989), Irigaray accounts for female hysteria as a form of rebellion against the strictures of patriarchy and its demands of a normative heterosexuality. Psychoanalysis, while offering descriptions of sexuality and sexual development that reinscribe patriarchy, nonetheless, provides the concepts and framework that feminist theorists need in order to articulate an antisexist perspective against not only psychoanalytic but all discourses. Psychoanalysis interprets heterosexual female sexual development, femininity, according to three possibilities: first, by the woman accepting her castration ("normal" femininity); second, by refusing her castration to consider herself "phallic" (the "masculinity complex"); third, by renouncing her "inferior" clitoral pleasures and refusing to convert her sexual organ and orientation to vaginal (paternal) heterosexuality ("frigidity") (Grosz, 1989, 133). Grosz argues that the third option is little discussed or understood in its structural similarity to hysteria as an attempt to remain within the preoedipal, maternal relation, and also a recognition of the patriarchal reality of women's *social* castration.

Irigaray adopts the terms and logic of psychoanalysis and then turns them back against that discourse to expose what it cannot acknowledge about women and femininity. Regarding hysteria, Irigaray analyses it to be an option of feminine sexuality that can be viewed as a form of unconscious rebellion in refusing patriarchy's demands *and also* in accepting patriarchy's reality: neither giving up on the primary relation with the mother (and by implication all women) *and also* accepting the social (rather than sexual) castration of women. Rather than the commonly held view of anorexia nervosa as compliance with the heterosexual ideal of femininity, from this proto-feminist perspective, Nyasha's eating disorder can be seen as a refusal of feminine passivity as well as a form of feminine compliance that results in an overcompliance with patriarchy's expectations. As Grosz puts the anorexic's proposition: "This is what you want; but what you'll get is much more than you bargained for" (1989, 136). We can see this tactic on display with Nyasha at the dinner table where she is required to sit and eat the food that she does not want that has been served via Maiguru's submissive role-playing as the compliant wife. However, in being forced to do so, Nyasha complies excessively with the requirement by rapidly and noisily stuffing her face with all the food on her plate before proceeding to the bathroom to vomit.

Irigaray does not advocate hysteria as a form of feminist consciousness or as a practice of rebellion for women. Rather she adopts it herself as a textual strategy in her own writing in miming the hysteric in her manner of "psycho-analyzing" or reading the discourses of patriarchy. In that sense, we can say that "Irigaray mimics the hysteric's mimicry" in her writings (Grosz, 136). The hysteric's rebellion, particularly the female hysteric's, is not a winnable strategy that results in triumph for her; it is a tactic that is potentially fatal. However, to observe the miming of patriarchy's demands can result in exposing and unsettling the structures of violence and brutalization that force another way of encountering the system by rendering it unworkable. In that regard, we can view the dangerous nature of Nyasha's hysteria as a proto-feminist rebellion against the forces of patriarchy that are doubly violent in their Shona and English embodiment by Babamukuru.

Nyasha's hysteria is also somewhat a doubly unspoken proposition in that she is corporeally speaking back to her father's own miming of the English colonial master as sovereign head of his household. Despite the tangled dimensions of Shona and British patriarchy embodied by Babamukuru, Nyasha's rebellion against him does not occur during those instances at the homestead making decisions about male and female members of his extended family and the direction of activities on the land. Rather, it occurs when he is the presiding patriarch of the nuclear family seated at the dinner table of the mission home miming the colonial, middle-class ritual based on the pretense that the bounty has been possible only because of the hard work and generosity of the patriarch. As Tambu came to realize after she arrived at the mission, her aunt too had a postgraduate qualification equal to her husband, and she too works hard at the school as well as undertakes the arduous role of feeding the extended family when it gathers at the homestead. In one of her private moments with Tambu she tells her that her uncle "wouldn't be able to do half the things he does if [she] didn't work as well!" (Dangaremba, 101).

Nyasha's hysteria expressed as anorexia in the micro-system of her familial household is disturbed and unsettled by her eating disorder. In taking her overcompliance with her father's demands to the point of mental and physical collapse, the members of her family are forced to reexamine the conditions of violence to which it as a member of the black colonial elite gives its consent. That reexamination does not occur in the time frame of the novel, but given Nyasha's breakdown and hospitalization, where she faultingly and half-sensibly attempts to articulate her proposition by speaking of "them" and "they" and what "they" have taken, "their lies" and the "traps" (Dangaremba, 201)—variously referring to her parents and the colonial system—Dangaremba focuses the target where change will come.

"Re-worlding"

Dangaremba has rendered the key mother-daughter relations of Tambu and Mainini and Tambu, and Maiguru and Nyasha as conflicted. Mainini attempts to dissuade Tambu from an education because it will not provide her with the lessons in life needed to cope as a woman: "With the poverty of blackness on one side and the weight of womanhood on the other. What will help you my child is to learn to carry your burdens with strength" (Dangaremba, 16). Tambu witnesses her mother's strength being sapped from her due to the grief of losing her status as the mother of a son—four babies, three of whom were sons, died in infancy before Tambu's birth, and then her only living son Nhamo died in adolescence. Mainini's earlier encouragement of her daughter's potential has given way. She now has no sense of her motherhood except as the mother of dead sons rather than as the mother of three living daughters. Tambu looks to Maiguru, her educated aunt, as a source of inspiration for her own development: "Maiguru was driven about in a car, looked well-kempt and fresh, clean all the time... I decided it was better to be like Maiguru, who was not poor, and had not been crushed by the weight of womanhood" (Dangaremba, 16).

Tambu's decision about the kind of woman she would identify with is entwined with her understanding of "progress" that Nyasha repeatedly warns her to be more questioning of. However, Nyasha's insights to colonialism, and the way its forces work within the family structure, diminish her relation with her own mother because of Maiguru's angelic role-playing and capitulation to supporting her father's authority as the patriarch while making herself invisible. From the perspective of each of the daughters, their mothers, for all their difference of social position and status, are stifling their daughter's development *as women*. However, Tambu's experience of Nyasha's insights combined with the crisis of her breakdown, force Tambu to put her own position of personal progress into a wider context of ideological forces. She belatedly comes to respect her mother's insights: "Mother knew a lot of things, and I had regard for her knowledge. Be careful she had said" (Dangaremba, 203). Similarly, Nyasha, even during her mental collapse, distinguishes between the system that has produced her parent's toadying to colonialism, and the ways that its forces work on girls and women through patriarchy within the family: "I don't hate you Daddy... They want me to, but I won't"... "I can't sleep. Mummy will you hold me?" (Dangaremba, 201).

Luce Irigaray not only analyses how discourses perpetuate sexism, but also how patriarchy is perpetuated through the relationships between women. She identifies the mother-daughter relationship as the "darkest of dark continents," that is the "most victimized [and] the most obscure relationship" where the real identity of both the girl/woman and the mother is lost (Irigaray, 1985–1986: 31). She further claims that the relationship between mother and daughter, as a prototype of relations between all women, forms the "silent substrate" or infrastructure of society, and while it has been annihilated under patriarchy, it contains the latency of overwhelming the social order "when it returns" (See Irigaray, 1991a; Irigaray, 1985–1986: 31). Irigaray claims that patriarchy annihilates the desire between mother and child, allowing only for the satisfaction of need. Such desire between mother and daughter, according to Irigaray's interpretation of psychoanalysis, is necessarily repressed in order for the law of the father to intervene and for the establishment of the symbolic order.

The imaginary order and the symbolic order are two important spheres in conceiving subjectivity. In psychoanalytic theory, the former is the realm where there is an inter- and intra-subjective identification between an ego and its other (Laplanche and Pontalis, 1980: 210). Irigaray expands the conventional psychoanalytic account of this realm by viewing the imaginary domain as the unconscious of Western, male thought, and also as a domain yet to be created from the residue, the remnants and traces of the feminine buried in the symbolic order. The latter realm is the domain of representation that is structured and regulated according to the law; that is, all that has not been repressed and is available to representation. The imaginary order for Irigaray contains both the passive or negative elements of what is unspoken and unspeakable along with the affirmative potential of speech and symbolization by women of a woman-defined symbolic order. These two orders of subjectivity or selfhood operate for Irigaray as intertwined registers of identity formation in viewing the imaginary as the precondition of identity, and the symbolic order as confirmation of that identity. To the extent that gaining entry to the symbolic order for an ego occurs through the acquisition of language, clearly, women under patriarchy achieve this entry, but they accede to a masculine symbolic order based on a masculine imaginary. Conversely, women exist in the symbolic order as nonspeaking subjects without a feminine imaginary, and thus without a feminine identity. On this view, Irigaray argues that woman remains in a state of nature, not yet a feminine subject; instead, she is an object of man's specularization, an image of man's self-representation. Phallocentrism, understood as patriarchy's standard of value based on the masculine symbol of the phallus, relies on woman serving as a mirror to man's identity. Through Irigaray's framework we can see why Babamukuru's fragile identity demands more from girls and women than the boys and men in his family to support his identity as patriarch.

To demonstrate her claims about the lost relation of desire between mother and daughter, Irigaray relies on a counter-myth to the truth of patriarchy as that truth is expressed by scientific discourses such as psychoanalysis. She puts forward the myth of the matricide of the motherlover, the woman who desires and creates, to counter the myth of patricide that Freud suggests in Totem and Taboo as the founding violence that establishes patriarchy. For Irigaray, the social order of patriarchy requires that the bodily encounter with the mother, with the desire and creativity that the relationship represents, remain forbidden and excluded, and that maternal power is viewed as a phallic threat or, at best, a reproductive function (Irigaray, 1991b: 39). Both Tambu and Nyasha view their mother as castrated: the woman in the mother is overwhelmed by her maternal role whether that role is "primitive" or "modern," such that her sexuality as a woman is rendered invisible.

Irigaray's raids on myth form an important strand within her method of exposing the limits of discourses' truths and what is beyond their field of vision. The absence of symbolization between mothers and daughters, an absence of a woman-defined love of the mother as the possibility for the love of the self, creates neuroses between women. Without positive symbolization, woman's specificity is valued and represented by the formula of "1+1+1," which is a nonindividuation between women, or a sameness between women, who are quantified but without qualitative differentiation within our sex, and without positive, qualitative differentiation from other women. A lack of qualitative differentiation results in rivalry and violence between women. In *Nervous Conditions*, Mainini blames both Babamukuru and Maiguru for the death of her only son, but expresses her anger explicitly toward Maiguru when the news of Nhamo's death is conveyed. When Lucia's fate is being determined through the judgment of Babamukuru and other men on the homestead, she vents her rage at Maiguru for the Shona protocol of female exclusion from the scene of judgment by demanding that Maiguru take sides with her against her husband's authority. Tambu reflects on the incident:

> With Lucia insisting that Maiguru take sides, come out in the open, we were in a very delicate situation... It stung too saltily, too sharply and agonizingly the sensitive images that the women had of themselves, images that were really no more than reflections. But the women had been taught to recognize these reflections as self and it was frightening now to even begin to think that... as women [what] set them apart as a group, as women, as a certain kind of person, were only myths. (Dangaremba, 138)

Irigaray argues that the absence of identification between women based on love of self (and therefore of all other women who are both others to oneself and one's same sex) expresses itself through rivalry between women because women feel that they only have value in their relation to men, not in relation to each other. Arguably, the complex framework of woman-to-woman relations that Irigaray puts forward not only lends itself to drawing on myth to diagnose and reconstruct from the ruins of patriarchy. Fiction, too, shows how psychological, cultural, and political forces operate and intersect through its power to dramatize and focalize those forces through a single consciousness that is representative of a collective. While Mainini and Maiguru each disappoint their daughters within their respective relations, Tambu expresses her love for these women who are both fallible to rivalry and jealousy, but also sources of succor and support to each other within their harsh existence.

What makes Mainini and Maiguru structurally similar in their relations to their daughters, in spite of their vastly different positions under colonialism, is that neither woman has positive symbolic sources or references for their identity as women independent of men, or more precisely, independent of masculinity. In contrast to the mothers in the novel, the grandmother, Myubu, is a shadowy figure who gave away her eldest son to be educated without any guarantee that he would be the provider that he came to be. Myubu, exists prior to the time frame of the novel; she has no direct speech, and no other character refers to her. It is as if is she exists in Tambu's imagination alone. She provides Tambu with a backstory to the arrival and deceit of the English "wizards," as she calls the English colonials who took the best land from her forebears, but also shows the necessity of working with and through the colonial system to improve her and her family's position within that world. Myubu had given Tambu skills to cultivate the soil from which she makes a small income that directly enables her to acquire the early schooling that she so desperately seeks, and for which Shona culture gives preference to the son over the daughter. Unlike Mainini, Myubu is not reduced by the loss of her son; hers is an act that opens up a mode of survival for her descendants. Myubu gives Tambu the resources for developing her identity within her bicultural existence and the beginnings of a basis for a feminine imaginary along with the resources of her mother's wisdom and her aunt's education. It is through the narrative perspective that Tambu comes to adopt by the end of her journey and the status that Myubu has within her consciousness that I claim Dangaremba as "re-worlded" not only a potential anticolonial future, but an antisexist one too. Myubu is not presented as a resolution to the patriarchal forces working in the novel, but through the lens of Irigaray's feminist framework she can be viewed as an indicator of what female relations demand under patriarchy. Irigaray locates women's impoverishment irrespective of their race, caste, class, or ethnicity, in the global absence of a female-defined imaginary under patriarchy. While the apparent universalism of this claim has invoked criticism of Irigaray's philosophy, aspects of which are justified, Irigaray's framework is a powerful one that can be modified by feminists in racially, ethnically, geo-politically, and socioeconomically specific contexts.

Works Cited

David, Deirdre (1995) *Rule Britannia. Women, Empire, and Victorian Writing*. Ithaca, NY: Cornell University Press.

Dangaremba, Tsitsi (1988) *Nervous Conditions*. London:The Women's Press.

Dangaremba, Tsitsi (1993) In interview with Rosemary Marangoly George and Helen Scott. *Novel. A Forum on Fiction* 26, no. 3, 309–319.

Grosz, Elizabeth (1989) *Sexual Subversions. Three French Feminists*. Sydney: Allen and Unwin.

Heidegger, Martin (1971) "The Origin of the Work of Art." In *Poetry, Language, Thought*. Translated by Albert Hofstadter. New York: Harper and Row, 17–86.

Irigaray, Luce (1985/86) "Language, Persephone and Sacrifice." *Borderlines*, no. 4, 30–32.

———. (1991a) "Women-Mothers, the Silent Substratum of the Social Order." In *The Irigaray Reader*. Translated by David Macey. Edited by Margaret Whitford. Oxford: Basil Blackwell, 47–51.

———. (1991b) "Bodily Encounter with the Mother." In *The Irigaray Reader*. Translatd by David Macey. Edited by Margaret Whitford. Oxford: Basil Blackwell, 34–46.

Laplanche, J. and Pontalis J-B. (1980) *The Language of Psychoanalysis*. Translated by D. Nicholson-Smith. London: Hogarth Press.

Meyer, Susan (1996) *Imperialism at Home. Race and Victorian Women's Fiction*. Ithaca, NY: Cornell University Press.

Sartre, Jean-Paul (1967) "Preface," to *The Wretched of the Earth* by Franz Fanon. Translated by Constance Farrington. London: Penguin Books, 7–26.

Spivak, Gayatri Chakravorty (1999) *A Critique of Postcolonial Reason. Toward A History of the Vanishing Present*. Cambridge, MA: Harvard University Press.

Spivak, Gaytri Chakravorty (1985) 'Three Women's Texts and a Critique of Imperialism,' *Critical Inquiry* 12, no. 1, 243–261.

9

Teaching World Systems: How Critical Pedagogy Can Frame the Global

David B. Downing

The main problem with teaching a World Literature class is that you can lose the world. Even with the best intentions in the world, the purpose of introducing students to the dramatic cultural differences reflected in various kinds of global literatures can defeat the very aim of negotiating those differences. Indeed, one of the most difficult problems of representing "World Literature" in some kind of survey class is that of decontextualizing the literary from the historical: removing most meaningful elements of geopolitical history in order to focus on a select group of representative literary texts from around the world. Strange literary texts become exotic exhibits, spectacular others, strangers in a strange land. The pressure to package literary texts as conveniently objectified and discrete objects comes in large part from the very pressures of neoliberal capital to commodify knowledge as information. This essay aims to demonstrate ways to resist and transform these pressures by deliberately framing world literature classes through the use of world-systems analysis.

The Anthological Problem

The problem of social contextualization in world literature courses can be especially overwhelming because the historical frames have been so thinly formulated in most of the existing world literature textbooks on the market today. Inevitably, most teachers assigned to such a course turn to one of these textbook anthologies, and they do indeed contain an impressive array of literary texts from diverse geographical locations and varied historical periods. Given the massive scope of such a global literary field, one can easily understand why the historical context might be thin or sketchy at best. The anthologies themselves are often now supplemented by extensive online databases that aim to thicken the contexts of study. And they can be extraordinarily helpful as a resource.[1] Nevertheless, the problems do not easily go away, and I will briefly highlight the generic problems of decontextualization by turning to the most ambitious and the most widely used of these anthologies, the *Norton Anthology of World Literature*. I take the *Norton* as exemplary, in the best sense of that term, so even as I highlight some structural weaknesses, my critique should be taken not as particular to this one anthology but rather as paradigmatic of most extant world lit anthologies.

The *Norton Anthology* in its full, six-volume edition, is like no other, simply because it is so massive, but still the editors must appeal to a combination of geographical and historical categories in the effort to fulfill reasonable coverage goals. Even with the focus on major regions like Europe, India, China, Africa, the Middle East, and the Americas, this compendium clearly abandons any presumption that they might be able to cover all but the major nationalities. Needless to say, many teachers deploy the condensed, two-volume shorter version, but even those two volumes weigh in at 3000 pages. How to get from there to the much more condensed selections necessary for a course in world literature: that is the framing problem in a nutshell. Besides the headnotes and section introductions, *Norton*'s website tries to aid those framing problems by offering all kinds of teacher and student aids such as sample syllabi, critical overviews, discovery modules, timelines, and maps.[2] Such aids or designs are crucial because the simplest organizing feature of the *Norton* is linear, by author birth date, and by division into large geographical zones.

What I wish to highlight is that the *Norton* site explicitly proposes what appears to be exactly the right kind of help: that is, the huge array of menu-driven resources are all organized to help teachers and students "frame topics for writing and research." Framing is, indeed, the problem when it comes to any kind of historical understanding because the frame determines the kind of evidence highlighted in a given context. I will elaborate on that problem shortly, but what I want to highlight here is that despite all the many terms that *Norton* deploys to frame global literary history, there appears to be a glaring, but paradigmatic, omission: there is no systematic overview, theme, or frame based on the shift from the world system of feudalism to that of capitalism, and no frames that organize the phases or cycles in the development of the 500-year history of capitalism. In short, fundamental frames with respect to the political economy seem to have slipped out the back door.

It is not as if the word capitalism never appears in, for instance, the menu for "Themes, Genres, and Other Clusters" that provides resources to each of the major sections of the anthology itself. But it tends to be buried, occurring only as a term in the themes listed for Section 20: "Revolution and Romanticism," with the mention of Adam Smith and Karl Marx in the third and fifth listing of themes for analysis, where there is mention that "capitalist theories of money and economy began to be widely circulated." Of course, it was much more than theories that got circulated. And the reference to Marx has a dismissive element built into it: "The publication of Karl Marx's *Das Kapital* prophesized the fall of capitalism and the emergence of a working class"—a wording that almost makes his "prophecy" seem foolish in light of the near-total spread and adaptability of the capitalist world system.

Indeed, at the risk of being unfair to the editors of the anthology, who might well invite the theme of capitalist world systems, let me just point out a few key instances where it would seem especially appropriate to mention capitalism even though the term itself does not appear. For example, in the themes offered for the Renaissance, there is considerable talk about the rise of science, religious tolerance, humanism, and other literary/philosophical movements—but nothing about the emergence of the capitalist world economy, especially given the Italian/Genoese and Spanish explorations of the world and establishment of trade routes overseas. In the section of Native American literature, the focus is on missionaries and colonialism, but no mention of capitalism with its pressures for new lands and new resources to fuel accumulation of profit. On the section on China during the modern period, the economy is mentioned, the control of "European colonial powers," and the "opium trade," but again, no mention of capitalism. In the section on the European Enlightenment, the themes offered refer to "the massive—and often cataclysmic—social changes that violently reshaped Europe during the eighteenth century," forms of "new commerce" that permitted "new wealth," but no mention of capitalism or the rise of the bourgeoisie. "Realism and Naturalism" are seen as following the "upheavals" of the French Revolution, the fall of empires, and the rise of "the political and social aspirations of the middle class," and the Industrial Revolution, but the term "capitalism" remains offstage even here. The final section on the twentieth century highlights decolonization, but not capitalism as a system that organizes world hegemonies.

One could reasonably ask, why are these omissions of the discourse of capitalism so common despite the enormous influence of the political economy? But, more importantly, what might a student miss in his or her reading experiences without some sense of the large frame of the capitalist world system? The work of the world-systems analysts help us to answer those questions, and their work can be used to reframe the contexts of reading and understanding.

The Epistemic Tension between Embedding and Framing

Two seemingly contradictory impulses must be negotiated in virtually any course, but they are especially magnified in a world literature course: embedding and framing. Embedding I take from the great economist Karl Polanyi who used the term embedding in his magisterial book *The Great Transformation* to emphasize that economic analyses should not be disembedded from or made independent of the broader social context of values, meanings, and practices of a given culture. When disembedding occurs, the general frame becomes false, mythical, and anti-universal even as it claims to have universal status. That is, of course, exactly what our current neoliberal hegemony seeks to do: claim that the myth of the self-regulating, free market economy is so natural, so disembedded from social and political values that there are no alternatives except to see how best to make the capitalist economy work.[3] Likewise, in a world literature course, disembedding any literary text from the broader social contexts in which it was produced and disseminated runs the risk of decontextualizing the work.

The second term, "framing," I take from several sources, but most noticeably I follow Nancy Fraser's use of the term, and its correlative, "misframing."[4] In a basic way, framing names the necessary underlying preconditions for both cognitive and social understanding of meaning, and Fraser has a keen sense of both how and why in our contemporary global, cross-cultural contexts, we have such deep problems with our ability to map, or frame, any problem. This is especially urgent with respect to issues of social justice pertinent to a World Literature course. In this context, framing is similar to periodizing, and as Fredric Jameson put it in *A Singular Modernity*, "We cannot not periodize" (119). How we frame and periodize is thus the key question.

We have so many conflicting frames, and so many different groups of people, cultures, nations, and international bodies all framing problems in different, often incommensurable ways. The rise in the nineteenth century of the discourse of political economy framed this dialectic in terms of the relations and tensions between particularity and totality, and Karl Marx was certainly the most insistent on the resonation between particular modes of production and lived experience on the one hand, and, on the other, the social totality as represented by his analysis of the shift from feudal to capitalist world system, a shift that affected all subjects within the system. In the specific context of a World Literature class, the question becomes: What is the most fair way of framing a World Literature syllabus with respect to the main criteria for inclusion? The ethical issues get foregrounded for the obvious reason that framing is not a neutral activity. As Wallerstein puts it, it is a "real protest about the deep inequalities of the world-system" (xi). Framing the totality is thus an intervention, a dissent, from the dominant ways of misframing, and always challenges us to consider what is fair about this frame. These are difficult, but unavoidable, questions to answer for any theory, and the way we answer them deeply affects the politics with which we are affiliated, or embedded.

Our initial frames have been shaped by our own cultural lenses, our own heritages, our own acculturations, so we initially start all investigations by seeing the particulars of everyday living through our own inherited frames. But the good thing about framing and embedding is that they tend to be correctives of each other to the extent that they tend to move in opposite directions: framing moves from the specific and particular to the more general and totalizing frame; embedding ensures that the general frames resonate fairly with the particular details within the frames. Misframing and disembedding are then the key vices. What one tries to avoid with careful framing is to blindly recreate, as Linda Tuwuhai Smith puts it, "The procedures by which indigenous peoples and their societies were coded into the Western system of knowledge" (43), or as Wallerstein puts it, the anti-universal discourse of the West that falsely poses itself as universal.

Indeed, disembeddedness and misframing often produce devastating forms of social injustice. As Fraser explains, "misframing" is itself a form of social injustice when those in power exclude from both recognition and representation many of the people directly affected by the former's decision making. A brief example can help clarify: when international financial organizations such as the World Bank, IMF, and WTO frame all problems as economic market problems, disembedded from the social fabric and lived values of the vast population groups, such misframings authorized by a small percentage of wealthy powerful groups in the core nations deliberately disempower those in the peripheral nations who are excluded from decisions that affect their working conditions and social life. International credit and loan policies ensure that the precariousness of debt liabilities are burdened upon those least able to bear it. Misframing therefore perpetuates huge social injustices when the frames deployed disembed themselves from the lives of the people affected by those theories and policies. Misframing further creates the conditions for the mystifications (and lies) of ideological masking, making invisible the history of hegemony that so maldistributed world resources. A course in world literature ought to seek to avoid perpetuating those injustices.

The traditions of critical pedagogy, beginning with Paulo Freire, have tended to highlight the need for embedding: addressing the problems students and educators face in particular situations. Problem-posing education means embedding the issues addressed in any class in the experiences of the learners. It is, thus, student centered, (although that's a bit simplistic—because it is interactive). But critical pedagogy has more need for framing than one might recognize. Even though, as Freire put it, we are "suffering from narration sickness" (71), he was highlighting the dominant narratives of the market economy that seek through a vast educational and media complex to hide the traces of its own exploitation and production of inequities through a constant focus on consumption. We can't avoid narratives, but we had better have more accurate stories, ones that avoid the historical amnesia deliberately produced by mainstream ideology. World-systems theory protests exactly that historical amnesia.

Nevertheless, the strategic problem of framing as experienced by any teacher assigned to a World Literature course is daunting indeed. How can one possibly frame the world? How could a syllabus be designed so as to contextualize texts from different parts of the world, and still be done in a 15-week semester? First of all, since a "survey" or coverage model of world literature in a semester-long course is an impossibility, we can give up that unrealistic aim, and focus on exactly the kind of frames that thicken the embedded contexts of any proposed sampling of literary texts. Fortunately, we do now have tools available to help any instructor work with both embedding and framing, both the local problems and how they impact the global economy.

Framing World Systems

Framing the world does, indeed, call for some grand narratives. More than any other critics, those associated with world-systems analysis have not shied away from that task—foremost among them, Immanuel Wallerstein. After several books on political history in postcolonial Africa, Wallerstein began in the mid-1970s to deploy the term "world-systems analysis," and his work led to the development of the international intellectual movement identified with a number of major historians such as Giovanni Arrighi, Samir Amin, Andre Frank, and Beverly Silver among others. The distinguishing feature of this movement has been the insistence on the importance of long-term, and large-scale economic systems such as the transition from feudalism to capitalism in what they call the long sixteenth century, the period from the European discovery of the

Americas to the English Civil Wars of the 1640s, and the ensuing history of the capitalist world system.

Understandably, Wallerstein drew upon some key work by those associated with the Annales School of historians that developed in the 1930s in France. One of the second generation leaders of this school was Fernand Braudel, who from 1956–1968 was the editor of the society's journal *Annales d'histoire économique et sociale*. Braudel also wrote several major historical studies, and what distinguished his work was, first, its resistance to the disciplinary separation of history, economics, political science, and sociology, and second, his willingness to articulate a wide-angle view of history that included geography, social movements, political economy, and, especially, a concern for the marginalized and peripheral people often neglected in world histories. Much of the Annales School historians tended to focus on early, or pre-Modern periods, but they altered the way many people thought about history in terms of their willingness to articulate the grand, even if slow-moving, integration of social, geographical, political, and economic systems.

The Annales School flourished after World War II, but with the advent during the 1970s and 1980s of the poststructuralist and postmodernist distrust of totalizing and essentializing systems, the Annales historians tended to be ignored precisely because of their basic assumptions about large-scale economic frames. Jean Francois Lyotard offered his stunning critique of grand narratives, and Michel Foucault offered his version of the specific intellectual whose focus was on the event and the structuring of the longitudinal, or spatial organization of an episteme, rather than on the chronological and temporal dimension of economic systems. During that period, then, Wallerstein was somewhat of an exception among historical theorists, but the clarity with which he articulated the broadly interdisciplinary principles of world-systems analysis, and his lucid responses to his critics have greatly extended the influence and significance of this work. Looking back at his predecessors, the Annales School had been critical of the Marxist focus on class struggle, but Wallerstein adapted and incorporated many of the basic Marxist principles regarding the critique of capitalism and the dialectic between particularity and totality into his articulation of world-systems analysis, and, together with Giovanni Arrighi, they have focused much more on the contemporary world system and the global economy so it has become more relevant and important than ever.

A key distinction in the work of these theorists is that they reframe the unit of analysis from the nation-state to what they call the "historical system." They argue that such systems have "existed up to now in only three variants: minisystems; and 'world-systems' of two kinds—world-economies and world-empires" (Wallerstein, 16). The virtue of this analysis is that it is not difficult to understand the basic distinctions. Minisystems are those social systems that have a much smaller geographical location, even though within a region the overall social and economic organization can be quite systemic. Thus, for example, ancient Greek city-states were minisystems in that some of them developed new kinds of relatively democratic political structures integrated with their largely local agrarian market economy. World empires are much larger systems, constituting a "world" unto themselves even if they are not global. For example, the minisystem of ancient Athens led, by way of Aristotle's student, to the Alexandrian empire that then included within the system many different ethnic and racial differences, even though, again, it was not global. The advent of modernity began with the transition between the world system of feudalism and the emergence of capitalism.

The key distinction between a world empire and a world system is that the former exercises power through direct political force, often by the dominance of a central figure such as Alexander the Great, whereas the latter operates through the integration of economic, political, and social forces. But here's the key point: world systems are grand, in the sense of representing long historical periods and broad, even if not global, geographical territories. Braudel articulated what he called "structural time," or the "longue durée," by which he meant the overall time periods during which a system operated. But even then, the structural time of world systems such as capitalism was never anything like a transcendental, ahistorical framework. Indeed, the world system of capitalism might be 500 years old, but that's much different than an idealized sense of an essential human narrative of "emancipation" as a basic property of human nature and civilized progress toward heaven or freedom. In short, the longue durée is historical, not timeless. And there have been two main world systems in the West (feudalism and capitalism), and before that, many different world empires and minisystems. Syllabus construction and text selection for World Literature classes can be organized around these large historical frames subdivided, as they can be, with their internal phases of development and devolution, and thus embedded in both the local context and the global arena. As Wallerstein explains, "Generalizations about the functioning of such a system thus avoided the trap of seeming to assert timeless, eternal truths. If such systems were not eternal, then it followed that they had beginnings, lives during which they 'developed,' and terminal transitions" (18).

The longue durée of the current capitalist world economy directly corresponds with the rise of nation-states, especially since the Treaty of Westphalia of 1648, but unlike most analyses of class struggle and economics that focus on the nation as the unit of analysis, world systems function on the larger, global context that affects everyone in the world. The point of what's called "the long 16th century," from 1492–1640, is the unevenness of the transition to the new world system: there remained large pockets of feudalism even as the progression to a capitalist world economy was well underway. As Giovanni Arrighi and Beverly Silver argue, "the essential feature of historical capitalism over its longue durée, that is, over its entire lifetime, has been the 'flexibility' and 'eclecticism' of capital rather than the concrete forms it assumed at different places and at different times" (259). The point of calling it a world system, however, is that even the peasantry and the feudalist pockets were no longer independent of the larger, systemic changes in markets, exchanges, and geopolitical power structures. For example, even though at the time of the French Revolution, about 80 percent of the population in France and Great Britain was rural, they still all felt some varying degree of the effects of the international system of the capitalist economy, especially when the great migration from rural to industrial urban areas grew exponentially during the nineteenth century.

Nevertheless, (and this is a key characteristic) even a world system need not be global in its territorial scope. That is, the system constitutes a "world" to the extent that its organizational principles affect all individuals living within the large geographical context of the given system. Thus, feudalism can be said to be a world system even though it's primary geographical location was in the area now constituted by the European nations, and not, say, on the continents of North and South America. It is a system when the relations of persons affected are integrated primarily through the mechanisms of economic exchange, the division of labor, and the modes of production necessary for life-sustaining activities for people within the system.

In contrast, world empires are largely held together through political force and will of dominant individuals: consider the Alexandrian Empire, the Roman Empire, the Holy Roman Empire, or the Ottoman Empire. A key point is that world systems cannot be integrated with world empires. Indeed, efforts to try and convert the world economic system of capitalism into an empire, such as those imperial efforts of Napoleon or Hitler, have always been a failure.[5] The capitalist system could not exist within a world empire because the latter would mean that the political will of an individual could override the economic system.

The great advantage of the concept of world systems is their claim to be based on shared empirical evidence: they may be "grand" in their large-scale geographies and periods, but they are based on historical evidence and their reliability depends upon their necessary obligation to "reflect reality more closely than others.... To be against the concept of timeless structures does not mean that (time-bound) structures do not exist" (Wallerstein, 21). They make the claim to be accurate with respect to articulating the larger forces that affect specific, local histories. Indeed, such specifics are "embedded" in historical realities to the extent that any particular details of a local narrative will be affected by the forces at work in the larger system; if not, then that would be evidence that the system was inaccurate.

This evidentiary nature of world-systems analysis is its great virtue for World Literature courses: it can be articulated in simple, grand stroke narrative outlines which can, therefore, be shared even with beginning students. At the same time, particular literary texts and effects can then be seen to be embedded in, and thus affected by the larger framing narratives. In short, they allow for both embedding and framing. The periods of the capitalist world system can be categorized in terms of the concept of hegemony, that is, the power of a leading nation to dominate the flow of capital toward that nation.

Framing the Cycles of Capitalism

In the precapitalist, feudal world system that operated throughout most of western Europe during the Middle Ages, the family labor system was central. All able members of a family performed labor, and the goal of the system was to produce what they needed to consume: that is, labor provided the necessities of life such as food, clothing, shelter. There were markets, but the exchange of goods was to meet consumable needs in the basics. In practice, this meant that you could not fire your family members if they did not produce rapidly enough, because you still had to feed them. Wage labor took place in isolated ventures, but it was marginal, if not irrelevant to the system. And the basic organizing features of the feudalist world system consisted of various levels of landed aristocracy, weak or nonexistent national governments, peasantry dependent on the landowners, and the integration of production and consumption through large dependence on the household economy.

The emergence in the long sixteenth century of the capitalist world system changed all this by the basic practice of separating production from consumption through the dominance of wage labor and the increase of rent. Now, production was not tied directly to consumption, but to the production of more capital. As Wallerstein puts it, the goal of the capitalist world system is endless accumulation, which meant continuous expansion in terms of the escalating need for more labor and more natural resources. Owners of larger, non-household factories and farms could now fire workers during economic depressions and not have to be responsible, in principle, for their subsistence. In short, the goal of the capitalist world system was (and still is) to maximize the exploitation of surplus labor—the labor that would go to the production of more capital, rather than direct needs of workers for the consumption of basic sustainable living. Various texts of world literature reflect exactly these kind of material changes.

The 500-year longue durée of the capitalist world system can be periodized, or framed, by reference to the succeeding hegemonic powers that controlled the orchestration of capital and the division of global labor between core, semi-peripheral, and peripheral regions of the world. The capitalist world system determines the overall direction of the flow of capital from rural and peripheral regions in the south to the core, urban, hegemonic powers in the north. These transitions were uneven, geographically, just like the unevenness of the transition from feudalism to capitalism. Nevertheless, the four periods can be roughly periodized as follows: (1) the Genoese-Iberian, roughly 1492–1640; (2) the Dutch, 1640–1780; (3) the British, 1780–1940, and (4) the United States, 1940–2010.

The transitional dates are, of course, much more overlapping than the specific years might indicate, which serve only as approximate markers. The shifts of hegemony appear to have followed cycles of material expansion of the production of goods and commodities, followed by a shift to financialization and various kinds of financial deal making and securities exchanges rather than material production. And with each succeeding hegemony, the overall system expanded in each transition in terms of both scope and complexity. As Giovanni Arrighi and Silber explain, the

> leading complexes—the Dutch complex in the seventeenth century, the British complex in the nineteenth century, and the US complex in the twentieth century—have all acted as "tracklaying vehicles."...In leading the system in a new direction, they also transformed it. Under Dutch leadership, the emergent system of European states was formally instituted by the Treaties of Westphalia. Under British leadership, the Eurocentric system of sovereign states moved to dominion globally. And under US leadership, the system lost its Eurocentricity to gain further in reach and penetration. (261)

Clearly, these framing cycles resonate with our current situation whereby, especially in the North Atlantic nations, production has been outsourced to peripheral nations, and we have entered in the last 30 years into a period of extremely risky global financialization where even the core nations' economies are in crisis.

Conclusion: How to Implement the Frames

Given the theoretical focus of this essay, I can only gloss some of the possible ways of embedding specific texts in the general frames I have outlined. I have experimented in several different ways, but the point is that anyone assigned to teach a World Literature course will inevitably find himself embedded in a context that radically alters expectations and possibilities. And I have no doubt that many readers can be more inventive than me in terms of the imaginative uses of various kinds of texts and media resources. If the requirements of an assigned course call for a stretch from *Gilgamesh* to *Infinite Jest*, then the frames will be thin no matter what. My basic presumption is that once the frames are clarified, any teacher reading this essay can imagine how he or she can best select works for whatever course design they wish to implement. The wide-angle frames allow for adaptability and flexibility with respect to the inevitably idiosyncratic strengths and interests of the teacher, but now specific text selections are always justified and embedded within the larger historical frames. Transitional moments in the cycles of capitalism described by world systems create stress, chaos, and new movements: much global literature can be seen as responding to these stress points. Syllabi can thus be organized around these crisis moments and transition points, an organization that enables a resonance between the detailed contexts of the literary texts and the geopolitical transformations taking place on a much broader scale. I can only make a few suggestions along these lines, leaving it up to individual teachers to design their own selection of texts.

If you have considerable autonomy in course design, I recommend not using an anthology, partly because so many texts are now available online, and partly because you can better customize course design rather than purchasing huge anthologies where you're reading only a fraction of the available sources. I also think it is wise to emphasize the contemporary moment that seems appropriate given the current crisis, and the global nature of geopolitical struggles in the twenty-first century. Wallerstein's short book (90 pages), *World-Systems Analysis: An Introduction,* can be assigned at the beginning of the course, and, fortunately, it is accessible to undergraduates. But even so, it is crucial to use some carefully prepared sets of handouts outlining the key terms and the four main cycles of hegemony in the capitalist world system. It usually takes only about a week or two to establish this outline. Once these introductory materials have been set up, it is possible to design a curriculum that situates texts within the frames, and I suggest a focus on three of the four cycles. The first period can be represented by, for instance, key texts representing the contrasting arguments for and against colonialism between, on the one hand, the reactionary and well-funded conservative justification for the exploitive system by Juan Ginés de Sepúlveda's *Democrates Segundo: About the Just Causes of the War Against the Indians* (1545), and, on the other hand, the famous Dominican friar, Bartolomé de Las Casas's critique of the Spanish encomienda system in *A Brief Account of The Devastation of the Indies* (1552).[6] Las Casas's conversion came during his time in the Americas (beginning in 1502) when he saw the horrors begotten by the use of indigenous people for the economic and cultural purposes of the colonial powers. Although their arguments on the surface may seem cultural and religious in nature, the subtext is so clearly economic, and this factor now comes into clarity more in the world-system frame. During the third phase of the capitalist world system, when the British Empire dominates, the choices are, of course, vast in range but, for instance, Conrad's *Heart of Darkness* raises all the issues Wallerstein has outlined, and it can be contrasted with translation's of the oral tales of the signifying monkey insofar as the latter undermines the economic and political dominance of the colonizer. The last half of the class can then focus on more contemporary texts, especially highlighting the current crisis in global capitalism. For this purpose, texts such as (among many other possibilities) Chinua Achebe's *Things Fall Apart*, Ngugi Wa Thiong'o's *Weep Not, Child*, Bharati Mukherjee's *Jasmine*, Arundati Roy's *The God of Small Things*, and Mohsin Hamid's *Moth Smoke* all resonate with the current crisis even as some of them stretch backwards to less contemporary periods. I always tend toward a sampling of fewer texts, including several novels since they provide more detail and depth, and they are also highly engaging for most students. For this purpose, it is often useful to contrast texts from the core nations with those from the peripheral zones during the relatively same time period.

There are important reasons for the highlighting of the contemporary crisis in global capitalism. As Arrighi and Silver put it, "A sea change of major proportions is taking place in the historical social system forming the modern world, creating a widespread sense of uncertainty about the present and foreseeable future" (257). The current situation differs significantly from the transitional cycles of hegemony in the past, mainly because the US hegemony can no longer be indefinitely maintained. Even though China's GDP will surpass that of the United States within the decade, China has not chosen to duplicate the huge US investment in the military required to duplicate another cycle of hegemony. We may be witnessing the collapse of nation-state hegemony in orchestrating the world system. As Slavoz Žižek puts it in the title of his recent book, we are *Living in the End Times*. If so, we are living through a more radical kind of transition to a different world system, although it is not at all clear what that will be. What is clear is that the capitalist expansion based on endless accumulation has reached its limit to the extent that we are now witnessing the loss of further rural areas with cheap labor and the loss of natural resources from the environment. The economic world system of expansion and accumulation has no more frontiers to conquer or lands to colonize. As Wallerstein explains, "True crises are those difficulties that cannot be resolved within the framework of the system" (76). In his estimate, the transition to the next system might occur over the next 25 to 50 years, but, as in all transition periods, there are great uncertainties, volatilities, anxieties, and an increase in violence. Forms of extremism and fundamentalism are always on the rise in periods of great crisis and transition.

In short, focus on the contemporary crisis can serve as an important justification for teaching world literature in the first place. Any course that avoids the contemporary situation named by "globalization" will risk being irrelevant. The world systems theory frames address pressing needs felt by those embedded in the current crisis. They allow for an historical understanding of why this crisis is happening. Informed citizenry requires a knowledge of the destruction of the welfare state protections, the rush to privatization everywhere, and the concomitant shrinking of the public commons around the world. The reasons for the increasing gaps between the 1 percent and the rest of the world have magnified not just because of some momentary downturn in the "nature" of otherwise progressively expanding markets, but as political and policy changes in the capitalist world system that have been deliberately implemented by governments and international financial organizations to increase the power of the wealthy elite, by lowering wages, reducing taxes, deregulating capital restrictions, and increasing limitations on labor rights. Only on the basis of sound historical knowledge of these changes can we begin to hope that the countermovements to the current world system that we see in demonstrations all over the world can begin to reshape a different kind of world. World Literature courses can contribute to those movements.

Notes

1. One of the many remarkable online resources for "Multicultural and World Literature Anthologies" is the site compiled at George Mason University (http://mason.gmu.edu/~ayadav/anthologies). This site now lists 1425 various texts, and the headnote for the site explains the difficulty of the category of world literature itself. Many different geographical and linguistic categories are used to aid navigation of the site, but it clearly indicates the need for careful framing for anyone planning to use the generic category of "world literature" as an undergraduate course.

2. All of the various citations that occur in this essay can be located on this web site: http://www.wwnorton.com/college/english/worldlit2e/full/
3. All the evidence from the current crisis of capitalism suggests that these myths are more like lies. See, for instance Holland and Reich. Polanyi believed that the problem with the classical economists of the 19th century (Adam Smith, David Ricardo, Jeremy Bentham, etc.) was that they believed that they could isolate, or disembed, economic analysis from social values, and for Polanyi that was a terrible mistake.
4. Although I draw most directly on the recent work of Nancy Fraser, especially in her book, *Scales of Justice*, the term framing has a long history of uses that are also quite useful, and contribute to our understanding of the fundamental significance of framing to human understanding. See, for instance, Morton and Zavarzadeh; Goffman; and Lakoff.
5. Michael Hardt and Antonio Negri's trilogy, beginning with *Empire*—associates US global hegemony with the notion of empire, but their analysis clearly demonstrates that the U.S. dominance is maintained through the neocolonial economic system in conjunction with military power, and thus reflective of exactly Wallerstein's description of a world-system (as opposed to a world-empire). Although there are substantive differences, there are much wider shared understandings of the dominance of the current capitalist world system.
6. Las Casas book is available in translation through the Gutenberg Project. Sepúlveda's work is not available in translation, but it is accurately quoted and summarized in Las Casas's book. Only certain selections of this long work can be assigned for a class, but enough that the contrasting arguments become quite clear.

Works Cited

Achebe, Chinua. *Things Fall Apart*. New York: Anchor, 1994 (1958).
Arrighi, Giovanni and Beverly J. Silver. "Capitalism and World (Dis)Order." *Review of International Studies* 27 (2001): 257–79.
Fraser, Nancy. *Scales of Justice: Reimagining Political Space in a Globalizing World*. New York: Columbia University Press, 2009.
Freire, Paulo. *Pedagogy of the Oppressed*, 30th Anniv. edn. New York: Continuum, 2003 (1970).
Goffman, Erving. *Frame Analysis: An Essay on the Organization of Experience*. London: Harper and Row, 1974.
Hamid, Mohsin. *Moth Smoke*. New York: Picador, 2000.
Hardt, Michael and Antonio Negri. *Empire*. Cambridge: Harvard UP, 2000.
Holland, Joshua. *The Fifteen Biggest Lies about the Economy: And Everything Else the Right Doesn't Want You to Know about Taxes, Jobs, and Corporate America*. Hoboken, NJ: Wiley, 2010.
Jameson, Fredric. *A Singular Modernity: Essay on the Ontology of the Present*. London: Verso, 2002.

Lakoff, George. *Don't Think of an Elephant: Know Your Values and Frame the Debate*. White River Jct., VT: Chelsea Green Publishing, 2004.

Las Casas, Bartolomé de. *A Brief Account of the Destruction of the Indies*. Project Gutenberg. http://www.gutenberg.org/cache/epub/20321/pg20321.html.

Lawall, Sarah, et. al., eds. *The Norton Anthology of World Literature*, 2nd edn., 6 vols. New York: Norton, 2003.

Morton, Donald and Mas'ud Zavarzadeh, eds. *Theory/Pedagogy/Politics: Texts for Change*. Urbana: University of Illinois Press, 1991.

Mukherjee, Bharati. *Jasmine*. New York: Grove Press, 1989.

"Multicultural and World Literature Anthologies." (http://mason.gmu.edu/~ayadav/anthologies)

Polanyi, Karl. *The Great Transformation*, 2nd edn. Boston: Beacon Press, 2001 (1944).

Reich, Robert. "The Seven Biggest Economic Lies." http://robertreich.org/post/11329289033.

Roy, Arundhati. *The God of Small Things*. New York: Continuum, 2003 (1997).

Thiong'o, Ngugi Wa. *Weep Not, Child*. New York: Penguin, 2009 (1964).

Wallerstein, Immanuel. *World-Systems Analysis: An Introduction*. Durham: Duke University Press, 2004.

Žižek, Slavoj. *Living in the End Times*. London: Verso, 2010.

10

Object Lessons: Material Culture Approaches to Teaching Global Poetry

Hella Rose Bloom

In this chapter, I will make a case for the teaching of material culture in the world literature classroom. Before I do so, I would like to pose a series of questions: Why do we teach literature? Why do we teach world literature? The answers to these two questions are not the same. Let us ask the question in different terms: What compels an Anglo-American student to choose a British or American literature survey over a world literature survey? Perhaps she is moved by the promise of identity-fulfillment through origin-inquiry, through the re-search of familiar signs. In the opposite scenario she might have chosen world literature to the same end but through different means: perhaps she sees an opportunity for identity-fulfillment through the search into unfamiliar signs. This assumption would suggest that we teach world literature to encourage unsettling encounters between bodies that experience the sign disparately. But why force an encounter that is marked by *unheimlich*?

Most committed teachers of world literature would agree that their attempt to decenter literary studies from its western European hinge comes from a desire to transform their students emotionally; but what is transformation if it does not inform our students' work with objects and bodies beyond the safe conceptual space of the classroom? Indrani Mitra and Madhu Mitra point out that the recent curricular trend to teach expansive world literature surveys is part of a "pluralism" that risks suppressing "the very real sociopolitical contexts that frame these literatures," and they go on to say that "the current practice of including texts from the

Third World in literary anthologies assumes—somewhat naively—that any historically rooted text can be lifted and placed unproblematically in the American classroom" (Mitra). Due to the dangers of universalism, world literature pedagogy handles a different responsibility than simply "literature" pedagogy, the latter of which terms I am admittedly using to represent the teaching of the canon. The uncomfortable conceptual encounter that oft accompanies our reading of foreign texts is in vain unless it has the potential to relocate to the material realm. Concrete political understanding and subsequent transformation is and must be the end to teaching ethnically and geographically estranged texts.

How do we begin the process of transformation given the daunting limitations of translation and strange metaphors? A foreign text's relationship to the materials it represents is familiarizing as well as alienating. In a world literature class, our students can understand palpably the connection between their self and their *stuff*, but they are often baffled by the varied types of objects and responses to those objects recorded in the strange and plural literature they are expected to encounter. Poetry can be especially challenging to deal with, as, unlike fiction, readers of poetry are not introduced to objects gradually—objects are not narrated to the same extent that they are in fiction. However, the often itemized list of objects we encounter in poetry can be generative, according to Wolfgang Iser's theory of "impeded ideation," in which he states

> runs counter to our habitual inclination to degrade the knowledge offered or invoked by the text during the process of moulding the imaginary object...we are simultaneously induced to imagine something in the offered or invoked knowledge which would have appeared unimaginable as long as our habitual frame of reference prevailed. Although we are caught up in the images we build while reading, their very collision makes it possible for us to relate ourselves to what we are absorbed in. (189)

Poet and teacher Dorothea Lasky believes that "poets, more than any other artists besides dancers, are always engaged in the work of felt experience...a connection between thought and the body, between the mind and the action of thinking and feeling simultaneously" (167). She goes on to say that students must discover how to "physically get into language" (167), and she fosters this through exercises that promote a deep engagement with words, actual objects, and physical activities. Due to poetry's unfettered love affair with objects, I would like to suggest that as a medium it is conducive to a materialist approach to world literature. In a world literature class, if we understand words as objects, we foster an empathetic understanding of the self and its response to the textual object. Training our students to understand the text tangibly prepares the way for them to transcend the page to act more perceptively in their world. Ideally, poets *doing* things with objects become models for students *doing* things with a heightened awareness in their respective communities.

This chapter will draw from theories that understand objects as animate extensions of daily life, and as things inextricably part of a private and public conversation, through which individuals articulate a sociability that is always already culturally, politically, and economically mediated. In it, I will offer a teaching method that heeds the demanding presence of objects in global poems, suggesting that by focusing on the artifact as both an inscription of memory and an invitation to experience empathy, an empathy which will always remain partially untranslatable and incomplete, one can streamline a disordered and problematic discourse. The chapter will examine three dominant theoretical approaches to literature: Marxist, psychoanalytic, and affective theories. I will argue that each of these schools of criticism is accounted for in material culture discourse. Despite their similar heuristics, the study of material culture remains a separate discipline from literary studies—it is typically relegated to the field of anthropology, yet they are having the same conversation in different rooms. This chapter will bring the two together through a pedagogy of the world literature survey. I will punctuate my arguments with selected excerpts from the poetry of Marilyn Chin, Yehuda Amichai, and Kishwar Naheed in order to concretize the pedagogical importance of the literary object as a social and psychological center in global poems.

The Marxist Inquiry in Material Culture

Marxist critics are interested in social ordering through *stuff*, whether that stuff manifests as possessions, sustaining resources, or commodities that bear value far removed from their labor source and conditions of origin. Marxist and postcolonial critic Gayatri Chakravorty Spivak has suggested that high Western theory, such as that advanced by Foucault and Deleuze, "ignores the international division of labor" and "is incapable of dealing with global capitalism" (67). Under these terms, it would seem that theories of power alone do not do enough to understand objects and subjectivities within their capitalistic frameworks. In an undergraduate world literature classroom, students are often asked to explore metaphor as though it exists in a vacuum. However, metaphors cannot sustain themselves, especially when the cultural conditions producing their meanings are of an alien sort.

How do we deal with poetic objects without simply doing close readings? How do we avoid the risk of over-analyzing metaphor to the detriment of meaning? Further, how do we express to our students the problems with bringing the canonical, fresh-out-of-secondary-school self to bear on the marginal, without disallowing their identities in the process? Theories of material culture step in to partially answer these questions with which high theory struggles, as the discourse of material culture accounts for the movement of artifacts between human hands in addition to the larger political and theoretical dimensions that define and are defined by its meanings. To this end, Arthur Asa Berger writes

> In order to manufacture clothes, furniture, automobiles, appliances, machines of one sort of another, we need factories and a huge industrial base. Ironically, then, it is the economic system hidden behind the artifacts and objects we purchase that plays so important a role in shaping our consciousness of ourselves and the world. (64)

Contemporary global poetry can reconnect the disengagement of objects from labor by recontextualizing it in unfamiliar margins. The abrupt destabilizations confuse our attentions, forcing us to investigate its origins and its constantly pluralizing contexts. By the process of a necessary reducibility, eventually we must strip it down to its madness; we must imagine its thingness, its sensation, and its journey from the factory to the memory of the poet. By the poet's manipulation, the object becomes a language. In his essay "Cultural Nationalism and Moral Regeneration," John Hutchinson asserts:

> Each language is not simply a way of expressing universal values. Rather, it is the manifestation of unique values and ideas.... Language is the property of the community, but it stretches beyond any one generation.... A language is not an arbitrary collection of utterances.... [These] arguments can be extended much further if all other human activities are understood as sorts of languages. Dress, architecture, customs, ceremonial, song, law: all these and many other activities can be understood in the same way. (105)

It we unite Berger's and Hutchinson's assertions, we can assume that commodities have a unique language. I would like to suggest that commodities are like euphemisms or commonplace words that efface their genesis at the service of mystification; but when poets employ them, they demand attention to the detriment of mystification.

The poetry of Marilyn Chin demonstrates how reprocessing American commodities in the context of poetry violates the system of mystification by drawing attention to their role in her alienation. Chin, a Chinese immigrant whose writing deals with themes of contemporary Chinese American life, represents the expanding generic borders of world literature through hybridity. The poetry of those who technically live within the borders of a nation but live displaced symbolically is especially interesting to teach material-culturally, as the disaffection in which capitalism is so invested palpably manifests in the poets' estranged relationship to the objects that surround them. Exposing this dynamic in poetry unmasks the commodity, and in order to lead our students to this reality, they must first understand the relationship between the speaker and her physical environment.

In *Identity Poem*, Chin's speaker interrogates the marginalized self, using objects to negotiate her hybridity: "Are you the only Chinese restaurant in Roseburg, Oregon? / ... Are you earphones—detached / Left dangling on an airplane jack to diaspora? / Are you doomed to a childhood without music? / Weary of your granny's one-string, woe-be-gone *erhu* / Mewling about the past" (ll. 2–9). Chin's poem demonstrates how commodities become not just signifiers of oppression and labor imbalance but also words for negotiating subjectivities. In the confines of a global poem, they speak a language that an American undergraduate student can understand, if not directly through a shared experience, then at least through an analogous pain or pleasure. We should have our students ask themselves: What is this *thing* doing in this poem? In Chin's case, the Chinese restaurant, the earphones, and the erhu (a stringed Chinese instrument) stage cultural signifiers for some purpose. We then ask, where does this *thing* come from? For Chin, the objects come from competing worlds—American consumerist life and Chinese tradition; additionally, one of the objects—the earphones—gets displaced in between these boundaries, on the airplane. This becomes a metaphor for the exilic feelings of being part of a diasporic group.

Further we ask, does the object cause the speaker pleasure or pain (what is the speaker's relationship to it)? For Chin's speaker, the objects seem to cause tension and resentment, perhaps for their role in mobilizing cultural stereotypes, objectifying the speaker, and frustrating the speaker's pursuit of a substantive identity. Finally, we would have our students ask themselves, does the poetic object cause me pleasure or pain? How does its re-contextualization draw attention to its role in a larger economy of injustices or freedoms? Once they have attempted to answer these questions, they can ask themselves how the stuff circulating in their world repairs or does violence to their subjectivities. Through a material cultural approach to poetry, informed by an understanding of the commodity and the cultural signifier, students ideally arrive at empathy.

Psychoanalytic Approaches to the Object

The introduction to this chapter invites us to question why we teach world literature, and how the answer is uniquely bound up in political transformation. It concludes that we teach world literature to encourage unsettling encounters between bodies that experience the sign disparately, and that this constitutes a forced encounter marked by *unheimlich*. Being "not at home" is a feeling we encourage in the classroom that engages with foreign texts. This is both a necessary component of transformation as well as a dying vehicle in a rapidly urbanizing world. Zygmunt Bauman expresses this loss beautifully:

> Whatever has come to be known as the "local community" is brought into being by this opposition between "here" and "out there," "near" and "far away."... The so-called "closely knit communities" of yore were, as we can now see, brought into being and kept alive by the gap between the nearly instantaneous communication *inside* the small-scale community...and the enormity of time and expense needed to pass information *between* localities.... [Now,] cheap communication floods and smothers memory rather than feeding and stabilizing it. (15–16)

Bauman's treatise reveals how what he terms the "time-space compression" eclipses the uniquely local, happening as a result of globalization, increasing mobility for communities of means, and the rapid transmission of information. To extend Bauman's melancholic argument, the time-space compression also threatens the generative power of *unheimlich*. Necessary to feeling "not at home" is the knowledge of the near/far binary. A binary that has the power to make the unfamiliar familiar has been replaced by a truncated way of seeing the world, where a 500-year sampling of the world's literature can be relegated to a single anthology and a single academic term, where our students can believe they know what is happening in China after a quick Google search or a glance at a scrolling headline. It is easy to see why Bauman marks this generation with memory loss and confusion. Reading global texts as locally specific artifacts *representing* locally specific artifacts can help bring us back to an awareness of geographical distinctiveness. A rigorous approach does not yield a quick or cheap read. A good reading will engage us corporeally rather than cyber-frantically. This is not to say that we must not then position its meanings in relation to centralized power.

Globalization has foretold the "withering away" of nation-states, which in turn threatens our assumption of "being in control" (57). For material culturalist and art historian Mimi Hellman, the moment we begin to unravel happens earlier than Bauman seems to suggest. For Hellman, who takes a Freudian approach to the artifact, we unravel at the dawn of industrialization and international trade. According to Hellman, in the eighteenth century we begin to see the psychological imperative for an object or commodity to stimulate psychological and environmental control by expressing its madeness. Specifically referring to the ostentatious and often bizarre eighteenth-century porcelain garnish, she asserts that these central household objects articulate the Freudian concepts of condensation and displacement, where viewers enjoy pacification through an object's artificiality—it announces its ornate handiwork and "worldliness" while it distorts any real gesture to the natural world, including the true "orient" it represents (39). By foregrounding "madeness," Hellman makes the decorative object important by moving away from an artist-centered analysis and instead turning it back on the viewer, showing us what the object says about *us* and our fears—in this case, the fear of finding ourselves alienated at the hands of proliferating industry, imperialism, and now globalization.

In global poetry, the loss of control is palpably rendered in poetic objects. In the classroom, I argue that we use Hellman's framework and look not just at the object being rendered, but also at the subjectivity it fashions. We must ask what kind of kind of trauma we and/or the speaker discovers when confronted with the demystification of the commodity, when the same object can be used for both mythmaking and guileless utility, and when the difference plays a role in human division. Yehuda Amichai's *Jerusalem* is a stunning place to start. In this poem the speaker describes a view of the Old City from a roof. He sees "laundry hanging in the late afternoon sunlight: / the white sheet of a woman who is my enemy, / the towel of a man who is my enemy, / ... In the sky of the Old City / a kite. / At the other end of the string, / a child / I can't see / because of the wall. / We have put up many flags, / they have put up many flags. / To make us think that they're happy. / To make them think that we're happy" (ll. 2–16). Amichai's poem demonstrates Meeta Chatterjee's point in her work on "khadi," in which she argues that cloth is a powerful economic, literary, political, and social marker (105). Amichai exhibits breathtaking scope through the use of cloth. The humanizing images of a woman hanging a sheet, a man using a towel to wipe his sweat, and the bodiless child holding a kite and a string, flare out to the national flags, which represent the highest register of the symbolic for the speaker. The final couplet (ll. 15–16) then exposes the symbolic as a construction. The speaker's exposé leads the reader back down the ladder of the symbolic to the white sheet again, which is a subtler symbol of poverty and labor, revealing a cavernous system of suffering and conflict that announces no immediate resolution. At this point, students may have experienced the Marxist trauma of knowing.

In his chapter "Wo es war: Marxism, the Unconscious, and Subjectivity," from his larger work *Psychopedagogy*, Daniel K. Cho questions whether students resist learning potentially traumatic knowledge, such as that of social, political, economic oppression and state-sanctioned murder (71).

He reminds us how bringing Marxist theory to the classroom can be psychologically challenging for students. Marxism reveals how the system in which they reside and that which they have been taught is the best of all possible systems necessarily operates on exploitation. It teaches, he says, how "exploitation was not avoidable collateral for capitalism but part of its integral structure, its very underside, that is, how the accumulation of capital is only possible if human misery also increases" (72). When we teach students to focus on the poetic artifact, examining all its symbolic registers, its role in constructing the subjectivity of the speaker, how it articulates his/her public and private self, and finally how it effaces or announces its role in global capitalism, we need to be sensitive to the possibility of trauma.

As Cho aptly states, "The overside of capitalism is obviously its various productivities: wealth, commodities, etc. These are easy enough to imagine (and desire) and therefore present no problem to any student studying capitalism…The underside however is not so inviting. It is of course the necessity of human misery" (74). He goes on to point out the omnipresence of the capitalistic economy: "While empirical individuals may not care about the economy or politics, the economy and politics care about empirical individuals" (84). Cho's position is actually central to material culture understanding; material cultural theorists maintain that, because of their intimate relationship to the body as well as to the economy and the political symbolic, objects articulate public meanings whether we care to listen or not. Economy and politics imposes itself on the text, notwithstanding the author's intent. The poetical objects in the poet's world must be understood as deliberately and accidentally political—players in an economy of subject-making, sociability, and trauma.

The Affective Turn and Material Cultural Understanding

The growing pedagogical interest in trauma correlates to a larger theoretical shift in understanding global causes and effects, where, according to Patricia Ticineto Clough, twenty-first-century thought has turned to articulate "a new configuration of bodies, technology, and matter" (2), in which a "psychoanalytically informed criticism of subject identity, representation, and trauma [moves] to an engagement with information and affect"; we have moved, she says,

> from privileging the organic body to exploring nonorganic life; from the presumption of equilibrium-seeking closed systems to engaging the complexity of open systems under far-from-equilibrium conditions of metastability; from focusing on an economy of production and consumption to

focusing on the economic circulation of pre-individual bodily capacities or affects in the domain of biopolitical control. (2)

Clough asserts that one of the results of this turn is that inquiry has become geopolitical rather than comparative (2). What this new global affective approach implies for contemporary world literature is that we can no longer read world texts within the confines of their culture and call it a day before we move on to the next geographical "boundary." We must understand global experience as an organic whole with plural experiences, where the central power (from which American students obtain their privilege) can no longer claim absence in areas "remote," where geographical phenomena are like impulse transmission—at once painfully local and only partially locally accountable. Fostering a greater sense of responsibility in our student readers who benefit from centralized power is increasingly necessary if we are to properly engage with global texts.

The affective turn also implies a material culture line of thought. There has been a shift from the relatively simple Marxist critique of commodity exchange to the more complex systems where objects and subjectivities are caught in a web of neocolonial values; in other words, where new forms of colonization—that is, corporate and cosmopolitan—at once connect us to global subjects through financial hegemony and alienate us via the stratifications of privilege. Objects must be read affective-globally rather than affective-locally. Students may feel responsible for their feelings on top of the feelings of the text. They may no longer feel they can read the materials circulating in their world without an accompanying guilt. The feeling of responsibility toward one's things and the clothes one wears is a necessary casualty of sociopolitical awareness, which happens as a result of the examination of the material culture of the global text. Again, poetry's obvious affective relationship to artifacts makes it a particularly strong vehicle for empathy.

Let us consider Pakistani poet Kishwar Naheed's fabric motifs, which, when taken as a whole, begin to look like "mesmerized immersion" resulting from the trauma of a Marxist exposé of the textile industry (Clough, quoting Leys, 6). The poem *We sinful women*, translated by Rukhsana Ahmad, is an example of Naheed's dominant conceit, where a female speaker negotiates power through fabric and etiquette by positioning herself in their symbolic economies—economies of both oppression and mobilization. "It is we sinful women," she writes, "who are not awed by the grandeur of those who wear gowns / who don't sell our lives / who don't bow our heads / who don't fold our hands together / . . . while those who sell the harvests of our bodies / . . . become distinguished / become the just princes of the material world. / . . . who come out raising the banner of truth" (ll. 1–13). The speaker resists the fantasy of western wealth, implied by "the grandeur of those who wear / gowns," and instead picks up the banner (evoking fabric or paper) for a different cause: that of "truth."

Fabric, paper, speech, and writing are nearly interchangeable instruments of power in Naheed's oeuvre. In order to understand what the "truth" of her poetry feels and looks like, students must do a material culture reading of the objects of the poem and this inquiry should culminate in an affective reading.

In order to understand the metonymy of the "gown" and how it affects the speaker, students need to go beyond the economy of production; we know based on our Marxist reading that the gown speaks to the exploitation of women and children tilling cotton fields and wielding the needle in a heinous unequal distribution of labor and compensation. We should go further to encourage students to inquire how their bodies operate in a larger system of etiquette that may be beyond their control, and how Naheed may be commenting on this. Naheed's demystification of "gowns" is a point of departure to talk about what that mystification is, how it operates, and how we are implicated in that system. Gargi Bhattacharyya criticizes the "fiction of white subjectivity as self-authorship [where] fashion is one technique of this self-authorship, and, on occasion, is the technique most available to women" (417). In other words, the "gown" is actually a coerced symbol of autonomy and status, and when worn, postures as self-authorship but shapes the Western female body according to preordained norms. Affective teaching helps our students understand this paradox. Affective approaches to global poetry asks more than "How does this make the speaker feel?" Like material culture, it attempts to see objects within their deeply rooted, systemic, biopolitical registers; meaning, it attempts to see them as they literally shape and wield the body and cause the body to act, in excess of the body's intent.

Naheed is a nice case study for material cultural theorists, as her conceptual critique, which hinges strongly on representational textile artifacts and the role of textiles in disempowering or empowering women, actually materializes in her work with Hawwa, a non-profit handicraft and textiles co-op owned and operated by women learning to become financially independent of their husbands. Naheed, Chin, and Amichai give students an opportunity to "physically get into language" (Lasky, 167). Of particular interest to material cultural critics is the idea of text as both an object itself and a vehicle for an author's firsthand experience with objects. Poet and pedagogue Dorothea Lasky writes, "Objects are the literal manifestation of the constant reconfiguration of elements in the mind, which happens in the creation of poetry" (166). Lasky's method for teaching students to write poetry is a useful framework for teaching students to read poetry.

In her classroom, students create "cabinets of curiosities" for their poetic repertoires. They choose a word that announces itself as a thing, they find a set of five objects that connect aesthetically to that word, spend time with each object touching it, write down the "feeling-memory" the object conjures, and seal their experience in a poem (167–168). To Lasky, all poets are materialists interested in the very tangible nature of words. I would like to suggest that in the contemporary world literature classroom, we make like the materialist poet and physically *do* our poetry. When we drive our cars, put on our shoes, button our shirts, put in our earphones, pick up our clementines in crates, we are *doing* global economy. In an American college classroom, we are mostly *doing* privilege. Poetry can help us reconnect intellectual thought to bodily response by focusing on the artifact's role in consumption and play.

Conclusion

In this chapter, I have advocated for the teaching of material culture in a contemporary world literature classroom, and have shown how poetry is a generative medium in this pursuit. Taking inspiration from material culture theorist Henry H. Glassie, who inverts the Saussurean convention that we register words before images in our minds, I ascribe to his contention that "only some of the thinking of some people gains presence in the record when linguists reduce social interactions to speech or historians find evidence only in stripes of inscription" (44). Less directly, I have also taken inspiration from Margaret J. M. Ezell and Katherine O'Brien O'Keeffe, who, in their work on *Cultural Artifacts and the Production of Meaning*, assert that "where language and the body of the text meet, the visual is political" (9). Ezell and O'Keeffe refer to the physical transmission of the text, using the example of Emily Dickinson's heavily edited and time-altered scraps; however, I would extend this to say that for comparative texts, media images representing exotic spaces, too, become the physical transmission of the global text. Often in tandem with dustcovers depicting foreign artifacts and forms, transmission also comes to the students wrapped in exotic visual rhetoric like the bright colors and dusty backdrops of CNN, Fox News; or, more ideally, through the somewhat contrived stimuli of cultural diversity events. Due to the constant threat of misrepresentation, it is important to have our students physically get into global poetry, probing its engagement with artifacts using multiple frameworks of seeing. In this chapter I have specifically examined three: Marxist, psychoanalytic, and affective theories. Ultimately, material culture draws from all three (and more) to understand "texts."

Hopefully I have achieved pedagogical transparency when I have asserted my expectations of the global text: the uncomfortable conceptual encounter generated by our reading of foreign texts is in vain unless it has the potential to transfer to the material realm. Concrete political understanding and economic transformation is and must be in partnership with emotional transformation. I have necessarily burdened global poetry with this prospect. The Marxist influence in material culture studies causes us to see how contemporary global poetry can reconnect the disengagement of objects from labor by recontextualizing it in unfamiliar margins. Marilyn Chin demonstrates how reprocessing American commodities in the context of poetry does violence to the system of mystification by drawing attention to their role in her speaker's alienation. Chin's *unheimlich* experience with American commodities is not unlike our defamiliarizing experience with foreign objects and texts. An excerpt from Homi Bhabha is relevant here:

> If the ambivalent figure of the nation is a problem of its transitional history, its conceptual indeterminacy, its wavering between vocabularies, then what effect does this have on narratives and discourses that signify a sense of "nationness": the *heimlich* pleasures of the hearth, the *unheimlich* terror of the space or race of the Other; the comfort of social belonging, the hidden injuries of class; the customs of taste; the powers of political affiliation; the sense of social order, the sensibility of sexuality; the blindness of bureaucracy, the strait insight of institutions; the quality of justice, the common sense of injustice; the *langue* of the law and the *parole* of the people. (307)

The feeling of being "not at home" in a space with objects that alienate us, in their language and their *thing*ness, is a necessary mode; it is at the service of generative difference. It is when we ignore, confuse, or repress difference that we deny the opportunity for empathy. We have to reposition the concepts of near and far and retrieve the local while not effacing its global vibrations. A concrete point of departure is the tangible object we invest with national and private meaning.

The psychoanalytic connection to material culture helps us to see how we invest the object (real and representational) with powers of control. Objects express their madness (artificiality) at the same time as they efface their conditions; we invest them with these qualities as an exercise in control, keeping the Marxist trauma and the trauma of globalization (per Bauman) at bay. For example, Yehuda Amichai uses fabric to expose the national symbolic as a construction, demystifying its powers of psychological control, revealing a cavernous system of suffering and conflict that announces no immediate resolution.

In this chapter, the discussion of trauma leads into affective theory and what material culture has to say to and about affective teaching. The Affective Turn is interested in bodily response as pre-individual process. The metonymy of the "gown" in Kishwar Naheed expresses affects beyond Marxist trauma, beyond the economy of production; we know based on our Marxist reading that the gown speaks to the exploitation of women's and children's labor. Affective readings go further to express how our bodies operate in a larger system of etiquette dictated subconsciously by biopolitical control. Nuanced exercises in reading and writing poetry, which hinge on a materialist-affective approach using physical drills, reconnects intellectual thought to the way we write, yield, and perform objects.

Filling the gap between the object in its material state and the literary representation of the object is the very material transformative possibility of the text—the possibility that a text can inspire more considerate relations between bodies. The text is derived from an inspired visual and tactile encounter with an object, and it cycles back through a mediated reencounter via the body of the reader. I question whether we should perceive a gap at all, and I encourage a more fluid understanding of the text's proximity to the body.

Works Cited

Amichai, Yehuda. "Jerusalem." *The Norton Anthology of World Literature*. Second ed, vol F., Gen ed., Sarah Lawall. New York: Norton, 2002. 2797. Print.

Bauman, Zygmunt. *Globalization: The Human Consequences*. New York: Columbia University Press, 1998. Print.

Berger, Arthur Asa. *Reading Matter: Multidisciplinary Perspectives on Material Culture*. New Brunswick and London: Transaction Publishers, 1992. Print.

Bhabha, Homi. "Narrating the Nation." *Nationalism*. Eds. John Hutchinson and Anthony D. Smith. New York and Oxford: Oxford University Press, 1994. 306–312. Print.

Bhattacharyya, Gargi. "Fashion." *A Companion to Racial and Ethnic Studies*. Eds. David Theo Goldberg and John Solomos. Blackwell, MA: Blackwell, 2002. 416–422. Print.

Chatterjee, Meeta. "Khadi: The Fabric of the Nation in Raja Rao's Kanthapura." *New Literatures Review* 36 (2000): 105–113. Print.

Chin, Marilyn. "Identity Poem (#99)." *Rhapsody in Plain Yellow*. London: Norton and Co., 2002. 83–84. Print.

Cho, K. Daniel. "Wo es war: Marxism, the Unconscious, and Subjectivity." *Psychopedagogy: Freud, Lacan, and the psychoanalytic theory of education*. New York: Palgrave Macmillan, 2009. 71–94. Print.

Clough, Patricia Ticineto. "Introduction." *The Affective Turn: Theorizing the Social*. Eds. Patricia Ticeneto Clough and Jean Halley. Durham, NC: Duke University Press, 2007. Print.

Ezell, Margaret J. M. and Katherine O'Brien O'Keeffe. *Cultural Artifacts and the Production of Meaning*. Ann Arbor: The University of Michigan Press, 1994. Print.

Glassie, Henry H. *Material Culture*. Bloomington and Indianapolis: Indiana University Press, 1999. Print.

Hellman, Mimi. "The Nature of Artifice: French Porcelain Flowers and the Rhetoric of the Garnish." *The Cultural Aesthetics of Eighteenth-Century Porcelain*. Eds. Alden Cavanaugh and Michael E. Yonan. Farnham: Ashgate, 2010. 39. Print.

Hutchinson, John and Anthony D. Smith. *Nationalism*. Oxford and New York: Oxford University Press, 1994. Print.

Iser, Wolfgang. *The Act of Reading*. Baltimore: Johns Hopkins UP, 1978. Print.

Lasky, Dorothea. "A Word is A Thing: Teaching Poetry Through Object-Based Learning and Felt Experience." *Poets on Teaching, a Sourcebook*. Ed. Joshua Marie Wilkinson. Iowa City: University of Iowa Press, 2010. 166–169. Print.

Mitra, Indrani, and Madhu Mitra. "The Discourse of Liberal Feminism and Third World Women's Texts: Some Issues of Pedagogy." *College Literature* 18.3 (1991): 55–63. *MLA International Bibliography*. EBSCO. Web. 28 Sept. 2011.

Naheed, Kishwar. "We Sinful Women." *The Distance of a Shout*. Ed. Asif Farrukhi. Trans. Rukhsana Ahmad. New York: Oxford, 2004. 74–77. Print.

Spivak, Gayatri Chakravorty. "'Can the Subaltern Speak?' Revised Edition, from the 'History' Chapter of Critique of Postcolonial Reason." *Can the Subaltern Speak?: Reflections on the History of an Idea*. New York: Columbia University Press, 2010. 21–78. *MLA International Bibliography*, EBSCO*host*. Web. 7 Aug. 2012.

Part II

Praxis

11

A Gun and a Book: Teaching Naguib Mahfouz's *The Thief and the Dogs* in a Time of Revolution and Occupation

Jessica Chiccehitto Hindman

In April of 2011, two months after Egyptians celebrated the end of Hosni Mubarak's regime and five months before the first Occupy Wall Street protesters set up their tents in lower Manhattan, I stood in front of a lecture room in a Dallas suburb and attempted to convince two dozen undergraduates that Naguib Mahfouz's *The Thief and the Dogs* is a novel that transcends its place and time—Cairo in the years following the 1952 revolution. To anyone familiar with Mahfouz's work, the dangers of a postrevolution society in late 1950s Egypt—corruption, complacency, and return to the prerevolution status quo—have obvious similarities to the challenges faced by a post-Mubarak Egypt in 2011. As I reread *The Thief and the Dogs* in preparation for my lecture, the jubilant images of triumphant Egyptians in Tahrir Square were still fresh, and I felt confident my students would be eager to make connection between Mahfouz's protagonist thief Said Mahran, and the college-age bloggers who helped organize the 2011 demonstrations. How lucky was I to be teaching a novel with so much potential to give depth and context to a recent world-changing event!

Five minutes into class time, a brief survey revealed that only 5 of my 22 students had heard about the recent revolution in Egypt. Like young college students in Egypt—who relied on Facebook and Twitter for vital information about when and where to protest—the majority of my students get their news from social networking sites. The 2011 Egyptian Revolution had simply failed to show up in their Facebook News Feeds. (A few weeks later, when Osama bin Laden was killed, every one of my 22 students reported first learning of the news on Facebook). And why should it have? What did the 2011 Egyptian Revolution have to do have to do with them—college students in Texas?

Granted, if every teacher of World Literature succumbed to the student complaint "What does this have to do with me?" we would teach nothing but Facebook News Feeds. Further, young Egyptians utilized social media for organization in the face of overwhelming government censorship, while my students use it for party invites, photo-sharing, and yes, the occasional link to a news article. But what I came to realize during the two class sessions (approximately 200 minutes) that I allotted to Mahfouz in this survey course was that the novel itself demanded a different approach than the one I had prepared. My initial class plans called for a 20–30 minute lecture on the historical context (a crash course in Egyptian history from the pyramids to Nasser), followed by close reading of passages which I hoped would demonstrate Mahfouz's work as an allegory for the return to corruption, complacency, and anger in Egypt after the 1952 revolution. At the end of our discussion of the text, I planned to argue that the fictional Said Mahran's feelings of anger and betrayal could parallel the feelings of post-Mubarak Egyptians if the interim military government failed to put the ideals of the revolution into practice.

But after I realized that most of my students had no idea that the 2011 revolution had just happened, something about my pedagogical approach seemed wrong. I was never going to succeed in cramming in all of the history, culture, religion, and political context of Egypt that my students would need in order to approach Mahfouz's novel as a window into Egypt per se. In this sense, my quandary was universal to the experience of teaching a World Literature Survey course at a public university wherein many undergraduates have never traveled out of the state, let alone the country. A survey course in which I was expected to cover everything from seventeenth-century Chinese epics to nineteenth-century French poetry to twentieth-century essays by Native Americans. In short, there was something about my students' ignorance of the 2011 Egyptian Revolution which made me feel the full weight of the semester's teaching challenge: How can anyone teach 400 years of World Literature in 15 weeks? What is the point?

Which is not to say that I didn't barrel right along with my initial plans, at a loss for how to reinvent an entirely new teaching strategy for Mahfouz's novel on the spot. During the first class period, I blazed through Egyptian history—condensing 4000 years into 25 minutes—beginning with what my students knew from their K-12 years (Ancient Egypt) and moving quickly to what they did not (everything else). Though I would now do things differently, it is important to note that even a paltry dose of historical context can be utilized by students during in-class textual analysis. Mahfouz's ingenious ability to work in multiple time frames—something that most students will miss during a first read—becomes evident with even the scantest sense of Egyptian history. Take, for example, the following passage, wherein Said Mahran remembers first meeting his wife, Nabawiyya:

> She was always so nicely dressed, much neater than the other servant girls, which was why she'd been known as the "Turkish lady's maid." The rich, proud old Turkish woman, who lived alone at the end of the road, in a house at the center of a big garden, insisted that everyone who worked for her should be good-looking, clean, and well dressed. So Nabawiyya always appeared with her hair neatly combed and plaited in a long pigtail, and wearing slippers. Her peasant's gown flowed around a sprightly and nimble body, and even those not bewitched by her agreed that she was a fine example of country beauty with her dark complexion, her round, full face, her brown eyes, her small chubby nose, and her lips moist with the juices of life. There was a small green tattoo mark on her chin like a beauty spot. (91)

One of the greatest pleasures of reading Mahfouz is to see how he personifies Egypt as a woman. In *The Thief and the Dogs*, every female character can be read as Egypt personified. Egypt is alternately the terrified child, the beautiful servant, the treacherous adulteress, the loving prostitute, the dying mother. In the backstory to the novel, Nabawiyya divorces Said Mahran and remarries his former business underling and friend, Illish Sidra, all while Said is stuck in prison. Said's rage at Nabawiyya and Illish's unfaithfulness is the impetus for all the events that occur in the novel. But in the scene excerpted above—the only description we get of Nabawiyya in the entire novel—Said has just met Nabawiyya, who is a young, beautiful servant. This much will be clear to students. Not as evident will be the reasons behind Mahfouz's choice to have Nabawiyya's employer be a "rich, proud, old Turkish woman." Why is her employer Turkish? Reminding students that Egypt was very much the servant of the Ottoman Empire will begin to illuminate the multiple time frames that Mahfouz is working in. Once students begin to see that Mahfouz's text can be read as an allegory not only for the 1952 revolution but ancient, Ottoman, and colonial times as well, the text will immediately become more complex. Why does Nabawiyya have a green tattoo on her chin? Well, where is Lower Egypt? (In the north). If we see Egypt as the ancient Egyptians did, what is on its "chin?" (The Nile Delta—a green mark on a round, brown face with juices—the Mediterranean—on its lips). "Country beauty" indeed.

For Mahfouz, the questions of Egyptian identity are so immediate that the decade before and after Nasser's revolution is naturally tied to Egypt's past, and throughout the novel there is a blending of ancient and modern (Said's last stand as a modern revolutionary takes place in an ancient graveyard). And the experience of everyday life in Egypt is itself a study in shocking contrasts between the very old and the very new. When I lived as a student in Cairo in 2001, I saw aristocrats in luxurious SUVs share the same roads as men on donkeys, barefoot guides in Giza use advanced cell phones (not yet widespread in the United States) to translate and calculate their fees, hungry-looking children selling Kleenex underneath the bright neon lights of advertisements for Digital Pocket Qurans (long before any sort of advertising for digital texts was common in the United States).

And yet, in providing these anecdotes and the scope of Egyptian history to my students, I began to wonder if I was doing more harm than good. After we finished the close reading of the Nabawiyya scene, in which I pointed to all the historical layers I could possibly think of, the first student question came out like this:

"So, do the women wear veils?"

And with that question, I realized that the othering of Egypt—the orientalized place of the ancient and the new—would do little to bring the novel's relevance to my students, many of whom had never met a Muslim, many of whom had never been out of Texas. Fearing that the conversation was about to move into the tired territory of headscarves (in just minutes I would be arguing that the socioreligious choice to wear a headscarf was tame in comparison to Western socioeconomic choices like breast implants) I tabled the question about veils ("We'll discuss it when we get to Nawal El Saadawi") and soon after, the class period was over. My students' assignment was to finish the novel before the next class. My assignment was to make Mahfouz's novel seem close to them, rather than far away—a novel less about Egypt and more, as Mahfouz intended, about the human condition in general, which in our case meant the condition of Texas college students in 2011.

I began our second and last class devoted to Mahfouz by directing my students' attention to the protagonist's rage, which causes him to embark on poorly planned burglary and assassination attempts. Said Mahran attempts to murder his enemies for revenge, but instead kills only innocent bystanders. Even with this lack of luck, and his eventual transformation into a celebrity criminal, Said learns that the Egyptian populace is on his side. I asked my students if they were also on Said's side despite the fact that he is a thief who murdered innocent people, and if so, why that might be.

My students, like the Egyptian population depicted in the book, were indeed sympathetic to Said, and to better understand our own sympathy for him we delved into all the ways in which Said attempted to do good before he was consumed with the rage that led him to murder. In the first scene of the novel, Said is failed by the courts (it is implied he will never win custody of his daughter, and, at any rate, these are the same courts that put him in prison for four years). Next, Said goes to see his father's holy man, Sheikh Ali al-Junaydi. The scenes with the Sheikh—whose cryptic advice exasperates Said—are emblematic of a religion that offers vague answers but no practical benefit to a man with pressing worldly concerns. In other words, Said is failed by religion, which has little to offer to him in terms of immediate assistance. After the Sheikh, Said visits Rauf Ilwan—a former revolutionary turned aristocrat—who incites Said's rage the most. Rauf's crime, in Said's view, is hypocrisy. Rauf gave Said books (an education) and encouraged him to take part in the revolution by stealing from the rich, which leads to Said's imprisonment. In one of the novel's flashbacks, Said remembers Rauf's words:

> "What does a man need in this country Said?" and without waiting for an answer he said, "He needs a gun and a book: the gun will take care of the past, the book is for the future." (59)

But when Said goes to see Rauf after his release from prison, what Said really needs is a job, which Rauf refuses to provide. And so, by the end of the novel (the book!), neither Said's education nor his gun is enough to save him. Said is a man who, despite his learning and intelligence, has no future—a metaphor for Egypt where the local joke (funny only for its accuracy) goes that all the taxi drivers are doctors and lawyers.

After we discussed the ways in which society had failed Said Mahran—law, religion, education—none are enough to save him, I asked my students if they ever felt like society had failed them. After a few moments, when no one answered, I became more specific:

> "For example," I asked, "How would you feel if, after all the work you've done in this course, after all the work you've done in your other courses, you finally graduate only to find out that a college education is no longer enough to get a job in America?"

This worked. I immediately experienced one of those moments that every teacher dreams of, the moment when students who have been silent all semester nearly jump out of their seats with eagerness to join the discussion:

> "I'd be pissed off!" yelled one male student from his seat in the back row.

What ensued was a discussion that, to an outsider, might seem to have very little to do with *The Thief and the Dogs*, Mahfouz, Egypt, or Arab Literature, but was, in fact, a way of getting to the novel's core argument. But before we could get to that, we had to discuss a few things that made us "pissed off":

"I have $50,000 in student loans."

"I don't know if I should be an English major—I'm worried it's not practical."

"None of us are going to get jobs so you should just major in what you like."

"Sometimes I feel like everything promised to us—like if you get good grades and go to college you'll get a good job and have a nice house and a car—that it's a lie."

"Everyone I know who has already graduated lives with their parents."

This conversation went on for 20 minutes or so. The more we talked about the possibility of a college education not being enough to secure a middle-class American life, the more obvious it became that my students had a lot of anger about the systemic failures of American society in 2011. Government, religious organizations, higher education—none were offering suitable protection against unemployment and poverty. Obviously, we had no idea that in just a few months, students on our campus would set up tents in protest of growing inequality and student debt. We had no idea that the protests on other campuses would grow large and menacing enough for universities to call in armies of riot police. We had no idea that Occupy Wall Street protesters would use the images of the 2011 Egyptian Revolution as inspirational slogans and internet memes or that the interim military government in Egypt would justify violence against civilians by citing Mayor Bloomberg's violent crackdowns against protesters in New York City (Read). All of this was months away. What I—we—*did* know was that *The Thief and the Dogs* provided us with a way to be angry, to see the ways in which multiple societal systems can fail and sabotage an individual, until the individual begins to act in irrational, despicably violent ways. Mahfouz's novel provides a safe way of discussing violent revolution precisely because it shows how violence always harms the innocent (even if the bullet is meant for the guilty).

The anger in my classroom grew until someone made a tired joke about having always wanted to develop his waitering skills anyway. Everyone laughed nervously and the anger dissipated somewhat. With a few minutes left, it seemed like a good time to return to the end of the book, where Said's anger also disappears. He has been fatally shot, and the last words of the book are his last thoughts before he dies:

The darkness was thicker now and he could see nothing at all, not even the outlines of the tombs, as if nothing wished to be seen. He was slipping away into endless depths, not knowing either position, place, or purpose. As hard as he could, he tried to gain control of something, no matter what. To exert one last act of resistance. To capture one last recalcitrant memory. But finally, because he had to succumb, and not caring, he surrendered. Not caring at all now.

Only a literature class affords the space to look at the repetition, placement, and verb tense of the word "caring." Marwan only surrenders when he stops caring—and caring is a persistent state of being—present participle (in both English and Arabic). The last sentence's lack of subject, emphasized with the word "now" suggests that the danger for Egypt post-1952 revolution is complacency. Not caring at all now. Complacency is arguably the greatest obstacle to revolution, as it causes people who are deeply dissatisfied with their condition to believe that nothing can be changed. Asmaa Mahfouz (no relation to Naguib), the young activist whose Facebook video sparked the massive protests on January 25, spoke about this complacency in her now-famous video:

> Whoever says it is not worth it because there will only be a handful of people, I want to tell him, "You are the reason behind this, and you are a traitor, just like the president or any security cop who beats us in the streets."

After her success in Egypt, Asmaa Mahfouz went on to join the Occupy Wall Street protesters in New York, where she told Democracy Now, "Many U.S. residents were in solidarity with us. I am here to be in solidarity and support the Wall Street Occupy protesters...they will succeed in the end."

My students' ignorance prevented their solidarity with the Egyptian protestors during the 2011 revolution, and they still may not care much about Egyptians or the revolution, although now, at least, they know it happened. When I first introduced them to *The Thief and the Dogs*, I tried to use the book as a way of developing empathy in my students for the plight of their college-age counterparts in Egypt. Maybe this happened, at least for some of my students. But what I came to realize is that Mahfouz's novel demands far more than the easy, action-less sympathy of Westerners sitting comfortably in a classroom. It demands that we care about the injustices that take place right under our noses, here and now, in our own Facebook News Feeds, on our own campuses. Caring now.

Works Cited

"An American Tahrir." Photograph. *Visualize Conversation: An Image Blog*, 16 Nov 2011. Web. 29 Nov. 2011.

Mahfouz, Asmaa. "Meet Asmaa Mahfouz and the Vlog that Helped Spark the Revolution." Translated by Iyad El-Baghdadi. Subtitles by Ammara Alavi. *Youtube*, 1 Feb. 2011. Web. 29 Nov. 2011

Mahfouz, Naguib. *The Thief and the Dogs*. 1961. Trans. Trevor Le Gassick and M. M. Badawi. Cairo: American University in Cairo Press, 1984. Print.

Read, Max. "How Egypt Justifies Its Brutal Crackdown: Occupy Wall Street." *Gawker*, 20 Nov. 2011. Web. 29 Nov. 2011

"Stand Like an Egyptian." Poster. *Visualize Conversation: An Image Blog*, 27 Nov 2011. Web. 29 Nov. 2011.

12

Magical Realism: A Gateway out of America and into the World

Tessa Mellas

A salesman turns into an insect and is shunned. The corpse of an inordinately handsome large man washes into a village. A girl grows wings and takes to the circus trapeze. Though these plots are canonical and beloved across the world, Franz Kafka, Gabriel García Márquez, and Angela Carter are new to most undergraduate students. But those stories' strangeness is what piques students' minds. Because magical realism features the fantastical and unreal, students embrace that which is foreign because they see it as a vehicle of the imagination. Once hooked, they enter a genre spread over the world, a feature that makes it an ideal unifying theme for a global literature course. And because magical realism creates meaning differently for each culture, it enables students to understand how the means of creating and processing narrative reveal differences in ideology that lead to oppression and inequality. This teaching note will explain how to structure such a course so that students can build the analytical skills needed to dissect the assumptions, beliefs, and values of various cultures, a journey that will reveal the rich and diverse ways in which magical realism is used across the globe.

When introducing undergraduates to magical realism, I start in their own backyards with contemporary American magical realism. Students can readily identify the conflicts in texts that use the grand narratives of their own culture and will be able to focus on learning to analyze those structures without the additional task of researching the culture first. Further, it is valuable for students to dissect their own culture's narratives for what they reveal about their ideologies, power structures, and means of making sense. Given that students are most familiar with a Western canon, it is important that they understand how European literary forms utilize a Western mentality centered on fundamentals such as capitalism, Christianity, science, and logic. Such analysis introduces them to the concept of constructedness, and they will come to see their own American reality as subjective, governed by the language Americans use, the stories they tell, and the ways those stories are perceived.

To get students to understand the constructed nature of reality, I ask them to define magical realism for themselves. The story "Miracle" by Judy Budnitz is ideal for this. After reading and discussing it, students are able to conclude that magical realism combines our reality with a bizarre circumstance that could not happen in real life. This observation is at the heart of how meaning is created in Western magical realism. As a literary device, magical realism positions that which is judged normal against that which is judged fantastical. By juxtaposing mundane and strange circumstances, magical realism questions what is considered real. Likewise, by treating something strange as normal, magical realism asks why a culture judges certain circumstances as strange. Readers will suspend disbelief—in the case of "Miracle" believing that a black baby is the biological child of white parents. In doing so, they will entertain a different way of viewing reality, one that illuminates problems with that culture's reality. Students can be taught to locate constructed aspects of American culture by asking questions about magical realist texts: *What is strange? Why do we see it as strange? Which of our social systems tells us this is strange? What does that say about our culture? Is there an alternative way of constructing our world?*

A second literary device central to Western magical realism is metaphor. George Lakoff and Mark Johnson's book *The Metaphors We Live By* is infinitely useful in introducing this concept. The book examines the prevalence of metaphor in speech, discusses how metaphor influences conceptual systems and defines everyday reality, and breaks down the ideologies that underlie metaphors. Lakoff and Johnson explore how metaphors such as *"Argument is war,"* and *"Time is money"* influence language and thinking. To illustrate the concept of metaphor further, I ask students to draw a metaphor stemming from this sentence: *I feel like _____.* Various expressions come to mind: *I feel like I was hit by a bus. I feel like a rat. I feel like a million bucks.* We dissect the assumptions upon which these metaphors are based and imagine narratives built around them. Next, we transfer this metaphorical perspective to literary analysis. Kevin Brockmeier's story "The Ceiling," in which the sky descends as a man's marriage falls apart, is apt. After the previous activity, students piece together that the protagonist feels like the sky is coming down on him because he has realized his wife's adultery. Such analysis illuminates metaphors used unconsciously in speech, their unstated ideologies, and the ways such ideologies influence thinking and behavior.

I discuss Western magical realism first because the genre functions quite differently in non-European cultures. Western magical realism and the way it makes meaning contrasts starkly with a different kind of magical realism, a kind that expresses magic as a natural element of a culture's reality rather than utilizing the fantastic as a literary device. In *Magic(al) Realism*, Maggie Ann Bowers explains how forms of magical realism have been differentiated in certain scholarship. Bowers identifies the form discussed above, the Western form, as epistemological and scholarly, taking "inspiration for its magical realist elements from sources which do not necessarily coincide with the cultural context of the fiction, or for that matter of the writer" (91). Bowers identifies the other form as ontological and folkloric. The latter often originates from colonized nations or marginalized cultures, and "has as its source material beliefs or practices from the cultural context in which the text is set" (Bowers, 91).

Louise Erdrich's novel *The Antelope Wife* can be excerpted as an example of the latter ontological form. When three women drift to the edge of a Native American powwow, disappear into the night, and turn into antelopes, it is not because Erdrich has some metaphorical meaning in mind. Rather, it is because the mythology of antelope women is engrained in her Ojibwa culture, a culture that doesn't see humans as separate from the natural world (as the Western world does) but instead possessed with qualities of sacred animals. For students to understand what is being expressed in ontological magical realism, they must research the cultural narratives that the text is utilizing, ask how the author has reimagined those narratives, and reflect on how that culture's realities derive from their unique historical context. Erdrich's work is also useful in showing students how epistemological and ontological forms of magical realism come together in the same text when a writer is influenced by multiple literary traditions that unite as a result of violent cultural clashes.

Once students have an understanding of the various ways that magical realist texts create meaning, the course can stretch out across the globe: to Latin America, (with Borges, García Márquez, Carpentier, Allende, Fuentes, and Cortázar), to Europe (with Kafka, Calvino, Grass, Gogol, Kundera, Carter, Rushdie, Winterson, and Ionesco), to writing whose magic stems from Africa (with Achebe, Morrison, Okri, Oyeyemi, and Brink) and from Asian (with Hong Kingston, Yoshimoto, and Ōe). In organizing the course, it makes sense to group authors geographically, and to discuss the political and social contexts of each region as prelude to its authors. These authors open discussions on a range of rich topics that can even segue into an introduction to critical theory. Here are some useful topics: ways of categorizing, ordering, establishing and defending boundaries; colonialism and postcolonial theory; power struggles, class structures, capitalism, socialism, communism, and Marxism; sexuality, gender, feminist theory, and queer theory; religions of the world, their influence on politics, religious oppression, and religious conflicts; Western versus Eastern philosophies, mysticism, romanticism, and surrealism versus science, reason, logic, and binary thinking; issues of authorship, intertextuality, genre, and oral versus print narratives. Such content makes for a challenging but intellectually rewarding course, one that will leave students and their entire thinking process changed.

Work Cited

Bowers, Maggie Ann. *Magic(al) Realism*. New York: Routledge, 2004. Print.

13

Making the Familiar Unfamiliar: Teaching Origin Myths, Material Conditions, and "the Bible as Literature"

Hillary Stringer

The first time I taught a world literature course, I encountered an expected but frustrating snag: students willingly analyzed foundational mythologies from around the ancient world—the *Popol Vuh*, Ovid's *Metamorphoses*, *Gilgamesh*, the Koran—but they resisted applying a similar critical reading to the Christian Bible. Teaching this class in northern Texas, I anticipated that I would have a few students who considered any questioning of the Bible blasphemy. What I did not anticipate was that even the students who claimed they did not regard the Bible as a holy text were still quite uncomfortable calling it "mythology"—a term they did not hesitate to use with mythological texts safely in the realm of "Other." And while not all students, even in Texas, may have this allegiance to the Bible (and some may feel the same discomfort deconstructing the other foundational texts listed above), origin "myths" are not confined to the sphere of religion. Instead, they often define state, nation, and ethnic background. Deconstructing and analyzing the formation of these "myths" highlights for students the way in which "nationality" or ethnicity—concepts that they often take to be inherent—are in fact constructed by and for a variety of reasons. As Homi Bhabha argues in his introduction to *Nation and Narration*, all cultures are hybrid and the idea of an originary moment that creates identity is in fact only a fiction used in order to make certain identity claims. Since World Literature One often introduces students to cultures at the very beginning of their written and recorded languages, it provides an opportunity to examine the material conditions that allow for the development of each language, literature, and "nation." Students can use this approach to find the "third space of enunciation"—both the "this" and the "that"—which is the first step in recognizing hybridity. Additionally, students can see how the foundational ideologies of their own cultures provide the lenses through which they view other cultures, ancient and modern.

As instructors, we must begin by making the familiar unfamiliar, moving in the opposite direction of twenty-first-century all-embracing and leveling multiculturalism.[1] Before they can approach or interrogate "originary moments," students must locate the hybridity inherent in their own cultural constructs and ideologies. They must understand the intended audience of these texts and what arguments their authors make. Finally, they must be aware of the material conditions that structure the creation and transmission of origin myths in early civilizations. In my teaching of World Literature survey courses at the University of North Texas, I use a combination of creative and critical writing activities to showcase the role of language in constructing identity, and vice versa. I will demonstrate my methodology through the use of an example taken from a World Lit One course on the ancients through the Early Renaissance (1620 CE). The materials used span broad swaths of time and space: *Gilgamesh*, ancient Egyptian poetry, and selections from the Hebrew Bible. I taught the following unit in three days, but the classes each spanned an hour and 50 minutes since this was a condensed summer course.

On the first day, I divide my students into groups and ask them to create a vocabulary for a new language. I allow use of letters or pictographs, but ask that they come up with a working alphabet. Then, they use this alphabet to write a sentence (or two) that reflects the most important "value" about their group's invented "culture." I give them examples of religion, finances, fashion, sports, and so on. I encourage them to take time to discuss and debate their value system. (I also tell them that if they disagree, that is okay, but that they must reach a compromise.) Finally, I have students reflect on this process, writing down whether or not they found the activity easy or difficult (and why) and why/how their group agreed (or not) on what to write about with their chosen sentences. I instruct students to write their sentences on the board, and we then discuss their responses as a class. This exercise reveals the interconnected nature of language, cultural values, and "material" conditions. Although I did not instruct students to create symbols that tied into each "culture's" value or belief system, many do so (soccer balls for a sports-loving culture, hamburgers and French fries for a junk food–loving culture). The activity of creating a linguistic community places students in the same position as the cultures that they are about to begin studying, charging them with the tasks of meaning-making and communication. At the same time, the process showcases the difficulty of creating a written language and highlights the fact that no one can ever write about "just reality"—material conditions or ideas formed by value systems underlie everything.

With this critical perspective in mind, students begin their course reading. For the second class, students read ancient Egyptian poetry and selections from *Gilgamesh*. I provide students with information and background on the composition and discovery of the *Gilgamesh* epic of Sumeria along with Akhenaten's poem "Hymn to the Sun" and a selection of Egyptian "Love Songs." I start with these texts so that students begin with the histories and mythologies of civilizations with which they might not be as familiar, providing a base of knowledge from which they can later compare and contrast these texts with the Hebrew Bible. I also begin by comparing these texts in order to model the comparative and analytical processes that I would like students to utilize.

In my lecture, I establish that scholars believe *Gilgamesh* to be a compilation of material from various sources, and that the epic poem was almost lost because it was not translated from cuneiform to other languages. I also provide a brief description of the gods and goddesses that figure in the epic. I then discuss the historical background of ancient Egyptian poetry, highlighting that the major difference between Egyptian texts and other ancient literatures that come from an oral tradition (such as the Bible or Greek epics) is that Egyptian writing is mostly from primary sources; if not the very first copy, something likely created during the author's lifetime. Students break into small groups to answer and respond to discussion questions, including a comparison of Egyptian poetry and *Gilgamesh* that examines the differences between monotheism and polytheism evident in these texts, the role of the "lover" and the "beloved," and the usage of fame and immortality. With these questions, I foreground the topics we will touch upon again when comparing these texts with selections from the Hebrew Bible.

My emphasis on the material conditions of the origins of the *Gilgamesh* and ancient Egyptian poetry is purposeful; I wish to show students the role that culture, linguistics, and geography play in determining when and how some ancient texts become canonical and what happens to the texts that are buried (literally in this case) under the sands of time. When teaching the unit on Egypt, I show students pictures of hieroglyphics that translate to one of the love songs in the Norton and the papyrus that was common. I also ask students to consider the differences between a culture whose legacy comes to us in poetry and one whose prose survives, the role of the translator, and the "situated-ness" of their initial reactions to these ancient texts and cultures. Students read the following selections from the Norton Anthology for homework: an introduction to The Bible (The Old Testament), and parts of Genesis, Job, the Psalms, the Song of Songs, and Jonah.

On the third day of class, I begin by summarizing the flood narrative of *Gilgamesh* and other themes that allow me to highlight the similarity between the epic and Genesis. Students are already familiar with the biblical tales—omnipresent in American popular culture as well as in religious teachings—and it is easy to use Genesis to showcase the way that ancient texts drew from a core group of ancient oral myths that spread from the earliest civilizations in Mesopotamia to the nomadic Hebrew tribes and the grand kingdoms of Egypt. Below is the trajectory I trace:

1. In *Gilgamesh*, Utnapishtim survived the great flood and was given immortality. Enlil, the warrior and consoler God, is given the task to destroy the world because the people are making too much noise (35). Ea, God of the waters and the bolt that bars the sea, warns Utnapishtim and so he builds a boat. Unlike the Hebrew God, Enlil is punished for bringing the flood's destruction on the people "without thinking"(37). Moral responsibility is applied even to the gods, who agree to temper their powers after this disaster and to make Utnapishtim their equal in immortality.
2. This way of conceptualizing divinity paves the way for the sun pharaoh Akhenaten in Egypt, whose monotheistic relationship with Aten the sun god eventually placed him in the position of both prophet and living incarnation of Aten.
3. Then, the Hebrew God comes onto the scene. In the first section of Genesis, there are echoes of an older polytheistic tradition: "Let us make man in our image, after our likeness," (57) and "Go to, let us go down, and there confound their language, that they may not understand one another's speech"(63). Like the Sumerian God Anu, this God has the ability to create the world through the power of speech.
4. As the biblical characters start to make their many famous mistakes (eating apples, listening to snakes, killing brothers, etc.) they often engage in long and personal conversations with the Hebrew God, who corrects their behavior.
5. What is revealed in these dialogues is an emphasis on morality and motives, instead of outward actions: God does not accept Cain's sacrifice because he can tell it has been made meanly; God sends the flood to punish wickedness: the Hebrew God "saw that the wickedness of man was great in the earth, and that every imagination of

the thought of his heart was only evil continually. And it repented the Lord that he had made man on the earth, and it grieved him at his heart" (60).

The goal of drawing these parallels is to allow students to see that, like the texts of ancient Egypt and Sumeria, the Hebrew Bible is part of a continuum of meaning-making that connects "gods" with mortals. Rather than singling out one text as "true" and others as "mythologies," these comparisons seek to place the familiar biblical stories into the—for students—unfamiliar contexts of the ancient world that composed these myths. I then provide a historical background of the assemblage of the Hebrew Bible and show students an image of a parchment scroll. This emphasis on materials highlights how part of the concept of creating the Hebrew God had to do with the diasporic nature of the Jewish people and the collection and transcription of materials that occurred during the Babylonian captivity.

I finish this unit by dividing students into groups and asking them to engage in their own critical and creative enterprise. I begin by reading a passage from *The Flood*, a creative retelling of the biblical flood story by David Maine. Then, I ask students to compose a revisionist version of one of the following sections, which they will share with the class: Genesis 4 (the story of Cain and Abel and the First Murder), Genesis 22 (the story of Abraham and Isaac), Genesis 25–27 (the story of Jacob and Esu), or Jonah. Finally, I ask them to reflect on their process of composition, keeping in mind that the Bible was rewritten many, many times over the centuries. I ask them to explain what changed and what remained the same in their retellings, and how they think this process might be similar or different from what the King James translators did (keeping in mind that Norton continues to use the King James version because it has been most influential on the canon of Western literature, even though there are more accurate translations from Hebrew available).

This creative activity accomplishes several objectives. Much like the "create-your-own-language" exercise, it allows students to again occupy the same position as those who "composed" or recorded the origin myths of the Bible. It also draws attention to the fact that each time the stories in the Bible were (re)recorded, the writer or translator added (or subtracted) according to the context or culture that defined their view of what was important in the story. Each "character" that emerged from this activity now spoke in early twenty-first-century English, and the switch from King James-era English to the modern variety sometimes changed the meaning or subtext of the story entirely (Abraham's attitude underwent a remarkable shift at the hands of my students; he was now pretty "pissed off" about what God had done to him). Additionally, allowing students to have hands-on manipulation of the text foregrounds the situatedness of the composing process, and the inherent hybridity or heteroglossia that underlies all composed or "finished" works of literature. By rewriting the Bible, students can see the literary elements (tone, pacing, structure, etc.) at work as they (re)create them.

Finally, I revisit this unit by allowing students to choose from a selection of short paper topics. My requirements for short essays are that they be longer than one but not more than two pages in length (500–1000 words). For each essay, students should formulate a central interpretive idea about the text through one of the following methods: analysis of literary elements (theme, symbolism, characterization, satire, etc.), "situating" the work within the historical context of the unit introduction and other works in the unit, drawing attention to a bias or contradiction within the text, or discussing the broader implications of the text. The topics listed below can be reformatted in various ways, but the goal is to ask students to formulate arguments that interrogate the texts discussed in class. (Note: Following this unit, students read the Norton Anthology's "Ancient Greece and the Formation of the Western Mind," Sappho of Lesbos's *Lyrics*, Plato's *Apology of Socrates*, and Aristotle's *Poetics*. These texts are included in their short paper topic choices.)

1. All of the texts that we have examined thus far address the idea of fate—or of being "chosen" to act in a certain way by a God or higher power. Choosing two or three of the flowing texts, discuss the similarities and differences between Gilgamesh, Akhenaten, one or more of the biblical characters (Noah, Jacob, Joseph, and Jonah), and Socrates's relationships to God(s), destiny, and free will.
2. Examine the role of love in an Egyptian Love Poem, a selection from Song of Songs, and Sappho's "Like the very gods in my sight is he" or "Some there are who say that the fairest thing seen."
3. Discuss the dream sequences in Joseph and *Gilgamesh*. Are their purposes similar or different in the plot of the stories? What thematic function do they serve?

After students become (mostly) comfortable with deconstructing the Bible as a work of literature, beginning a unit on an "unfamiliar" culture can seem less daunting. They are now equipped with the tools to examine why and how a text or story is told. Sometimes the parallels are strong. For example, I use the method of drawing attention to how language itself and materials affect the content of texts when I discuss ancient Chinese poetry written on oracle bones, where characters sometimes look like pictorial renderings of the words and concepts that they represent. Another example, of course, is the role of the printing press in bringing about the Reformation in Medieval Europe. There are countless other instances where material conditions—from writing materials to canvases—determine how and why certain "origin" stories become "familiar" to Western students, while others remain foreign or obscure. Reversing this process, simultaneously making the familiar "unfamiliar" and the unfamiliar "familiar," showcases the constructed nature of all texts, which points in turn to the narrative underpinnings of culture.

Note

1. My pedagogical approach draws from Barry Kanpol's *Critical Pedagogy, An Introduction*, (Westport, CT: Bergin and Garvey, 1999), where he argues that teachers and students must acknowledge that Western, upper-class Anglo-Saxon culture is posited as dominant over other cultures and worldviews. Both instructors and students must strive to locate points of empathy with contextualized cultures and literatures from groups traditionally subjected to stereotype. Reflection on the creation of such stereotypes and the location of commonalities of experience between the "self" and the "Other" will ideally create an opening for understanding of experiences outside of one's own worldview and culture.

Works Cited

"Ancient Egyptian Poetry." Trans: John L. Foster. Norton Anthology of World Literature, vol. A, 2nd expanded edition, 2003. New York: Lawall and Mack, 41–52. Print

Bhabha, Homi. *Nation and Narration*. New York: Routledge, 1990. Print.

"Gilgamesh." Trans: N. K. Sandars. Norton Anthology of World Literature, vol. A, 2nd expanded edition, 2003. New York: Lawall and Mack 10–41. Print.

Kanpol, Barry. *Critical Pedagogy, An Introduction*. Westport: Bergin & Garvey, 1994. Print.

Lawall, Sarah and Maynard Mack, eds. *The Norton Anthology of World Literature, Beginnings to A. D. 100*. Volume A. 2nd ed. New York: W.W. Norton and Company, 2002. Print.

Maine, David. *The Flood*. Great Britain: Canongate Books,, 2004. Print.

"Papyrus Specimen." artlex.com. ArtLex, n. d. Web. 29 June 2010.

"Parchment Scroll." artlex.com. ArtLex, n. d. Web. 29 June 2010.

"The Bible: The Old Testament." The King James Version. Lawall and Mack 52–103. Print.

"The Love Songs of the Chester Beatty Papyrus I." Egyptology.com. n.p. n.d. Web. 29 June 2010.

14

Cycles of Opportunity: On the Value and Efficacy of Native American Literature in Teaching World Literature to Millennials

Marnie M. Sullivan

The Millennial College Student

There is a large volume of research from scholars and research institutes, administrators in higher education, and industry, about the cohort of students currently attending college. Altogether, this research paints a surprisingly coherent portrait of the generation known as the millennials. Like generation Xers before them, millennials are savvy with technology, productive collaborators, and exhibit a highly evolved, if intuitive, media literacy. Like the baby boom generation before gen-X, millennials are a large generation that is confident, team-oriented, and involved in their communities. They come to college more respectful of norms and institutions than previous generations and may be less prone to activism or the appeal of radical movements. According to a recent Pew Foundation report, millennials were among Barack Obama's strongest supporters in 2008, backing him for president by more than a two-to-one ratio—that's more than the older generations by about 15 percent (Taylor and Keeter, 3).

Millennials have enjoyed the benefits of inclusive and multicultural education throughout their lives in schools, communities, and from the media. Their attitudes reflect an interest in, and acceptance of diversity in all private and public spaces. Tolerance of diversity is often manifested as acceptance of single-parent households and same-sex couples, interracial and blended families, and cohabitation without marriage. In addition to being the beneficiaries of multicultural education and programs since birth, millennials are also the most racially and ethnically diverse generation in American history. Nearly 35 percent of millennials identify themselves as nonwhite and Latinos (of all backgrounds) are the largest minority group; this is the first generation in US history in which blacks are no longer the largest racial or ethnic minority group (Strauss and Howe, 85). To these demographic shifts, add the fact that one in every five millennials has at least one immigrant parent (Strauss and Howe). Progressive college educators who support multicultural practices, curriculum, and programs but who fail to address the unique needs of millennials risk entrenching reform into new categories of social isolation, political apathy, and worse, the perpetuation of injustice around the globe.

Persistent patterns of global power inequities, economic disparities, and environmental degradation conspire to create reluctance among college students to identify their own positions of relative privilege. Students come to class with a full range of stereotypes and unexamined assumptions about the other, and are often uncomfortable when they feel excluded or alienated by narratives and aesthetics that are not familiar, or that do not accommodate them. Educators must move beyond tolerance as a goal of world-centered curriculum, and toward the development of critical awareness of the complex interaction between and among personal, social, cultural, political, and economic identities. An ongoing and rigorous exploration of the ways in which the twentieth century has been experienced differently by Western and non-Western peoples is necessary. Essential concepts must be defined from multiple perspectives and reinforced throughout the term. Relevant terms may include: art, beauty, context, culture, colonialism, domination, exploitation, feminism, knowledge, literature, modernism, modernization, neocolonialism, postcolonialism, postmodernism, progress, tolerance, and so on. Instructors must provide a structured curriculum that requires students to share responsibility for learning about world cultures. The methods I discuss can help educators reimagine the purpose of world-centered curriculum from cultural sensitivity, to what Okokon O. Udo refers to as "cultural competence," whereby students move beyond simply having knowledge of, or even a deep respect for other cultures to cultivating a critical awareness situated intellectually, emotionally, and spiritually among many ways of viewing the world.

Best Practices for Engaging Millennials in the Classroom

Millennials respond well to teachers who are enthusiastic about teaching, who challenge them intellectually, and who are responsive to students. Strategies that will most likely lead to successful learning will:

- require collaborative learning and small group work, both spontaneous in-class activities and formal assignments;
- provide opportunities for role-playing exercises, experiential learning, and the exploration of character profiles and case studies;
- incorporate technology and online components in assignments, activities, and class time—as long as you can do it well!
- use student response systems (such as clickers, text messaging, social networks).
- reinforce meaningful themes and concepts;
- emphasize time on task;
- permit flexibility in the delivery of course content, course requirements, and classroom policies.

Teaching World Literature

Literature is both a means to connect people across time and space and an ideological or political production situated within a particular moment in time and space. Dynamic strategies that help students reconcile this seeming paradox and identify aspects of a shared humanity expressed in literature while compelling them to challenge assumptions of universal experiences must be forged. Feminist pedagogy provides methodology and rationale that is appropriate across disciplines and particularly effective with millennials because it is student centered, promotes collaboration and cooperation, and fosters a democratic creation of knowledge. In the classroom, feminist teachers strive to challenge existing power structures, dominant paradigms, and privileged epistemologies in assignments, discussions, and activities. Whether in the composition or literature classroom, feminist teachers embrace diversity and inclusivity, often by seamlessly centering marginal voices.

Best Practices for Teaching World Literature to Millennials

Instructors who successfully engage millennials consistently communicate high expectations to students, acknowledge multiple ways of knowing, and support diverse talents in the classroom. Strategies that will most likely enhance teaching effectiveness will:

- encourage contact between students and faculty;
- cultivate student community;
- offer prompt feedback;
- foster reciprocity and cooperation among students;
- promote active learning;
- connect course work to things that matter—especially linking global implications to student career plans and lifestyle choices;
- promote balance between required curriculum and student-driven learning.

World Classics at Mercyhurst College

World Classics (ENG 144), is one of two introductory survey literature courses required of all Mercyhurst College students. In this course, students read, analyze, write, and speak about representative twentieth-century, non-Western texts from Asian, Arab, Islamic, Hebrew, African, and Latin American traditions. Extensive and active reading is required and students are expected to practice critical analysis, research, and documentation by completing various oral and written performances. Mercyhurst College is a small, Catholic, liberal arts institution that takes seriously its core values to produce students who are socially merciful, globally responsible, and compassionately hospitable. These commitments influence all aspects of campus life from an 18-course world-centered, interdisciplinary core curriculum to a campus-wide commitment to service and faculty involvement in the community. The cost of tuition necessities that the majority of our students are from affluent families, however, the college has significant minorities of local students and international students. The methods I discuss in this chapter have been successful in World Classics classes on Mercyhurst's main campus as well as with adult students in a community center setting.

Native American Literature and World Classics

Many world literature classes like World Classics require teachers to cover multiple, unrelated, and distinct cultural traditions in a relatively short period of time. This has been a particular challenge within Mercyhurst College's 10-week trimester system. Therefore, I have developed a systematic comparative approach for choosing literature that promotes a controlled dialectic between student and text. For each culture studied, students read at least one text from the early twentieth century and one from the latter half; for every one masculine voice, one feminine voice;

and so on. I incorporate a variety of narratives including graphic novels, film, and music.

Native American literature is not formally included in any literary survey at Mercyhurst; however, I have had great success incorporating it as a frame for the course. I begin and end the term with Native American literature because it provides many opportunities to both stimulate and challenge millennials. It confronts mainstream Western assumptions about culture and literatures, requires recognition of "otherness," and encourages tolerance for ambiguity. The Navajo "Night Chant" is an ideal introduction to a world-based literature class because what is seemingly familiar to students is made unfamiliar. The Navajo Night Chant or "Night Way" is part of a vast interlocking cosmology of origin stories that date back to 1000 BCE when it was performed by people living in eastern Arizona. It is the most sacred of all Navajo healing ceremonies and also the most demanding to learn and difficult to perform because it requires the memorization of hundreds of songs, dozens of prayers, and several very complicated sand paintings. A young man who leaves home to visit the gods predicates it. Once there, he learns their ways and upon his return, he shares knowledge with his people. Those lessons and the ones carried by a study of the work as literature, remain valuable for twenty-first-century millennials.

In her essay, "Mapping Contests in Unknown Locations," Paula Gunn Allen discusses the consequence of self-serving stereotypes associated with Native American. She remarks that "Americans, when they think of us at all, prefer us to be objects of pity...impoverished beyond even the lower limits of impoverishment" in order to bolster the feel-good moment of sending "used clothing to the poor Indians at the mission" (18). While millennials accept diversity and multiculturalism, most millennials unquestioningly accept this dynamic as well and are therefore completely swept away by Leslie Marmon Silko's "Yellow Woman." The story is about an unnamed Laguna Pueblo woman who goes for a walk along the river and meets a man who claims to be a ka'tsina spirit. He calls her Yellow Woman, a character she knows from her grandfather's stories. She follows the man and engages in behavior that is both seductive and unsettling. They traverse a landscape that is circumscribed by boundaries and passages. They part after a violent exchange with a white rancher and the woman returns to her husband and family, hoping to meet the man again.

Silko transforms traditional Laguna Pueblo stories into new versions that address contemporary realities. Like much contemporary Native American literature, her work exhibits tropes and techniques from multiple traditions. The Western canon offers predominantly individualistic and secular perspectives, linear plot development, monologic or dialogic appeals, the promotion of hierarchical social organization, and critiques of dominant culture. Literature from Native American and other world perspectives may be communal in orientation, metaphysical in focus, cyclical in structure, conversational or multivocal, and critical of colonialism. These categories are neither oppositional, nor exclusive, but rather, relational thereby helping reduce resistance to marginal perspectives.

Materials

The lesson plans outlined below were developed for two 90-minute class periods.

Both "The Navajo Night Chant" and Silko's "Yellow Woman" are available in *The Norton Anthology of World Literature: The Twentieth Century* (2002).

First Class

These lesson plans are preceded by a class—usually the first class of the term—when I define culture as an integrated and shared system of values, beliefs, behaviors, and norms; I also explain that literature is comprised of text and subtext, and that context helps readers make sense of both. Finally, I make a case for literature as a vehicle that both reflects and informs culture. I use images from many cultures to demonstrate these points.

1. Instructor provides a brief context for the "Night Chant." The introduction in the *Norton Anthology* is sufficient, and I highlight the following points:
   A. This is literature from an oral tradition, the earliest form of literature in all cultures.
   B. This is a healing ceremony that integrates chanting, drumming, dancing, painting, sweats, and rituals that last for 9 days.
   C. The "Night Chant" attends to ailments of the head, reconnects individuals with their communities, and restores a connection with nature.
   D. Ceremonies take place in the fall and begin in the evening, the beginning of the Navajo "day."
   E. The "Night Chant" is the most popular ceremony practiced, today.

2. Instructor divides students into groups of 3–5, and gives each group a section of the "Night Chant" to read. The recommended version of the "Night Chant" has numbered lines that can be divided into sections to accommodate seven or more groups. It's awkward and halting at first as students become familiar with one another and get accustomed to speaking in unison. They stumble over tongue-twisting phrasing and driving cadences before reading it together, aloud.
3. After one complete reading, the instructor should systematically review the sections and explain some of the aesthetic attributes such as repetition of sounds and words, the ritualistic pairing of images, and the incremental development of each movement, as well as relevant themes including references to balance, beauty, and interconnection. The instructor invites students to share their observations and responses before moving on.
4. Students read the "Night Chant" aloud a second time: This time, the instructor asks them to identify images and themes that reveal or suggest the values, beliefs, behaviors, and norms of Navajo culture. Topics that students may mention during the discussion include the importance of family and community, the fecundity of nature, the valuing of the dream world, and performances of masculinity and gender. Additional topics that can be covered include issues of reading in translation, differences/commonalities between oral and written literary traditions, and the social roots of beauty.
5. Follow-up activities/assignments:
    A. play Voyager's Golden Record of the "Night Chant" recorded by Willard Rhodes and discuss the aesthetics of an original recitation;
    B. listen to the information about the Navajo language and hear words spoken at Smithsonian Native Languages website and discuss the intersections between language and culture;
    C. share contemporary Native American artists who incorporate traditional themes and techniques in modern performances, such as Jim Pepper, Joanne Shenandoah, and Robbie Robertson.

Second Class

For instructors with some knowledge of Native American studies, the introduction in the textbook combined with Dr. Fidel Fajardo-Acosta's online study guide of Silko's "Yellow Woman" (http://fajardo-acosta.com/worldlit/silko/yellow_woman.htm) provide sufficient background and context to conduct this class. Instructors should be prepared to define the following terms as necessary: ka'tsina, trickster character, Yellow Woman and the corn sisters, borders, border crossers, and border theory, colonialism, postcolonialism, and postmodernism. Biographies of, and interviews with Silko as well as critical readings of "Yellow Woman" are readily available and generally reliable online (choose .edu and .org sources over others). In advance of the class outlined below, instructors should show or assign students the downloadable video "Running on the Edge of the Rainbow," which introduces Silko's definition of storytelling as gossip that connects people to each other, to their culture, and to their history. Later, this discussion will help challenge implications of student perceptions of literature as the "high art" of Western people.

1. Instructor provides context for Silko's work and a brief introduction to "Yellow Woman." I highlight the following points:
   A. Silko is a Native American poet, novelist, short story writer, and essayist. She is also identified as a postmodern writer.
   B. She has deep roots in Laguna Pueblo society and believes that storytelling is more than entertainment and more than a method to pass on values and traditions. Storytelling is a necessary ritual that links people to each other and to larger realities.
   C. She preserves traditional stories and storytelling techniques by making them relevant to modern readers.
   D. She is a vocal activist who is critical of historic and current domination of whites (who profit) and governments (that enforce) domination over nature and people of color; she is similarly critical of men's domination over women.
2. Silko, like many non-Western writers, must negotiate the Western world of literature while maintaining and promoting an alternative to those traditions. Instructors may segue from the archaic "Night Chant" to the postmodern "Yellow Woman" by analyzing Silko's poem "Lullaby." The class discussion should examine how Silko translates oral traditions into written ones.
3. Students will need help with text as well as context. Therefore, following the overview above, the instructor should lead a discussion that identifies and analyzes the plot, setting, and characters of "Yellow Woman."
4. Thematic topics include gender, relations between men and women, personal and cultural identity, the natural world, the tension between individual desire and the needs of the community.
5. Instructor should link relevant course concepts by guiding a discussion on Western and non-Western perspectives, colonization

and postcolonialism, narratives of resistance, strategies used by the "other" to code or cloak criticism of dominant culture, narrative point of view, and the role of ambiguity and complexity in literature.
6. Follow-up activities/assignments:
   A. students can be instructed to research and compare Yellow Woman stories from various North, Central, and South American indigenous peoples;
   B. students can be assigned to map their own personal and cultural identities using methods described by Peter Prevos's "Cultural Identity" and Ulrike Meyer's "In the Name of Identity: Teaching Cultural Awareness in the Intercultural Classroom";
   C. students can circle back to Native American literature with James Welch's *Fools Crow* at the end of the term. Chapters 7 and 8 are available in several anthologies and could be covered in one 90-minute class session. Or, students could be required to produce a literary analysis essay in response to the entire novel. Published in 1986, *Fools Crow* tells the story of the early contact with European colonizers and consequently, the "end" of a tradition Native American way of life. Like Silko, Welsh successfully utilizes Western conventions while interweaving details from a Blackfoot physical, emotional, and spiritual quest. Students strongly identify with the "coming of age" story of the hero. However, Welsh privileges the native perspective. For example, words are sometimes translated, sometimes not and complex names are not abbreviated or simplified.

Resources

Meyer, Ulrike. "In the Name of Identity: Teaching Cultural Awareness in the Intercultural Classroom." Paper presented at "Changing Identities in a Globalized World." Vilnius University. November–December 2007. Web.

Lawall, Sarah, ed. *The Norton Anthology of World Literature: The Twentieth Century*. Volume F. 2nd edition. Gen. New York: WW Norton and Company, 2002. Print.

"Poet Sherman Alexie Talks 'Faces' and 'War Dances.'" The News Hour with Jim Leher. Judy Woodruff, host. October 22, 2009. Web.

Prevos, Peter. "Cultural Identity." Lecture. Foundations of Social Science. Maquarie University, Sydney Australia. August 2004. Web.

"Running on the Edge of the Rainbow: Laguna Stories and Poems with Leslie Marmon Silko." Words and Place: Native Literature from the Southwest. University of Arizona. Web.

Silko, Leslie Marmon. "Lullaby." *Storyteller*. Self-published: 1981. Print.

Recommended Readings

Alfred, Gerald R. *Peace, Power, Righteousness: An Indigenous Manifesto.* Don Mills: Oxford University Press, 1999. 80–113. Print.
Andrews, Tracy and Jon Olney. "Potlatch and Powwow: Dynamics of Culture through Lives Lived Dancing." *American Indian Culture and Research Journal.* 31.1 (2007): 63–108. Web.
Beck, Peggy V., and Anna Lee Walters. *The Sacred: Ways of Knowledge, Sources of Life.* Tsaile: Navajo Community College, 1977. 49–95. Print.
Cajete, Gregory. "Philosophy of Native Science." *American Indian Thought: Philosophical Essays.* Ed. Anne Waters. Malden: Blackwell Pub, 2004. 45–57. Print.
DeLoria, Phillip. *Indians in Unexpected Places.* Lawrence: UP of Kansas, 2004. Print.
Elliott, Michael A. "Indians, Incorporated." *American Literary History* 19.1 (2007): 141–159. Web.
Fixico, Donald Lee. *The American Indian Mind in a Linear World: American Indian Studies and Traditional Knowledge.* New York: Routledge, 2003. 1–61. Print.
Grande, Sandy. *Red Pedagogy: Native American Social and Political Thought.* Lanham, MD: Rowman and Littlefield, 2004. Print.
Hafen, P. Jane. "Indigenous Peoples and Place." *A Companion to the Regional Literatures of America.* Ed. Charles L. Crow. Blackwell Companions to Literature and Culture Number: 21. Malden, MA: Blackwell, 2003. 154–70. Print.
Jenco, Leigh Kathryn. "What Does Heaven Ever Say?: A Methods-Centered Approach to Cross- Cultural Engagement" *The American Political Science Review* 101.4 (2007): 741–755. Web.
la Duke, Winona. "Masks in the New Millennium." *Cultural Representation in Native America.* Ed. Andrew Jolivette. Lanham, MD: Alta Mira Press, 2006. 61–73. Print.
Petrone, Robert and Robert Gibney. "The Power to Speak and Listen." *The English Journal* 94.5 (2005). Web.
Stewart-Harawira, Makere. "Cultural Studies, Indigenous Knowledge and Pedagogies of Hope." *Policy Futures in Education* 3.2 (2005): 153–163. Web.
Vizenor, Gerald. *Fugitive Poses: Native American Indian Scenes of Absence and Presence.* Lincoln: U of Nebraska P, 2000. Print.
Zitzer-Comfort, Carol. "Teaching Native American Literature: Inviting Students to See the World through Indigenous Lenses." *Pedagogy* 8.1 (2008): 160. Print.

Works Cited

Allen, Paula Gunn. "Mapping Contests in Unknown Locations." *Cultural Representation in Native America.* Ed. Andrew Jolivette. Lanham, MD: Alta Mira Press, 2006. 13–26. Print.

Taylor, Paul and Scott Keeter, eds. *Millennials: A Portrait of Generation Next*. Pew Research Center. February 2010. Web.

Strauss, William and Neil Howe. *Millennials Rising: The Next Great Generation*. New York: Vintage Books, 2000. Print.

Howe, Neil and William Strauss. *Millennials Go To College: Strategies for a New Generation*. Washington DC: American Association of Collegiate Registrars and Admissions Officers, 2003. Print.

Jolivette, Andrew, ed. *Cultural Representation in Native America*. Lanham, MD: Alta Mira Press, 2006. Print.

15

"The Speculation of Schoolboys": Confronting the Academy in *Ulysses*

Matthew McKenzie Davis

We face an inherent paradox as instructors of world literature. Although we present our students with texts that often challenge the norms of formal academic discourse, we simultaneously ask our students to respond to these texts in written assignments that enforce the very same norms. Requiring students to embrace these norms in their own writing often undermines the authors under consideration; enforcement of the formal academic standard foregrounds the underlying Western value system—clarity, directness, linearity, and so on—that many authors in the world literature cannon resist. Moreover, the formal standard mitigates the revolutionary potential of the ideas presented in world literature by reinforcing the type of intellectual training that, Lynn Bloom argues, "promulgates the middle-class values that are thought to be essential to the proper functioning of students in the academy" (656).[1] Within our curriculum, then, we must locate opportunities where students can enact—not merely observe—techniques and writing strategies that complicate the implicit values of formal academic discourse; we must locate opportunities where students can demonstrate their understanding of a text not by merely recycling a prescribed form, but by authoritatively establishing their own voice.

To be sure, an infinite combination of texts and assignments could successfully present students with a project that results in an intense interaction with the style and ideas of an author from outside their culture. My interest and research has lead me to offer James Joyce's *Ulysses* to my students as an example that both challenges formal academic discourse, and depicts the type of resistance that students can expect to encounter from the academy when they steer their writing away from that academic standard. Using *Ulysses* in this capacity also affords instructors the opportunity to discuss why Joyce, who is most often included in courses on British literature, should be discussed alongside authors from non-European countries. Although Joyce was born in an Ireland still under England's colonial rule, critics have long sought to frame Joyce as an apolitical aesthete. In his definitive biography, Richard Ellmann lays the foundation for this view by juxtaposing examples of Joyce's partisan stands alongside examples of political indifference. Ellmann reports, for example, that Joyce supported a call for "an economic boycott of Britain" in 1907, but he immediately undermines this action by citing Joyce's concession that his socialistic leanings were "'unsteady and ill-informed'" (238–239). Ellmann goes on to assert in summary that Joyce "continued to pursue the question [of socialism] with great energy, but decreasing confidence in prevailing nostrums" (239). This perspective set the tone for a generation of critics who emphasized Joyce's aesthetics over his politics.[2]

This critical approach overlooks the fact that Joyce's politics and aesthetics are in fact deeply interrelated, and it is this interrelation that we lead our students away from when we assign formal academic essays that mimic the form and content of literary critics. In his work, Joyce engages England's oppressive colonial control over Ireland on two fronts: he utilizes the political conflict as a source of confrontation between the characters within the narrative, and he challenges the influence of English literature with innovative stylistic techniques. Often, he pushes back against British political and aesthetic influences simultaneously. In "The Dead," for example, we can call our students' attention to the way that the destabilization of the point of view overlaps with the realization by Gabriel—whom Vincent Cheng describes as "a qualified representation by Joyce of a potentially oppressive patriarch in symbolic collaboration with the ruling masters of the English colonial empire"—that his wife will never love him as she loved the definitively Irish Michael Furey (130). Thus, Joyce undercuts the traditional value placed on a stable point of view and an Irish character who has fully embraced British rule in the same moment.

The interconnected resistance of Joyce's style and content continues in *A Portrait of the Artist as a Young Man*, which combines Joyce's use of the free-indirect style with—among many examples—a critique of England's role in the downfall of Irish politician Charles Stewart Parnell.[3] As the novel draws to a close, Joyce again pairs stylistic deviation with political declaration, abruptly shifting from the narrator's point of view to Stephen's journal in order to deliver the well-known penultimate sentence of the text: "I go to encounter for the millionth time the reality of experience and to forge in the smithy of my soul the uncreated consciousness of my race" (213). The obvious significance of the shift into the journal format here is that Stephen makes his famous assertion in exactly his own words. We can invite our students to read this shift as Stephen finally speaking without the mitigating influence of the narrator and articulating his own identity in the closing pages of a novel that has seen him experiment with identities based on both religion and aesthetics adopted from English colonizers. It is no coincidence then that Stephen frames his ambition in nationalistic terms. Having renounced the dogma of the church, Stephen now disavows the dogmatic influence of English literature. In stating that he intends "to forge...the uncreated consciousness of my race," Stephen announces that he does not intend to craft a piece of literature that will fit in among the works of the British canon, but to craft one that will reorient Irish literature away from the influences of its colonizer.

In *Ulysses*—a text that draws its structure from Homer and that mocks the nineteenth-century English novel—Stephen continues to place himself in opposition to English literary influences.[4] Although Joyce does not offer a sample of Stephen's writing in this text, Stephen does provide students with an example of the difficulty one faces when attempting to establish a perspective that counters hegemonic thought. In the "Scylla and Charybdis" episode, Stephen posits a theory that challenges Shakespeare's standing as the untouchable genius of English literature by suggesting that the salacious details of the bard's life could be discovered in his greatest works. Namely, Stephen suggests that Shakespeare's wife was unfaithful and that his own brothers were included among her numerous lovers. In a long and thoroughly cited exposition, Stephen alleges that "the murdered father" in *Hamlet* represents Shakespeare, "the dispossessed son" Shakespeare's dead son Hamnet, and Ann Shakespeare "the guilty queen"; that the "spurned lover in the sonnets" should also be read as a stand in for the author; and the use of the names of Shakespeare's brothers, Richard and Edmund, in *King Lear* and *Richard II* demonstrates the tension between siblings (*Ulysses*, 209–210; cited hereafter as *U*).[5] The connections between Shakespeare's life and art that Stephen formulates are speculative, but the value of his theory lies in the argument underpinning the specific claims: Shakespeare was a man like any other—English or otherwise—and his work—and English literature more broadly—should not be treated as a separate entity removed from the culture and man who produced it. In short, Stephen argues against the unquestioned level of acclaim Irish intellectuals award Shakespeare, which precludes his work from the level of scrutiny given to other English imports.

Joyce underlines the intended audience of Stephen's argument by setting the "Scylla and Charybdis" episode in Dublin's National Library, and by giving Stephen an audience of Irish literary scholars. Each of these figures has received an education steeped in English literature, and, predictably, each of them responds with skepticism to Stephen's interpretation.[6] The most aggressive rebuke comes from George Russell, who summarily rejects Stephen's theory by likening it to a "discussion of the historicity of Jesus" (U, 185). Russell asserts that the sole concern of art is "to reveal to us ideas, formless spiritual essences," and "all the rest is the speculation of schoolboys for schoolboys" (U, 185). He concludes that readers should enjoy "the poetry of *King Lear*" instead of concerning themselves with "how the poet lived" (U, 189). We should point our students' attention to the deliberate construction of Russell's response, which Joyce uses to outline the exact view of English literature that Stephen seeks to refute. Moreover, Russell demonstrates the rhetorical approach often used to suppress work that contradicts dominant views within the academy (like papers that resist the rules of formal academic discourse). As Russell accuses Stephen of pursuing a futile argument, so will our students be accused by most professors of veering off topic if they connect their analysis with their own experience. And as Russell likens Stephen to a schoolboy, so will our students be dismissed as immature or even ignorant for writing in their own voice.

Russell punctuates his complete dismissal of Stephen's argument by walking out before Stephen has a chance to finish. Although the remaining scholars hear Stephen out, their rejection of Stephen—and his acceptance of that rejection—demonstrates the kind of self-effacing attitude that the academy expects from students. The scholars let Stephen finish, but ultimately undercut him when they ask, "Do you believe your own theory?" (U, 213). This question recognizes the rhetorical success of Stephen's argument while also challenging him to fully align himself with his ideas. Having no other way to counter Stephen, the scholars force him to either back down or shift his argument from an interesting exercise to an ostracizing stand against an overwhelmingly dominant view of Shakespeare. Stephen recognizes this and immediately backs down, denying his theory without equivocation. Of course, the complexity and thoroughness of the argument Stephen has presented indicates that, despite his denial, he does believe what he has put forth, yet the power of the academy forces him to conform. For our students, the conformity imposed on Stephen offers a lesson in the forces they will encounter when contradicting the formal academic standard of writing. If they choose to pursue a style of writing that successfully subverts the expectations of the formal academic standard, the academy will force them to stake their reputation (i.e., their grade) on that choice. We must emphasize that most students simply conform to the expectations of the academy since they are not willing to lose their place within it.

Having outlined this reading of the text, the question then becomes: How can we guide our students through a reading of *Ulysses* that encourages them to respond to Joyce in the same individualized way that Stephen responds to Shakespeare? To accomplish this, I invite my students to consider *Ulysses* as a text separate from its reputation. I push my students to find in the novel what T. R. Johnson identifies as "the openings, cracks, and fissures in every discursive act" (638). Johnson argues that these "fissures" reveal the specific rhetorical choices behind every piece of argumentative writing, while minimizing the "transcendental ideal of 'academic discourse'...which names, masters, and controls reality" (638). I utilize this approach with *Ulysses* by asking students to look for fissures within the text that illuminate the choices Joyce made in its construction. I ask them to locate passages that reveal Joyce's intended audience and the values he believes this audience possesses. Typically, students require some prompting in this discussion, so I begin by asking students, as an example, how the abundance of literary allusions Joyce employs in the "Scylla and Charybdis" episode reflect the assumed expectations of his audience.

Emerging from this discussion, I assign students what amounts to an exercise in translation—summarizing Stephen's argument about Shakespeare in formal academic language. I have my students complete this task in class so that they can then share their work in groups and talk about both the strategies they utilized and the differences in audience expectations that this exercise revealed. To employ the concepts we discuss in class, I give my students a writing prompt for homework that mirrors the kind of prompt one would expect in freshman composition: I ask them to argue for why someone should pursue whatever it is they have chosen for their major. But, unlike composition, I ask them to construct their response as though it was to be read by their friends on Facebook. I explain to them that one way to understand Joyce's style (or any author's for that matter) is to think of him as writing for authors in his peer group. Thus, the approach they take when building an argument for their friends is no different than the approach used by Joyce in *Ulysses* (and no less confusing for someone outside of their group). When students return to class with their completed prompts, I have them share their work again in small groups, and, building off their previous discussion, I then ask them to talk about the choices they made in their most recent writing and how those choices follow or diverge from those of Joyce. I encourage them to talk about whether or not it is possible for them to imitate Joyce in this assignment.

From this, I pivot the discussion toward an analysis of formal academic writing. I ask my students why, if they cannot merely imitate Joyce, the academy expects them to imitate scholars who write in the formal academic style. Why is this discourse—which is as constructed as Joyce's highly stylized and esoteric language—considered more appropriate for a college class than form that reflects a student's own voice? I ask them to consider what was lost when they translated Stephen's argument from a literary to a formal style. What was gained when they talked about their major in a way that was meant for Facebook instead of their professor? Of course, these questions must lead students to a discussion of the actual consequences of rejecting formal academic writing for a style that more closely reflects their own voice, and therefore more accurately conveys their ideas. I ask them to consider what would happen if they submitted a stream of conscious narrative in a history course where academic discourse was expected. Of course, the answer is obvious.

Notes

1. Bloom convincingly and thoroughly argues that traditional writing assignments in freshman composition promote self-reliance, responsibility, respectability, decorum, propriety, moderation, temperance, thrift, efficiency, order, cleanliness, punctuality, delayed gratification, and critical thinking.
2. For a thorough discussion of the critical progression from an apolitical reading of Joyce to a postcolonial reading, see the collection of essays Leonard Orr, ed., *Joyce, Imperialism, & Postcolonialism* (Syracuse: Syracuse University Press, 2008), specifically Orr's "From High-Modern Aesthete to Postcolonial Subject," 1–11, and Eugene O'Brien's "The Return and the Redefinition of the Repressed," 41–57.
3. Joyce presents the accusation of British culpability in the fall of Parnell made by Stephen's father in a scene in which Joyce removes all narrative distance so that the reader is left only with the perspective of a young Stephen, who is unable to grasp the argument and whose mind wanders to thoughts of the girl next door.
4. For an example of Joyce's critique of 19th century literature, direct students to the 'Nausicaa' episode, in which Cissy Caffrey views a man at the other end of an empty beach. Reflecting the influence of Romantic novels on her imagination, Cissy begins to dream of the idealized courtship and desexualized marriage that would follow if this man were to introduce himself. Joyce then switches to the perspective of the man. It is Leopold Bloom, and he is masturbating to the figure of Cissy in the distance.
5. Don Gifford, and Robert J. Seidman, *Ulysses Annotated: Notes For James Joyce's Ulysses* (Berkeley: University of California Press, 1989). *Ulysses* confirms that the facts Stephen presents about Shakespeare are consistent with those found in books available to Joyce by the historians George Brandes, Frank Harris, and Sydney Lee.

6. Interestingly, the critical responses to Stephen's theory mirror the dismissive attitude of the characters in the text. In a summary of the critical consensus on "Scylla and Charybdis," Katherine Mullin, *James Joyce, Sexuality and Social Purity* (Cambridge: Cambridge University Press, 2003) reports that Stephen's theory has been called "contradictory, irrelevant, historically inaccurate, a mere theatrical façade and of little literary value" (120).

Works Cited

Bloom, Lynn Z. "Freshman Composition as a Middle-Class Enterprise," *College English* 58, no. 6 (October, 1996): 654–675.
Cheng, Vincent. "Empire and Patriarchy in 'The Dead.'" *Joyce, Race, and Empire*. New York: Cambridge University Press, 1995. 128–47.
Ellmann, Richard. *James Joyce*, rev. ed. Oxford: Oxford University Press, 1983.
Gifford, Don, and Robert J. Seidman. *Ulysses Annotated: Notes For James Joyce's Ulysses*. Berkeley: University of California Press, 1989.
Johnson, T. R. "School Sucks." *College Composition and Communication* 52, no. 4 (June, 2001).
Joyce, James. *A Portrait of the Artist as a Young Man*. Oxford: Oxford University Press, 2000.
———. *Ulysses*. New York: Vintage International, 1990.
Mullin, Katherine. *James Joyce, Sexuality and Social Purity*. Cambridge: Cambridge University Press, 2003.
Orr, Leonard, ed. *Joyce, Imperialism, & Postcolonialism*. Syracuse: Syracuse University Press, 2008.

16

Reaching for the Other in Teaching Aleksandar Hemon's "A Coin"

Zach VandeZande

I teach my students theory. I am talking about college freshman and sophomores. I make no apologies about it. They're living in a world in which theory is being leveraged against them all the time, and it's in their best interest to start showing them early and often how to leverage it for themselves. If they roll their eyes at me when I bring up Foucault or Deleuze, if they look at me like I'm mad while I'm pounding down my dry-erase marker's felt nub against the white board to try and get them to see what's so cool about the signifier-signified relationship and how that undermines all of their ideas about how communication works, well, I'm okay with that. It's my right to seem a little crazy; I teach literature classes.

This approach is doubly important in a World Literature course, where the texts are going to seem often strange and impenetrable to many of the students, and where each day brings a new, sometimes wildly different cultural landscape for us to explore. Theory is the through-line in my globe-hopping syllabus. The problem with this approach is that it engenders a certain weariness in my students—an attitude that invariably comes up is that if everything is subject to destabilization or deconstruction, then why bother? When it was first asked of me, I didn't have a clear answer. A few classes later, though, we were covering Aleksandar Hemon's powerful short story, "A Coin," in which a young woman is harried by snipers in the besieged Sarajevo, and I found a solution to the problem.

"A Coin" is a deliberately alienating story, constantly playing with the reader's perception of distance between reader and author, author and subject, character and character's perception; this is precisely why it works so well as an entry point into talking about Othering, the subaltern, and the conflict between representation and re-presentation, as well as how we as readers are supposed to deal with those ideas once we know how to wield them. Hemon also happens to have the post-Raymond Carver immediacy of the modern short story writer that a young American audience craves. The stakes are immediate and ever-looming, as the story begins with the following line, "Suppose there is a point A and a Point B and that, if you want to get from point A to point B, you have to pass through an open space clearly visible to a skillful sniper" (119). The streets between the two points are littered with meaningless objects—a purse, a destroyed videocassette, a wet loaf of bread—the remains of real lives stripped of context; already a metaphor is emerging for the distance between the two narrators: Aida, the young woman trapped in Sarajevo with her family, and a fictionalized Hemon, who interjects often to discuss his life in his dim Chicago apartment waiting for letters from home.

Even an astute reader is likely to take this relationship at face value, despite the obvious metafictional conceit of Hemon so closely mirroring his own life in this piece—our Hemon surrogate waits on a letter, Aida sends a letter. They serve as each other's release valve, each trying to escape a reality from which there is no escape. But something interesting starts to happen as the story unfolds. Hemon says early on of Aida's letters, "What terrifies me is that, as I rip the exhausted envelope, she may be dead. She may have vanished, may have already become a ghost, a nothing—a fictitious character, so to speak...I dread the fact that life is always slower than death and I have been chosen, despite my weakness, against my will, to witness the discrepancy" (120). Here, Hemon is already revealing his true goal in writing this story: an exploration not of the horror of war, but of the tragedy of being unable to actually capture that war, despite his close connection to it.

This passage is followed closely by Aida's description of a dream in which she is trapped watching someone else perform her life "And then I realize—it's the language. I'm trapped within the wrong language" (123). If you ask a student to take this passage apart given what the story's offered us so far, she will likely talk about the literal distance of time and space and the way that Aida feels trapped by her situation. After a few weeks with me, though, my students are ready for my inevitable, ever-looming question: "Is that it?" We've already talked about how meaning is complex and difficult to pin down. When I first taught this story, I asked that question and they looked on for a minute, letting the uncomfortable silence settle into their bones. Then I asked them to read Hemon's next section, in which he says, "I think of all the things I could've told her or should've told her: how cumbersome I feel in English, sinking in syntax, my sentences flapping helplessly, like a drowning child's arms" and ends with "I used to believe words can convey and contain everything, but not anymore, not anymore" (124). The similarity between Hemon the character's thoughts and Aida's dream seems too neat, too clean for some of my students, and the brave ones will say so, possibly chalking it up to a flaw in the storytelling. Other students will grab on to the ending, which sounds like the kind of thing I may have said to them before when we spoke about how language works through the lens of de Saussure, of Levi-Strauss, of Derrida. This line becomes crucial to the reading I'm about to offer them, in which the various layers of interpretation and meaning fall away and the story becomes about one man knowing that he can't escape the prison of himself.

    I ask my students to skip ahead a little bit to a crucial passage, "Since April I have received no letters from Aida. From that time I had to make up her letters, I had to write her letters for her, I had to imagine her, because that was the only way to break the siege and stay connected with her. I'm sure she's alive, I'm sure that one of these days I'll have a bundle of her consecutive letters stowed in my mailbox, I'm sure she's writing them this very moment" (129). Here, the narrative comes undone and a question is raised: Which of these letters from Aida is real? What have we seen here that can justifiably be called *authentic*? It's a trick question, of course, and a nasty one at that. The students have to immediately process the facts of Hemon the actual writer, a young man who was trapped in Chicago during the actual siege of Sarajevo; the facts of Hemon as character (again, a young man trapped in Chicago during the siege of Sarajevo); and the facts of Aida the character, whose words may now be seen as Hemon the character's re-presentation of her from the woman he used to know and a photograph of her in a bulletproof vest that he has received; all while internally groaning at the sneaking suspicion that this whole story may be unmasked as a meaningless (to them) metafictional trick so that Hemon can indulge in the high intellectualism of language as a flawed system that never reaches the asymptote of true meaning.

    Which is, of course, the whole problem of postcolonial studies as I know how to tackle it, wrapped up in one question. If we are to accept the doubt that Aida's voice within the story has authenticity—that is, if we entertain that it is not actually her speaking—then we've hit upon the problem of the Other as an entity that is defined by the limit of the Self and that can only be perceived through the lens of the Self. I ask my students to look for other places where the two character's thoughts or the details of their lives collide, and they're able to find a dozen other moments of mirrored thought or rhyming action—Hemon in his apartment plays sniper with a cockroach running from point A to point B, for example, or Aida and he have the same thought about the bombed-out buildings: Hemon looking at pictures says "What was in the pictures was what was not in the pictures—the pictures recorded the very end of the process of disappearing, the nothingness itself" while Aida says "the places on our tour were between being a memory and being reduced to nothing but a pile of rubble. The camera was recording the process of disappearing" (128). The distance between the two characters is no longer about space and time; it is about the inability to understand what is outside of the Self.

From there, we can conclude as a class that Aida has no voice, and that Hemon is trying to make a statement about the subaltern in a wartime situation. Not only that, he is also trying to condemn himself as someone who has no power to give them voice; all he is able to do is what Spivak talks about in "Can the Subaltern Speak?": represent and re-present (70). In this reading, Hemon's use of sensational violence in places (a woman without arms or legs pleads to a camera, a dead aunt is eaten by dogs) seems less about authenticity than about a desire to *make* authenticity out of a situation he cannot understand or give voice to. And in a way, he must; after all, he's been selected, he's our Bosnian ambassador in the American literary scene (another point worth talking about with students).

Letting the students unravel the strings themselves is important, which is why I leave the ending to them. Hemon the character's last action in the story is to buy a Polaroid camera and take pictures of the things in his apartment, a quest to, as he says, "find out how space and things appear when I'm not exerting my presence on them...here's a dried cockroach; here's a glass, with still water not being drunk; here are my vacant shoes; here's my TV not being watched; here's a flash in the mirror; here's nothing." I ask my students, as I often ask my students: Why this? Of the infinite hundreds of choices that pop into a writer's head at any moment, why must this one thing happen right now? And how does it square with what happens next: Aida, in a letter, finally discussing what it feels like to reach point B, to feel too alive for a moment and then forget: "Once you get to Point B everything is quickly gone, as if it never happened. You pick yourself up and walk back into your besieged life, happy to be. You move a wet curl from your forehead, inhale deeply, and put your hand in the pocket, where you may or may not find a worthless coin; a coin" (134).

They don't know. I push them a little bit. One of them may have the guts to say that since Aida's passages are made-up, they're meaningless (this did in fact happen the first time I taught this story). I ask them: Why was I moved, why am I always moved at the end of this story, if I doubt that it's even happening within the fictional universe Hemon has created? Why were they maybe moved? Then they'll start to get it: it's about Hemon's pain at not knowing, Hemon the character's desire to step out of the frame and let Aida finally, really speak, and Hemon the writer's knowledge, that devastating knowledge, that by not being there he is unable to ever understand what became of his home.

That is important. That is why we're here in the classroom. "A Coin" illustrates so many of the central reasons why literature exists: to understand and be understood, to learn compassion, to try and communicate what it is to be alive with an imperfect medium, to know that you will fail, but to do it anyway, because it's the trying that matters, not the getting there. That's what the students paid money to understand. By engaging with the theory, and by using it as a filter for our close reading, we've opened up options for looking at this story, which in turn has allowed us options in looking at the pain underpinning it. The very destabilization that gave my students pause has opened up into a new understanding.

Works Cited

Hemon, Aleksandar. *The Question of Bruno*. New York: Vintage, 2000. Print.
Spivak, Gayatri. "Can the Subaltern Speak?" PDF file. Web.

Afterword

Masood Ashraf Raja, Hillary Stringer, and Zach VandeZande

The problem with a World Literature course, especially a World Literature Survey course, is the nagging suspicion that the whole endeavor of covering 400 or so years of *everything else* is, in and of itself, more than a little silly. How am I to move from a day of looking at Urdu poetry with my students to a day of Borges without revealing the disjointed, schizophrenic narrative of the modern English department—that this stuff is all relevant, even though it isn't British or American, which of course sets British and American literature apart in exactly the way a World Literature course is fighting against. A whiff of the old colonialist ethos exists in every syllabus, a combination of globetrotting tourist hours with an ill-prepared doctoral student at the helm (I am referring here to myself) and retreats to the safe harbors of the Russians, Marquez, and Achebe. No matter how animated the lecture, no matter how grandiose the claim that a particular culture's literary output is relevant and important and alive, the clever student thinks to herself, "Why are we talking about it for just an hour, again? And what of the next hour?"

This problem is not helped by the anthology model of course construction that most universities require graduate fellows and young professors to follow. The idea of a literary canon is never so flawed as it is in a world literature course, and the implicit assertion that world literature can be covered in six volumes—the same amount of space that is given to American literature alone—furthers a meta-discourse of nonessentiality. Add to this the fact that literary anthologies often privilege certain ideologies and readings in their introductions. The Norton Anthology of World Literature, for example, praises Chinua Achebe for writing *Things Fall Apart* in English while invoking the idea that Ngũgĩ wa Thiong'o has made a poor choice by writing in a native African language: "In contrast with writers such as Ngugi wa Thiong'o, who insist that the contemporary African writer has a moral obligation to write in one of the tribal languages, Achebe maintains his right to compose in the English he has used since his school days...By including Standard English, Igbo, and pidgin in different contexts, Achebe demonstrates the existence of a diverse society that is otherwise concealed behind language barriers" (2857). The subtext here is clear: world literature *written toward* a white audience has more value than world literature that tries to define a national culture on its own terms and for itself. The colonial model of the West as consumer of the world's cultural goods is reinforced throughout the Norton, and the implication that the rest of the world needs to feed themselves into that Western maw undercuts the instructor's goal to prove that these literatures have value unto themselves.

The problem is exacerbated by the placelessness that world literature occupies in many modern universities. It is not uncommon to see an English major's degree plan (at either the undergraduate or graduate level) require several classes in both American and English literature while relegating World Literature courses to the electives column. Often one or a small handful of professors will be thrust into the position of *the* postcolonial scholar(s) on the faculty while the rest of the department reinforces the privilege that Eurocentric models of teaching maintain.

In short, it is a frustrating time to be a scholar or teacher interested in presenting and studying postcolonial or worldly literature. It is also a crucial time, one that points to the very strengths of postcolonial theory that favors looking closely at liminal spaces, deconstructing power structures, and presenting multivalent readings of work that stress how literature works in a broader global discourse while trying to determine what sociopolitical work literature is able to accomplish within that discourse. As educators, we need a keen awareness of where we stand within the academic power structure, and we need a wide array of tools to leverage that position and help our students see not only why the world literature classroom space exists but also why it is one of the most important spaces in the university setting.

One of the goals of literature is to teach compassion, and world literature offers inroads into a broader, more compassionate understanding of our global culture that are not found anywhere else in the educational landscape. It's our job to be educators on the front line, pushing our students toward these understandings and making sure we do justice to the work in a system that is often designed in opposition to that end. We hope that these teaching notes and essays offer more tools for the educator's repertoire, so that she is better equipped to deal with the challenge of exposing Western students to viewpoints that are marginalized elsewhere in their education.

Contributors

Hella Rose Bloom, teaching fellow and an English PhD candidate at the University of North Texas.

Mark Bracher, professor of English and director of the Center for Literature and Psychoanalysis, Kent State University.

Linda Daley, senior lecturer in Literary and Communication Studies in the School of Media and Communication, RMIT University.

Matthew McKenzie Davis, teaching fellow—English, University of North Texas.

Jeffrey R. Di Leo, dean of the School of Arts and Sciences and professor of English and Philosophy at the University of Houston—Victoria.

David B. Downing, professor, director of graduate studies in Literature and Criticism, Indiana University of Pennsylvania.

Robin Truth Goodman, professor, English Department, Florida State University.

Jessica Chiccehitto Hindman, teaching fellow, English Department, University of North Texas.

Jonathan H. X. Lee, assistant professor of Asian American Studies, College of Ethnic Studies, Department of Asian American Studies, San Francisco State University.

Tessa Mellas, PhD candidate in English and Fiction, University of Cincinnati.

Swaralipi Nandi, PhD candidate, Department of English, Kent State University.

Mary Thi Pham, graduate student, San Francisco State University.

Masood Ashraf Raja, assistant professor, English Department, University of North Texas.

Kenneth J. Saltman, professor, Educational Policy Studies and Research, College of Education, DePaul University.

Hillary Stringer, teaching fellow, English Department, University of North Texas.

Marnie M. Sullivan, visiting associate professor of English, Mercyhurst College.

Zach VandeZande, teaching fellow, English Department, University of North Texas.

Kyle Wanberg, graduate student, University of California, Irvine.

Index

academic discourse, formal 213–14, 216
academic freedom 63, 70–3
Adorno, T. 120, 127–8
Afghanistan 9–11, 19–21, 23, 90, 92
 Afghan girls' education 21–2
 Afghanistan-girls-education-report 21–2
alterity 76, 82, 88, 90, 92
altruism 30, 34, 44
American students 76, 91–2, 173
analysis, world-systems 151, 156–7, 160, 162
Appiah, Anthony 27, 43, 94–5
appraisals 30, 39
 compassion-producing 30–1
arts 15, 45, 68–9, 72, 107, 125–6, 128–30, 147, 202,- 229
assignments 42, 184, 203, 207, 209, 213, 217
assumptions 21, 26, 29, 49, 59, 85, 127, 165, 170, 189–90, 203
authenticity 10, 223–4

Bauman, Zygmunt 62, 170, 176–7
behaviors 26–7, 29, 34, 42, 49–50, 191, 196, 205–7

Cambodia 98, 100–1, 103–4, 110–11
 American experiences 109–11
 American literature 97–8, 109
 Americans 97–101, 103–4, 107–8
 Cambodians 97, 99–101
capital 1, 3–4, 15, 20, 23, 157–9, 172
 cultural 55, 88, 95, 116
 neoliberal 1, 149

capitalism 3, 57, 95, 150–1, 154–60, 163, 169, 172, 190, 192
 consumer 53, 56–7, 60
 global 161, 167, 172
capitalist world economy 151, 157
capitalist world system 151–2, 155, 158–62
care 2–3, 10, 57, 59, 68, 137, 139, 172, 185, 187
China 79–80, 150–1, 161, 170
class 13, 26–7, 41, 67, 92, 119, 146, 151, 154, 161, 163, 193–4, 196–8, 208, 217
classroom 2–3, 15–16, 25, 93, 109, 113–15, 117–23, 125, 165, 170–2, 175, 186–7, 203, 225
commodities 159, 167–72
communities 36, 52, 97, 99, 101, 103–4, 109–11, 119, 138, 168, 170, 201, 204, 206–8
comparative literature 65, 78, 86, 88, 92, 94–6
compassion 28–34, 36, 39, 225
consumption 48, 57, 59, 87, 89–90, 154, 158–9, 172, 175
context, cultural 86, 89, 92, 191
corporate personhood 47, 57, 60–1
corporate university 64–7, 70–3
Corporate World Literature 63, 65, 67, 69–71, 73
corporations 47–51, 55, 57, 60–3, 65
corporatization 65, 71–3
cosmopolitanism 25–31, 33, 35–7, 39, 41, 43–5, 81, 90–1, 95
cosmopolitans 25–7, 29, 31, 54, 173
cosmopolitics 43–5, 130

critical pedagogy 3–4, 113–14, 118–20, 122, 149, 154, 199
critical theory 128–30, 192
Cultural Critique 61–2
cultural differences 81, 87, 92, 114, 149
cultural identity 93, 208–9
cultural productions 94, 103–4, 115–16, 123–4
cultural translation 114, 128, 130
cultures 11, 27–8, 79–82, 86–7, 89–92, 95–7, 99, 110–11, 116–17, 123–7, 137–8, 189–91, 193–7, 199, 204–8
  foreign 81, 86, 92
  popular 23, 35, 51–3

dehumanization 33, 35–6, 43–4
discourses 97–8, 115–17, 120–2, 138–41, 145, 151–2, 167–8, 176, 218, 228
diversity 43, 79, 91, 115–16, 118, 124, 201–3, 205
domination 40, 97, 115–16, 118, 202, 208
dreams 3, 128–30, 218, 222

economic systems 155, 157, 163, 168
economy 9, 11, 13, 15, 17–19, 21, 23, 60, 151, 159, 163, 172–3
  political 150–2, 155
education 10–12, 17, 19–23, 26, 31, 43, 53, 67, 73, 118, 120–1, 127, 129, 134–8, 185
  college 69, 185–6
  cosmopolitan 25–6, 28
  multicultural 201–2
Egypt 181–8, 195–6
  history 182–4
  poetry 194–5
  revolution 182, 186
emancipation 11, 122, 127, 129–30, 156
emotions 29–30, 32–3, 36, 38–40, 42, 44–5
empathy 2, 28, 30–1, 44, 49, 167, 169, 173, 176, 199

empire 89, 96, 124, 132, 139, 147, 151, 157, 163, 219
empowerment 3, 104, 109
encounter 25, 87, 91–2, 165–6, 214–16
English literature 79, 123, 214–16
exchange 84, 93, 117–18, 124, 157–8
exploitation 36, 40, 97, 154, 159, 172, 202

family 10, 54, 59, 98–9, 134–5, 137–9, 142–4, 158, 205, 207, 222
  extended 135–7, 142
feudalism 154, 156–7, 159
  world system of 150, 156
fiction 10, 22, 30, 51, 114, 121, 133, 145, 147, 166, 174, 191, 193, 229
film 47, 51, 53, 61, 205
foreign texts 25, 76, 81–4, 86–7, 89, 166, 170, 176
frames 117, 120, 149–50, 152–4, 160, 164–5, 205, 225
framing 41, 103, 119, 150, 152–4, 158, 162–3
framing problems 150, 152
freedom 2, 56–7, 62, 71, 83, 106–7, 122, 127–9, 156, 169

gender 9, 13, 22–3, 110, 119, 192, 207–8
Gilgamesh 193–6, 198–9
global literature pedagogy 114, 116–17, 124
global poetry 168, 171, 174–6
globalization 88, 93–5, 162, 170–1, 176–7
globe 91–3, 116, 126, 189, 191, 202

heal 97–8, 102, 107–9
healing 97–105, 107, 109, 111
healing narratives 97–8, 101, 103–7, 109
hegemony 94, 153, 158–61
Heidegger, Martin 126, 129
higher education 63, 66, 68–9, 72–3, 186, 201

INDEX

Higher Education and
  Neoliberalism 72-3
humanists 4, 65-6
humanities 26, 37, 40, 42, 63-73, 97, 100, 102, 105-7
hybridity 82, 168-9, 194, 198

identification 36, 51-4, 57, 60, 145
identity 15, 22, 43, 51, 54, 60, 99-101, 110-11, 117, 133, 144, 146, 168, 209, 215
identity formation 132-3, 144
ideologies 51, 114-15, 119, 122, 189-90, 194, 227
imagination 42, 101-2, 189, 196, 218
imperialism 19-20, 128, 147, 171, 218-19
inequalities 2, 4, 52, 121-2, 189
information 5, 32-3, 39, 42, 67, 92, 149, 170, 172, 181, 195, 207
information processing, guiding 40-1
information-processing routines 37, 42-3
injustices, social 120, 153
Intercultural Classroom 209
Islam 94, 126-8

Joyce, James 219
justice 26, 45, 51-2, 59-60, 97-101, 103-7, 109, 111, 163, 176, 228

Khmer Rouge (KR) 98-107, 109-10

labor 2, 15-16, 18-19, 23, 158-9, 167-8, 171, 174, 176
language 16-17, 25, 71, 86, 88, 94, 104, 113-14, 123-4, 128-30, 147, 168-9, 175-6, 194-6, 222-3
law 17, 47, 51-2, 58-9, 144, 168, 176, 185
liberal arts 67-72
  curriculum 69, 71
  education 68-9
literary imagination 28-9
literary study 26, 28, 30-2, 117, 125

literature 28-9, 31, 49-51, 77-9, 83, 97-9, 104-5, 107-9, 114-16, 124-5, 127-30, 198-9, 202-6, 208-10, 228-9
  national 76-7, 115
  non-Western 80-1, 116

Marxist 167, 174-5, 177
material conditions 193-5, 199
material culture 167, 173-8
metacognition 41-2, 45
metaphors 105, 167, 169, 185, 190-1, 222
millennials 201-3, 205, 211
Mortenson, Greg 9, 18, 23
multiculturalism 77, 90, 118, 127, 205
mystification 153, 168, 174, 176
mythologies 191, 193, 195, 197
myths 62, 95, 144-5, 152, 163, 193, 197

neoliberalism 10, 13, 61-3
Nussbaum, M. 26, 28-31, 44, 95

orature 114-16, 118, 123-5, 128
otherness 2, 80, 82, 91, 205

Pakistan 9, 11, 19, 21, 23, 92
paradigms 76, 81, 83-5, 90
patriarch 136, 138-40, 142-4
patriarchy 133-4, 136, 140-6, 219
pedagogy 47, 50-1, 60, 71, 76, 88, 96-101, 103, 105, 107, 109-11, 118-21, 127, 163-4, 210
  informed 4
  moving 113-15, 117, 119-21, 123-7, 129
perceptions 31-7, 39-40, 44, 69, 91, 109, 116, 136
postcolonialism 202, 208-9, 218-19
power 2-4, 40, 61-2, 68, 82, 88, 98, 107, 114, 120-1, 124-5, 137, 173-4, 176, 196
  hegemonic 159
psychoanalysis 140-1, 144, 147, 229

race   13, 88, 110, 119, 132, 146–7, 176, 215, 219
representation   19, 88–9, 114, 117, 124, 126, 133, 144, 153, 172, 222
revolution   181–3, 185, 187–8
Robbins, Bruce   26–7, 43–5, 130

Said, Edward   2, 126–7
schooling   12, 15, 20, 135–6
self   25, 31, 34–5, 45, 56–7, 59, 93, 99, 101, 104, 136, 138, 145, 166, 223–4
Shakespeare, William   73, 78, 94, 215–18
social cognition   32, 43–5
social justice   43, 88, 100, 105, 119–20, 152
society   43, 51, 60, 98–9, 103, 109, 121, 143, 153, 185, 228
solidarity   91, 187
Spivak, G.   5, 76, 89, 92–3, 96–7, 110, 130–1, 133, 147, 178, 224–5
subjectivities   14, 104, 107, 126, 130, 144, 167, 169, 171–3, 177
subjects   10, 32, 63–6, 135, 140, 152, 187, 221–2

transformation   11, 100, 111, 114, 119, 123, 125, 131, 165–6, 170, 184

translation   25, 76, 79, 81–2, 84, 96, 113–27, 130, 161, 163, 166, 197, 207, 217
acts of   117, 119, 122
trauma   102, 111, 171–3, 176–7

unheimlich   92, 165, 170

violence   20, 26, 35, 49, 51–3, 60, 83, 91, 132, 135, 138, 140–2, 145, 162, 186

Wallerstein, Immanuel   153–6, 158, 160–2, 164
workers, cultural   52, 127, 129
world citizenship   26, 28, 44
world literature   3–4, 75–81, 83–9, 91–6, 115–16, 124, 149–50, 152–4, 159–60, 162, 164–6, 182, 193, 199, 227–8
contemporary   95, 173
teach   165, 169–70
World Literature Anthologies   162, 164
world literature classes   156, 166, 204
World Literature courses   78–81, 86, 92, 149, 158, 162
world systems   156–7, 160–1
worlding   114, 126, 131–4
worldliness   2, 171